Arabic/English syntax in translation:

Equivalence at word and sentence levels

By

Dr Ahmad Khuddro

2014

Dedication

To Sammy, Melanie, Aemon, Rema and Lejane

And all members of my family

Contents

Preface:.. 10

PART I: Equivalence at word level... 25

Chapter One: Arabic word and its English equivalence 27

1.1. Functionality of Arabic word and its English equivalence 27

1.2. Arabic word acting as particle, verb or noun and its English equivalence 29

Some words in Arabic can be problematic as they can act as a particle, verb or noun 29

1.2.1. The word ما 29

1.2.2. The word هل 38

1.2.3. The words من and متى 40

Chapter Two: Arabic word acting as noun and its English equivalence 43

2.1. The defective noun الاسم المقصور ending with its contracted 'alif' ى alongside its English equivalence 43

2.2. The defective noun الاسم المنقوص that ends with ي alongside its English equivalence 46

2.3. Another type of defective noun الإسم المعتل and its English equivalence.................................... 47

2.4. Redundant Arabic prepositions and their English equivalence 51

2.5. Redundant Arabic semi-prepositions and their English equivalence 53

2.6. Functionality of Arabic pronouns and certain nouns along with their English equivalence... 57

3

2.7. Duality and gender in Arabic with their English equivalence 103

Chapter Three: Arabic word acting as verb and its English equivalence 111

    3.1. The five forms of verb الأفعال الخمسة and their English equivalence 111

3.2. The present aspect of defective verbs الفعل المضارع المعتل الآخر 114

3.3. The past tense of the Arabic verb and its English equivalence 120

3.4. Imperative forms of the verb in the SL along with their equivalence 123

3.5. Verbs in the present tense with the feminine 'n' نون النسوة or the emphatic 'n' نون التوكيد
and their English equivalenc 123

Chapter Four: Superseding auxiliary verbs النواسخ in the nominal SL sentence and their TL
equivalence 125

4.1. كان = verb 'to be' 125

4.1.1. Proper verb to mean 'happen' 125

4.1.2. Auxiliary to the nominal SL sentence: 126

4.1.3. Present participle or gerund 126

4.1.4. In a collocation 127

4.1.5. Redundant verb for exclamation 127

4.1.6. In a conditional form 127

4.1.7. In negation in the present tense 128

4.1.8. Being omitted from SL sentence 128

4.1.9. Being omitted alongside its subject or predicate 129

4.2. ظل = Be still or continue to do 130

4.3. أصبح = to become (but usually implies 'morning time') 130

4.4. أضحى = to become (but usually implies 'late morning time') 130

4.4.1. As proper verb 131

4.5. أمسى = to become or end up (but usually implies 'evening time') 131

4.6. بات = to stay (but usually implies 'all night long').. 132

4.6.1. As an auxiliary 132

4.6.2. As a proper verb 132

4.7. صار = to become (implying 'to transform') 132

4.7.1. Other similar auxiliary verbs with similar function and meaning to the verb صار = 'to become' 133

4.8. ليس = not to be 135

4.9. (لا) زال = to be still (implying 'continuity').. 139

4.10. انفك (ما) = to be still (implying 'continuity') 140

4.11. فتئ (ما) = to be still (implying 'continuity') 140

4.12. برح (ما) = to be still (implying 'continuity' 141

4.13. دام (ما) = to be so long as (implying 'for a certain period of time')............ 141

Chapter Five: SL verbs of appropinquation, beginning and beseeching (أفعال المقاربة والشروع والرجاء) functioning as auxiliary and their English equivalence 149

5.1. SL verbs of approximation, along with their equivalence................................ 149

5.1.1. كاد = To be about to or almost... 149

5.1.2. أوشك = To be about to 149

5.2. SL verbs of initiation and their equivalence: 150

5.2.1. شرع = To start to 150

5.2.2. هبّ = To start or to rush to 150

5.2.3. هلهل = to start to become... 150

5.2.4. جعل = to make someone do or to begin 151

5.2.5. طفق = To start to do or to do something suddenly 151

5.2.6. أخذ = To start to do or to begin 151

5.2.7. اخلولقت = To start or To be about to 151

5.3. SL verbs of beseeching and their equivalence 151

5.3.1. عسى = To hope to happen 152

PART II: Equivalence at sentence level 155

Chapter Six: Nominal SL sentence and its TL equivalenc 157

6.1. The subject in the nominal SL sentence and its corresponding equivalence in the TL 157

6.2. Where are the SL predicate and its corresponding TL equivalence? 167

6.2.1. The predicate in the nominal SL sentence with just one noun, and its equivalence 168

6.2.2. The predicate in the nominal SL sentence and its equivalence 168

6.2.3. Nominal SL sentence, whose predicate must be a clause, and its equivalence 169

6.2.4. Tautology or repetition of the subject for rhetoric, including intensiveness or

hyperbole 172

6.2.5. Repetition of the subject in the form of demonstrative pronoun, its predicate clause

and their equivalence 173

6.3. Predicate as prepositional phrase 173

6.3.1. Predicate with ف 174

6.3.2. Multiple predicates in the nominal SL sentence and their equivalence 174

6.3.3. Omission of SL predicate and its equivalence 175

6.3.4. Fronted or delayed predicate in the nominal SL sentence and its equivalence 177

6.3.5. Predicate is a verbal sentence in the ST 179

6.3.6. Subject and predicate in the nominal SL sentence defined and their equivalence 180

6.3.7. Subject strictly defined by predicate, or limited to predicate 180

6.3.8. Predicate with the ف 181

6.3.9. Predicate separated with a pronoun 181

6.3.10. Fronting the predicate in interrogative and its equivalence 181

6.3.11. Predicate limited to subject in the nominal SL sentence and their equivalence.................... 182

6.3.12. Subject undefined in the nominal SL sentence and its sentential or semi-sentential

predicate.. 183

6.3.13. The subject in the ST implicitly refers to a pronoun which acts as the predicate................. 183

Chapter Seven: Other superseding words functioning auxiliaries إنَّ and its sisters in

nominal SL sentence and their English equivalence 193

7.1. إِنَّ or أَنَّ = certainly/actually/definitely... 193

7.2. ليت = to wish... 196

7.3. كأنَّ or كأنْ = Just like/ as if/ as though 197

7.4. لكنَّ or لكنْ = But/however/yet 197

7.5. لِ attached to subject or predicate in nominal SL sentence and its equivalence..................... 197

7.6. Cases with combinations of أنْ and either قد – لم – لا – لن and their English equivalence.......... 198

Chapter Eight: 'No' which denies the whole genus لا النافية للجنس in the SL and its TL

equivalence.. 209

8.1. Undefined subject in nominal SL sentence and its TL equivalence.................................... 209

8.2. Defined subject in nominal SL sentence and its TL equivalence...................................211

Chapter Nine: Verbal SL sentence and its TL equivalence.. 217

9.1. Subject الفاعل 217

9.2. Pro-agent or subject of the passive voice نائب الفاعل 232

9.3. Object المفعول به and its types alongside their English equivalence 238

9.3.1. One direct object in the verb SL sentence and its straightforward equivalence 238

9.3.2. Accusative of specification or particularisation المفعول به على الاختصاص 258

9.3.3. Object for cautioning or instigation in the verbal SL sentence and its equivalence...............259

9.3.4.   Unrestricted object, or absolute object المفعول المطلق 265

9.3.5. Causative Object, also known as Cognate accusative المفعول لأجله 273

9.3.6. Adverbial object المفعول فيه, or adverb of time and place ظرف مكان وزمان with its TL

equivalence 276

9.3.7. Concomitant object المفعول معه 288

9.3.8. Denotative of state or circumstantial accusative الحال 289

9.3.9. Objective complement for distinction التمييز 297

9.3.10. Vocative...304

9.3.11. Exception and Restriction المستثنى 311

9.3.12. Wonder, praise and blame, or vituperative التعجب والمدح والذم.............................316

Conclusion 321

Bibliography 325

Appendices 329

Appendix I: Varieties, analysis of STs translated from English into Arabic 329

The use of the conjunction أو 'or' in the SL and its equivalence 329

Two clauses links with the conjunction و 330

The use of the word غير to be mean 'the opposite of' 331

Gender related matters when translating from English into Arabic 331

Homonyms in Arabic 331

Polysemous words in English and their Arabic equivalence 332

Appendix II: Practicals 333

Foreword: 333

Practical One 335

Practical Two 337

Practical Three 341

Practical Four 345

Practical Five 349

Preface:

This book is designed for all English/Arab students whose major is translation. The aim is to introduce students to English translation through their comprehension of the Arabic syntax, therefore, help them to understand how to think and translate into English. No theoretical concepts in translation studies are discussed here, the reason is to give way to practice because it is through practice that students learn best how to translate any text and not just through theories which are in abundance. But when it comes to applying them, they fail to assist students and professionals to learn properly the skill of a good translator, and cannot be implemented fully as tool to produce a cohesive and coherent target text that can be acceptable by the reader and fully informative and contextually correct in its situationality. That is with no translation loss semantically and with the same meaning and effect as the source text – though the ST might sound sometimes incomprehensible in the first instance to the translator. Theories in translation, though applicable in part every now and then, are by no means totally helpful in the marketplace – that is, outside the university campuses. Readers of this book need to be armed with the basics in English grammar and syntax, in order to follow how the meaning of each word, phrase or sentence is translated. It is important to point out that this is a syntactic analysis

11

at the word level, which shows how the word meaning changes due to its case and position in the sentence, and not to the word choice in a sentence with its polysemy. So the focus is not on whether the literal and non-literal (or figurative) meaning of a word in the SL is translated in the TL, though in most examples of this book the literal meaning is the one used, but rather how the syntactic position of the word in the SL can affect its meaning in the TL and therefore helps in finding its most appropriate equivalence. The term 'equivalence' is to be discussed later in this preface.

The book also attempts to show how the translation of a phrase or sentence is produced, and in the later chapters how source texts are analysed before they are being translated, in order to show the workings of the translator's mind and the research that needs to be done by the translator before putting pen to paper and translating a full text.

It is noticeable that students or translators fail to find equivalence at the level of phrase or sentence due to their poor analysis of the word in a unit in the SL – a phrase or sentence. This has prompted me to write this book that will hopefully help English/Arab students who are good in Arabic syntax, and non-native speakers of Arabic translate a simple unit properly with no obvious errors. This book shows the first steps that professional translators and students must take in order to understand the text. Now the major steps the translator and student need to take when translating any text, are first to wear the hat of the source reader, then the hat of the researcher looking for any terms or expressions that appear to be ambiguous or field-specific. The third hat is the hat of the translator, writing the target text (TT), followed by the job or task of the proof-reader, who checks if there is anything missing or not been translated or any incorrect equivalence in the TT. It is advisable to do the translation and stay away for it for a couple of days before you go back to it and do this task of checking or proof-reading. The final hat for the translator and student to wear is the hat of the target reader; this task must be done without looking at the source text (ST), that is to read the TT as if it stands on its own. Now this book cannot cover all these aspects or steps in the process of translation, but attempts to explain one of the tasks the translator must do while translating, which is when wearing the third hat – the translator's hat. A future project will hopefully be to probe more of these steps.

This book starts with the translation of words and sentences, as it is the first step students need to take before one attempts to translate paragraphs and eventually texts. So the main focus of the discussion throughout the book is on the practical approach so that students and professional translators benefit most from the examples, and get as it were hands-on experience in translation from the exercises of each section. In these exercises one sees how different translators approach the ST (the Arabic text) and produce their own translations.

It is rather amazing that non-native speakers of Arabic sometimes learn the language better than natives. The best examples are scholars of Arabic from Persia – Sībāwayh, Nufṭawayh and Khilyāwayh, to

13

name a few - and more recently Arabists such as Edward W. Lane and later Hans Wehr - and their well known dictionaries, *An Arabic-English lexicon* (in eight volumes) and *Dictionary of Modern Written Arabic*, respectively. Both dictionaries are considered by many as the best in the field. Other tools of translation are also necessary, so one needs to use English-Arabic dictionaries too, such as Hasan al-Karmi's *al-Mughni al-akbar*, as well as good monolingual dictionaries in both English and Arabic. The latter are certainly essential, such as *Webster online* for English/English, *al-Wasīt* and *Lisān al-'Arab* for Arabic/Arabic. s

Now not only native Arab students would benefit from this book, but also non-native students of Arabic may well benefit. Although it focuses at the beginning on Arabic and its equivalence, it still inadvertently improve the student's command of Arabic when translating from English into Arabic, as students are usually not aware of how to use diacritics in Arabic properly. English/Arabic students need to be fluent in their mother tongue and should have a good command and comprehension of the second language.

Although the book starts with examples and exercises at word, phrase and sentence levels syntactically, the intention here is to make sure that students understand the Arabic syntax as well and see how it changes the meaning of the Arabic phrase or sentence radically. So it is both the syntax and the semantic levels of the word, phrase and sentence, but not contextually as they are not fully fledged texts which are being discussed in this book and do not display their exact situationality. Therefore, they might appear as if taken out of context. One must

point out that words, phrases and sentences are translated from Arabic into

English, the reason is to show the Arabic syntax and how it affects the English

equivalence in translation, this is demonstrated using examples.

The translation adopted throughout the whole book verges on the

communicative translation and not the literal one. Peter Newmark points out,

> Admittedly, all translation must be in some degree both communicative
> and semantic, social and individual. It is a matter of difference of
> emphasis. In communicative translation, however, the only part of the
> meaning of the original which is rendered is the part... which corresponds
> to the TL reader's understanding of the identical message.... (p.62)

Newmark has previously adapted Nabokov's 'semantic translation' by defining it

"as an attempt to render, as closely as the semantic and syntactic structures of the

target language allow, the exact contextual meaning of the original ('only this is

true translation', Nabokov wrote)". Then Newmark contrasts this semantic

translation with his own 'communicative translation' as being "also true

translation, and much more in demand" (p.63). Then Newmark proposes two

other definitions:

> 1) Interlinear translation (Nabokov's lexical or constructional
> translation): the primary senses of all words in the original are
> translated as though out of context, and the word-order of the
> original is retained. The main purpose is either to understand

15

the mechanics of the source language or to constitute a pre-translation procedure for a complicated SL text.

2) Literal translation: the primary senses of the lexical words of the original are translated as though out of context, but the syntactic structures of the target language are respected.

The basic difference between semantic and literal translation is that the former respects context, the latter does not (p.63).

James Dickins in his book *Thinking Arabic Translation* (2000) also talks about various types of translation along similar lines,

In literal translation proper, the denotative meaning of words is taken as if straight from the dictionary (that is, out of context), but the TL grammar is respected ... the standard grammar and word order of English is respected... for most purposes, literal translation can be regarded as the practical extreme of SL bias (p.16).

He also mentions the 'interlinear translation' as "an extreme form of the much more common literal translation" which is used "to shed light on the structure of the ST" (p.16). But the method used in this book is the communicative translation which certainly respects the TT syntax, and the ST is being analyzed for the purpose of showing how it is transferred from the SL to the TL. Dickins writes, 'A communicative translation is produced, when, in a given situation, the ST uses an SL expression standard for that situation, and the TT uses a TL expression standard for an equivalent target culture situation' (p.17). It is what Jakobson calls 'interlingual translation' which is the translation proper but the 'idiomatic' type and not the literal one as Dickins calls it (pp.11-12). In this book the translation of the Arabic examples are all communicative and not literal, and the same can be said about the examples that are translated from English into Arabic in Appendix One.

Another point to be highlighted here is "the naturalness of a translation", as Peter Newmark calls it. He writes,

> Normally, the translator should write within his own idiolect or his conception of the SL text author's, always provided the text appears to be written naturally. The translator must not use a word or phrase that sounds intuitively unnatural or artificial to him (pp.128-29).

So in the analysis or evaluation of the translation of Arabic examples in this book, the word 'natural' is used only in the above sense.

With regard to 'equivalence', it must be noted here that the 'equivalence' used is not the one which

> denotes the relationship between ST features and TT features that are seen as directly corresponding to one another, regardless of the quality of TT... [but rather the] 'equivalence' [which] denotes the relationship between an SL expression and the canonic TL rendering of it... An influential variant of prescriptive equivalence is the 'dynamic equivalence' [Eugene Nida's] ... (p.19).

But that 'dynamic' one used here in the book is not to be considered, as Dickins indicates, "as giving carte blanche for excess freedom" in translation (p.19). So the 'dynamic' equivalence is used with extreme care; and one attempts "to avoid an absolutist ambition to *maximize sameness* between ST and TT, in favour of a relativist ambition to *minimize difference*" (p.20). [*emphasis in the original*]

17

In an attempt to facilitate the reading and comprehension of this book certain words in the examples are highlighted in bold as well as their TL equivalence in order to show how they affect the syntax of the sentence and therefore its semantic aspect. This proves that syntax plays a major part in the selection of the exact meaning of a polysemous lexeme. Also all examples used from the holy *Qur'ān* are written within inverted commas in order to differentiate them from other examples in the Arabic language.

The sections in this book are enhanced by a selection of examples mainly taken from Abdu al-Rājiḥī's grammar Arabic book (1988) *The implementation of [Arabic] syntax.* They are also organized in a similar manner to that used by al-Rājiḥī. This way the English/Arabic translator or student will understand the Arabic grammar well when analyzing the ST in order to benefit from this research most. So the purpose of this organization of these sections is to improve the translator's grammar in the ST, as well as show how the TT is produced by using many examples.

The translation of the holy verses is mainly taken from M.Haleem's *The qur'ān: A new translation* (2004/2010). Other translations of the holy verses are quoted only in the exercises and they are done from 'Abdullah Yūsuf 'Alī's *The holy qur'ān* (2007) and al-Hilālī and Khan's *The noble qur'ān: English translation of the meaning and commentary* (1404AH). In all examples and exercises words and phrases in question are highlighted in bold. An appendix is also included but, unlike all the sections which discuss the analysis of

Arabic syntax in the ST and its TT equivalence, this appendix discusses mainly examples from English into Arabic, that is why it is not considered as one of the main parts of the book.

Now it is vital to note that the syntactic analysis at the text level is not being discussed in this book due to time and space, as it needs to consider the seven standards of textuality. Robert-Alain de Beaugrande (1981/7th ed. 1994) writes about them in *Introduction to text linguistics*, and they are Cohesion, Coherence, Intentionality and Acceptability, Informativity, Situationality and Intertextuality. He describes them as follow:

> COHESION... concerns the ways in which the components of the
> SURFACE TEXT, i.e. the actual words we hear or see, are *mutually*
> *connected within a sequence.* The surface components **depend** upon each
> other according to grammatical forms and conventions... (p.3).
> COHERENCE... concerns the ways in which the components of the
> TEXTUAL WORLD, i.e. the configuration of CONCEPTS and
> RELATIONS which *underlie the surface text,* are *mutually accessible* and
> *relevant.* A CONCEPT is definable as a configuration of knowledge
> (cognitive content) which can be recovered or activated with more or less
> unity and consistency in the mind... RELATIONS are the LINKS between
> concepts which appear together in a textual world... (p.4).
> "INTENTIONALITY... concern[s] the text **producer**'s attitude that the
> set of occurrences should constitute a cohesive and coherent text
> instrumental in fulfilling the producer's intentions, i.e. to distribute
> knowledge or to attain a GOAL specified in a PLAN (p.7).
> ACCEPTABILITY...concern[s] the text **receiver**'s attitude that the set of
> occurrences should constitute a cohesive and coherent text having some
> use or relevance for the receiver, e.g. to acquire knowledge or provide co-
> operation in a plan. This attitude is responsive to such factors as text type,

social or cultural setting, and the desirability of goals (p.7).
INFORMATIVITY... concerns the extent to which the occurrences of
the presented text are expected vs. unexpected or known vs. unknown...
(pp.8-9). SITUATIONALITY... concerns the factors which make a text
RELEVANT to a SITUATION of occurrence (p.9).
INTERTEXTUALITY... concerns the factors which make the utilization
of one text dependent upon knowledge of one or more previously
encountered texts (p.10). [*Uppercase and bold in original*]

This book discusses in the main the cohesive element, and it touches upon other elements alongside it – when discussing the translations of the holy verses in the exercises only – mainly lexical and semantic elements (such as word choice, polysemous words and synonyms) as well as coherence and informativity when need be.

When giving exercises at the end of each section or concept, these exercises are taken from the holy verses in The qur'ān, and in most cases four translations are given, the last one is the author's own translation. The first three translations are numbered (a), (b) and (c) in each exercise, and the fourth one - translation (d) - is introduced only when there is controversy about the former three translations, in the eyes of the author. In addition, the last translation sometimes refers to non-syntactic elements when there is a lexical or semantic issue such as the word choice. Translation (c) is done by al-Hilālī and Khan and characterised by its exegetic technique with a number of brackets inserted to explain further the meaning of the ST. This technique, though informative for the reader, is rather distracting as the reader might struggle to know what the end product actually is. Translation (c) also uses a number of loan words from the ST (Arabic) and then explains them in the TT (English). This technique is useful only for those who are interested in the interpretation of *The qur'ān*. Haleem's translation is the least of all which has no brackets inserted in the TT, therefore can be considered the least distracting when it comes to knowing what the actual target text is saying, rather than inserting phrases and clauses to interpret a point in question. In this connection, Yūsuf 'Ali's translation – translation (b) – falls in between Haleem's and al-Hilālī and Khan's.

It must be pointed out that not all exercises have my translation, as one of the other three translations has already served the purpose; otherwise the inclusion of my translation will be redundant and mere repetition. Another point is that at times few exercises with all the translations (a-d) are self-explanatory and require no syntactic analysis. My translation of some exercises is to show the implementation of a certain Arabic rule discussed in its section and how the syntactic and at time lexical analysis helps in attempting to get the most appropriate translation of the ST.

Also, the discussion about the various translations of the holy verses by these three professional translators is an attempt to improve one's understanding of English translation in general. The discussion in the exercises does not undermine the significance and invaluable effort done by these translators but rather is a good training practice that will hone the skills of students and translators who are training themselves on how to translate. No one can deny the magnanimous treasure these three translators have provided, a treasure that certainly polish one's own translation technique.

Finally, the plan or outline of the book is to start the discussion by dealing with issues at word level and move to those at sentence level. In Part I, there is Arabic *word acting as particle, verb or noun*, then *defective nouns* and their English equivalence. This is followed at the word level by a discussion about Arabic *pronouns (connected, demonstrative, relative pronouns)* and their TL equivalence. They are followed by Arabic *verbal nouns* and their English equivalence. There are also Arabic *interrogatives, conditionals, compound nouns (for numbers) and miscellaneous nouns* alongside their English equivalence demonstrated by the use of examples and exercises. Then we will see issues with the SL *word in duality, word and gender* and then *redundant prepositions* and *semi-prepositions* as well as their TL equivalence in the form of examples too. They are immediately followed by issues regarding the SL *nominal sentence* and its TL equivalence. These are dealt with at sentence level and its TL counterpart.

In Part II, the Arabic *verbal sentence* is dealt and it is seen how its English equivalence is found demonstrated in the use of several examples. This is done by a discussion about Arabic *word acting as verb, five forms of verb, defective verb, verb in the past, in the present and then in imperative form*. These are all discussed alongside their TL equivalence. They are followed by Arabic *auxiliary verbs and appropinquation* in addition to their TL equivalence. All these are done, along with the discussions about the Arabic *subject, pro-agent or the subject of the passive, types of objects including absolute object, cognate accusative, concomitant object, denotative of state and objective complement for distinction, as well as exception and finally vituperative.* All the elements of the SL verbal sentence are discussed alongside their TL equivalence shown in the examples and exercises. This is done to see how the position of the word in a certain structure whether it is a phrase, clause or sentence affects its meaning and therefore its equivalence should be chosen carefully in order to convey the most appropriate meaning in the TL.

Finally, it must be pointed out that this textbook is by no means a reference book of Arabic grammar, but helps to understand how some syntactic elements in Arabic language can change the meaning of the text and therefore affects our decision in finding its most appropriate equivalence in English.

PART I: Equivalence at word level

Arabic/English syntax in translation

Chapter One: Arabic word and its English equivalence

1.1. Functionality of Arabic word and its English equivalence

The first problem encountered in translation is to look at not merely the lexical meaning of the word but at its functionality in a phrase or sentence in the source language (SL) and understand what that word or expression means before attempting to translate them into the target language (TL). It is true that one should not only translate a text at word level but also at a much higher level – at sentence, paragraph or eventually text levels. But the method adopted here at word level helps first analyse the functionality of a word in the SL syntactically before thinking of an equivalent in the TL. This method shows how the functionality of a word in a sentence, i.e. its position in the sentence, affects the sense of the whole unit – whether that unit is a phrase or sentence. This method helps break down the structure of the sentence in the SL, Arabic, to its basic structure, and therefore understand the meaning of the unit. To start with, students and professional translators might fail even at this simple level, that is why it is being discussed here.

When the translator overcomes this obstacle in his/her translation – the obstacle of understanding the functionality of words in a unit, then he/she can move to the level of understanding a paragraph and eventually a whole text. Understanding the SL is the first step towards translating it properly. After the syntactic analysis of the

Arabic text at the word and sentence levels to find its appropriate equivalence, it should be analysed as a text according to the seven standards of textuality explained by de Beaugrande in his book *Introduction to text Linguistics* which is based on its context, situationality and intertextuality and informativity, to name a few of these standards.

Now the main concern in this book is the cohesion levels of the word and then of the sentence. This is the first step, i.e. understanding the cohesion and coherence of just one word and its relation to the unit – be it a phrase or sentence. Understanding the context is a step that can only be used when translating a full text which consists of at least one paragraph. But at this level – at the functional level of a word - there is no context when it comes to such a simple unit, a phrase or sentence.

Although the semantic aspect of the SL word is significant, its functionality or position in the phrase or sentence is the one in question here, as well as how that functionality changes the sense of the phrase or sentence, and subsequently its TL equivalence changes accordingly. The reason for this focus is to narrow down the topic of the book.

Also, although the lexical aspect of a word (that is, which word in the dictionary to use in the TL to be the equivalent of an SL word) is important, but it is not in focus here. The reason for overlooking this aspect is also to narrow down the topic of this book. So the focus here is how the functionality of the SL word affects the structure of the unit, therefore the meaning has changed. This in turn affects the choice of equivalence in the TL.

1.2. Arabic word acting as particle, verb or noun and its English equivalence

Some words in Arabic can be problematic as they can act as a particle, verb or noun.

1.2.1. The word ما

The word ما in Arabic is polysemous, acting as particle, noun or verb. Pierre Cachia (1973, p.93) in his book *The monitor: A dictionary of Arabic grammatical terms - Arabic/English, English/Arabic*, points out that this word has many syntactic positions; that is why no single equivalence is used in this reference.

The word ما acting as particle

When acting as *particle*, the word ما has more than one meaning in the SL. It is used either for negation or has no function at all (al-Rājiḥī, 1988, p.12). This word is either translated into English as '*not*' or *dropped out altogether* as in the following examples:

1. ما جاء أحمد.
Aḥmad did **not** come.
2. "(وَقُلْنَ حَاشَ لِلَّهِ) مَا هَـٰذَا بَشَرًا." (*The qur'ān*, 12: 31)
    a. "He can**not** be mortal!" (Haleem, p.147)

29

b. "**No** mortal is this" (Yūsuf ʿAlī, p.272).

c. "**No** man is this" (al-Hilālī and Khan, p.307).

d. "**No human** is this" (*my translation*).

3.　　　"وَمَا مُحَمَّدٌ إِلاَّ رَسُولٌ". (*The qurʾān*, 3: 144)

a.　　　"Muhammad is only a messenger" (Haleem, 2010, p.44).

b.　　　"Muhammad no more than Messenger" (Yūsuf ʿAlī, p.75).

c. "Muhammad is no more than a Messenger" (al-Hilālī and Khan, 1404AH; Yūsuf ʿAlī, p.75).

4.　　　"فَبِمَا رَحْمَةٍ مِّنَ اللَّـه لِنتَ لَهُمْ." (*The qurʾān*, 3:159)

a. "Out of mercy from God, you [Prophet] were gentle in your dealings with them" (Haleem, 2010, p.46).

b. "It is part of Mercy of Allah that you do deal gently with them" (Yūsuf ʿAlī, p.78).

In the first three examples, the word ما acts as particle for negation in the SL and therefore its TL equivalence is the particle 'not' or 'no (not any)' to indicate negation. Moreover, in Example 2 the word 'بشر' is best translated in (c), because that Arabic word has the human aspect in it. One might propose translation (d), which seems closest meaning, and can be considered closer to the vital adjective 'بشر'. A more dynamic communicative translation would be 'He is above humans' (he is an angle). It is a rather free translation, for it reverses the negative aspect in the SL into a positive one in the TL.

In the fourth example, however, the word ما is redundant and has no function in the Arabic syntax; therefore, its TL equivalence is totally ignored totally. Further, translation (b) of Example 3 is syntactically closer to the ST, and therefore can be considered more 'truthful', though 'only' in translation (a) is the equivalence of 'no more than' in translation (b). But translation (a) in Example 3 is certainly more concise.

The word ما acting as noun

The word ما also can be a *noun* acting as subject in a verbal SL sentence, as in the following examples:

5.　　　　　"يُسَبِّحُ لِلَّهِ مَا فِي السَّمَاوَاتِ وَمَا فِي الْأَرْضِ." (*The qur'ān*, 62:1)
a. '**Everything** in the heavens and earth glorifies God' (Haleem, p.372).
b. '**Whatever** is in the heavens and on earth, does declare the Praises and Glory of Allah' (Yūsuf 'Alī, p.705).
c. '**Whatsoever** is in the heavens and **whatsoever** is on the earth glorifies Allāh' (al-Hilālī and Khan, p.759).
d. : '**All things** in the heavens and earth glorify God' (*my translation*).

Here the word ما is a noun, acting as subject; and its TL equivalence can be either 'a thing' or 'what'. Now it is clear that all three translations in Example 5 are close to the meaning, but the closest TL equivalence of the three is translation (a). al-Hilālī and Khan's translation (c) is the closest in its literalness. However, one might suggest a fourth version here which is more communicative than

31

Haleem's. This last version, translation (d), might be considered the closest of them all semantically and communicatively.

In addition to the TL equivalence mentioned in Example 5, the word ما when acting as noun can also be used in the interrogative case – i.e. to form a question to mean 'what' or 'how'. Here is an example,

6.   ما أدراك أن علياً قادم؟
a. **What** has <u>made</u> you realise that Ali is coming?
b. **How** do you know that Ali is coming?

The word ما in the SL is a *noun* acting as subject to the verb, and forms a question. Its TL equivalence can be the *wh*-structure which functions either as subject using 'what' as in translation (a) but can function as object using 'how' as in translation (b).   Translation (b), though less 'truthful' syntactically, is still concise and more 'natural' and appropriate than translation (a) as the former requires no extra verb which is used in translation (a) – namely, the verb 'to make'.

Here is another example in which the word ما is a noun acting as object to the verb in the sentence in both the SL and TL and is used to form a question as well,

7.   ما أكلت اليوم؟
What have you eaten today?

Not unlike the previous examples, the TL equivalence of the word ما is 'what' in its various positions in the SL sentence.

Another usage of the word ما in the SL is a *noun* acting as subject in a nominal sentence that needs a predicate. It is also used for exclamation. Its equivalence is the same as above - 'what' – which has a similar function in the TL as in the following example,س

8.   ما أجمل السماء!

What a wonderful sky!

So the TL equivalence of the Arabic word ما can vary from 'not' to 'what' and 'thing' depending on the syntactic analysis of the ST. More varied examples are provided by Wolfdietrich Fischer (2002) in his book *A grammar of classical Arabic* in support of the discussion above with regards to the function of the word ما and its TL equivalence 'what'. The best example is Example 9 below because it has the word ما in its two forms, acting as particle and then as noun,

9.   ما ترى رأيَ ما نرى

'You do **not** think **what** we think.' (p.218)

Here is an example with the word ما as noun acting as

10.   جمعتُ ما جمعتُ.

'I gathered **what** I gathered, i.e. a certain quantity.' (*Ibid.*)

11.   هم ما هم.

'They are **what** they are'. (*Ibid.*)

12.   فأعطاني ما كان عنده من خبز.

'Then he gave me **what** he had of bread.' (*Ibid.*)

Also, here is the word ما in negation,

13.   ما وجت مركبا قبل الذي أتيت به.

'I did **not** find a ship before the one in which I came.' (p.216)

In Example 14, not unlike Examples 10-12, the word ما is certainly not in negation, but as noun acting as object,

14. ‏إتفق على ما تطلبه الناس.‏

'He agreed as to **what** people asked.' (*Ibid.*)

In Example 15 the word ما is in negation,

15. ‏ما بلغت الباب حتى سمعت.‏

'I had **not** yet reached the door when I heard…' (p.224)

Here the word ما is used in the interrogative,

16. ‏ما فعلَتْ حتى استوجبَت القتل؟‏

'**What** did she do to deserve to be killed?' (*Ibid.*)

Further, it is a common mistake to back translate the word ما as 'ماذا' in a statement. This common error is repeated in Karin Ryding's (2005) *A reference grammar of modern standard Arabic*. When Ryding says 'يعرف **ماذا** يريد حقاً' and gives its TL equivalence, 'He knows **what** he wants' (p.327). In fact, the ST itself given above sounds like a translation from English, and not vice versa. The Arabic equivalence of the English text 'He knows **what** he wants' should have been 'يعرف ما يريد حقاً'.

Another similar point is in the following example by Fischer (2002) that shows the word ما being used in negation,

17. ‏والـله ما نبالي أين ذهب.‏

'By God, we do **not** care where he went.'(p.218)

The TL equivalence clearly shows negation, but again it appears as if the TT is the ST, because of the use of 'أين'. Here the Arabic can be

'والله ما نبالي **حيثما** ذهب', as the word 'where' in English has a more appropriate equivalence, namely 'حيثما'. Even a better equivalence is 'والله ما نبالي **مكانه**'. 'والله ما نبالي **المكان** الذي قصده' or 'المقصود'. This is the strategy when one encounters the *wh*-structure in an English statement, as it is not used in the interrogative. A further comment is Fischer's equivalence into English is still problematic in that the two tenses, present and past, are mixed in one sentence. The English should have been 'where he **has gone**.'

A similar example where the *wh*-structure is used is 'أريد أن أعرف **كيف** نفذ ذلك' with its TL equivalence 'I want to know **how** he has done that.' Now if we are to back translate the English, one might find a more appropriate equivalence such as 'أريد أن أعرف **طريقة** تنفيذه لذلك', 'أريد أن أعرف **طريقته** في تنفيذ ذلك' or 'أريد أن أعرف أسلوبه في تنفيذ ذلك'.

More varied examples but this time from Ryding in her book are,

18.   'في **ما** يتعلق بالزراعة.'
'In **whatever** relates to agriculture.'
19.   'ما لا نهاية.'
'Infinity' (p.326).

Now the translation of Example 18 is rather literal, but uses an appropriate equivalence to the word ما, namely 'whatever'. So from the syntactical perspective it is most appropriate, but from a stylistic and dynamic point of view that translation is rather poor. A more appropriate translation would be 'as regards agriculture' or 'regarding agriculture'; as it is communicative in its approach.

35

In Example 19 the translation is dynamic, a literal translation would have been 'what is endless'; as it shows the equivalence of the word ما. One can also say 'endlessness' but then this is very rare in English, and therefore one needs to use the more familiar expression – 'infinity'.

Further, in Example 19 the use of لا before the noun is worth discussing. In *Thinking Arabic translation*, James Dickins (2002) points out "standardized calques from English into modern Arabic [which] include... لا عنف" as an equivalence to the term 'non-violence'. In his discussion of cultural transposition, Dickins defines claque as "an expression that consists of TL words and respects TL syntax, but is unidiomatic in the TL because it is modelled on the structure of an SL expression" (p.31). Perhaps a more appropriate equivalence of 'non-violence' is 'وقف العنف' or 'نبذ العنف', the latter is a familiar term mainly in political texts. However, there are other terms like اللا مبالاة 'indifference' or 'carelessness' and 'لا رجعة فيه' 'irrevocable' or in writing amounts of money the term 'لا غير' meaning 'only' as in 'عشرون دولار لا غير' meaning 'twenty dollars only'. In classical Arabic the praise 'لا شلت يداك' communicatively meaning 'well-done', and one cannot say 'May your hands not be paralysed'. Another similar example is 'لا أشبعه اللـه أسئلة ومناقشات' meaning "insatiable is his hunger for questions and discussions!" ('Imād Zakī's Arabic novel *Tears on the Slopes of Glory*, 2003, p.18). This means, 'You have an insatiable appetite for questions and discussions' which is a communicative translation, and 'May God' is connotative in English but not so in Arabic. One can say in English 'May God not satisfy your insatiable appetite for questions' but it is rather a literal translation. However, a good example of standardized calques from English into modern Arabic would be 'الأتمتة' 'automatism'.

Ryding has given another equivalence for 'non' which is 'عدم' as in 'non-existence' with its equivalence 'عدم وجود' or 'instability' with its equivalence ' عدم استقرار', and there are similar examples given in her book *A reference grammar of modern standard Arabic* (pp.218-19). Here are also more example by Ryding which clarify the use of the word ما,

20.   شكرَه على ما قدّمه.
He thanked him for **what** he offered.
21.   وقال ما يلي...
(And) he said the following... ('**that which** follows) (p.326)

There are other usages of the word ما as an indefinite relative pronoun also beautifully highlighted by Ryding to mean 'one, some, certain or including' such as,

22.   'سيرجع يوما ما.'
'He will come back **one** day.' (or some day)
23.   'غيرت موقفها إلى حد ما.'
'She changed her position to a **certain** extent.'
24.   'لماذا تحب فناناً ما[؟]'
'Why do you like a **certain** artist?'
25.   'يجري اتصالات مع جميع الأطراف بما فيها حكومة إسرائيل.'
'He is in communication with all the parties **including** the government of Israel.' (pp.327-28)

To sum up, depending on its functionality in the Arabic unit, the word ما when translated can either be deleted completely when it is redundant, or have the TL equivalence 'not' in negation, or the TL equivalence 'thing' or the *wh*-structure 'what' – whether in a statement or in the interrogative. It is true that the word ما in the SL is polysemous, but how can the student or professional translator decide on which meaning to choose depends heavily on its syntactic aspect.

1.2.2. The word هل

It is another word in the SL (Arabic) which is considered as *particle*, but only used in the interrogative with its various equivalences in the TL (English). In nominal sentences, only the verb 'to be' is reversed in English to give the equivalence of the word هل as in these two examples,

1.   هل أنت متزوج؟
Are you married?
2.   هل حضر عليّ؟
a. **Is** Ali present?
b. **Was** Ali present?

It must be pointed out that only the present/past tense implied in the SL needs to be considered, and can be decided upon based on the context whether it is in the past or in the present.

But the equivalence of the word 'هل' can change to the verb 'to do' when the sentence is a verbal one but has no auxiliary verb in the SL.

The verb 'to do' in English needs to be used in either its present or past form as in this example,

3.   هل تريد مقابلته؟

Do you want to meet him?

4.   هل رأيته؟

Did you see him?

5.   هل تعرف الحل؟

Do you the solution?

Now the word هل can be problematic when the Arabic sentence refers to be both present and past at the same time which means that its tense in English would have to be the present perfect tense.   The equivalence of the word هل is to use the *auxiliary* verb 'to have' as in the following example,

6.   هل عرفت الحل؟

Have you found the solution?

It must be pointed out that this equivalence is only when the verb 'to have' in English is an auxiliary and *not* when this verb is not the main verb in the sentence. A good example for this note is 'هل تناولت الإفطار؟' and its appropriate equivalence is '**Did** you have breakfast?' This solution is mentioned above Examples 3-5.

Another English equivalence of the word هل changes yet again when the SL sentence has an auxiliary verb such as تستطيع or يمكن with its appropriate equivalence 'can' or 'could' as in the following example,

7.   هل بمقدورك القيام بهذا العمل؟

Can you do this work?

8. ‎هل بإمكانك رفع هذا الصندوق؟
Can you lift this book?
9. ‎هل يمكنك إصابة الهدف؟
Can you hit the target?
10. ‎هل تستطيع مناقشتها في الأمر؟
Could you discuss the matter with her?
11. ‎هلا فتحت النافذة؟
Could you open the window?

In short, the word ‎هل in Arabic is only used in the interrogative form, but its English equivalence can change depending on whether the sentence is nominal or verbal sentence. When the question is a nominal sentence, then the equivalence of the word ‎هل is the verb 'to be' reversed to correspond to the TL grammar. But when it is a verbal sentence the equivalence of ‎هل is either the verb 'to do' as auxiliary or other auxiliary verbs such as the verb 'to have' and 'can' and 'could'.

1.2.3. The words ‎من and ‎متى

These two words in the SL are also interrogative words in Arabic. But these two are *not* particles. They both are, according to al-Rājiḥī, *interrogative nouns* (1988, p.13).

The SL interrogative noun ‎من acts as subject and its equivalence is 'who'. But unlike the word ‎متى, it requires no reversal of the auxiliary verb, the approach followed above when using the word ‎ما in the interrogative. Here is an example,

12. ‎من حضر اليوم؟
a. **Who** has attended today?
b. **Who is** present today?

c. **Who was** present today?

d. **Who has** been present today?

It is noticeable that the noun من has a straightforward equivalence in English, because it is acting as subject for a predicate. Only the tense is a problem, in Arabic the verb حضر is in the past but can refer the present, but in English that verb cannot be used because it is an intransitive verb. Here one might wonder which translation (a), (b), (c) and (d) is more appropriate and why. Translation (a) is unacceptable in English due to the use of the verb 'to attend' which is intransitive, i.e. it requires an object in English, and is often transitive when in the passive sentence (See the definition of 'to attend' in *Collins*, 1985, p.92). Translation (a) breaks a rule in the TL grammar. Translation (b) is communicative. It is more appropriate, though the verbal SL sentence has a nominal sentence as its TL equivalence. This proves that a verbal sentence in Arabic can translated into a nominal equivalence in English, when the verbal English sentence is inappropriate or uncommon in the TL grammar. As for the tense translation (c) is the most appropriate as it links the present tense with the past tense in English.

The equivalence of the Arabic interrogative noun متى is 'when' which is simply a *wh*-structure but the English translation needs to follow the TL grammatical rule used for the word هل discussed above. That is to reverse the auxiliary verb when it is existent such as the verb 'to be' or 'to have'. Here is an example,

41

13.   متى حضر سامر؟
a. **When did** Samer attend?
b. **When was** Samer present?

In Example 13 there are two translations, one with a verbal sentence and the other is a nominal sentence. Also as discussed above in Example 12, translation (a) is inappropriate but unacceptable as it breaks the TL grammatical rule. Translation (b) is appropriate due to the use of the nominal sentence which follows the TL grammar.

Chapter Two: Arabic word acting as noun and its English equivalence

2.1. The defective noun الاسم المقصور ending with its contracted 'alif' ى alongside its English equivalence

This kind of noun is problematic in defining its syntactic position in an SL

sentence as vowel diacritics are often not used in modern Arabic books, unless

they are discussing grammar or syntax. The defective noun keeps the same form

or morpheme ('shape') in Arabic in the SL do not change when, though

assuming different positions, acting as subject, object or in a prepositional

phrase. Here are some examples with their equivalence to elaborate this point,

1. جاء فتىً.
A young man came.
2. رأيت فتىً.
I saw **a young man**.
3. مررت بفتىً.
I came **by a young man**.

Before doing the syntactic analysis here one needs to point out that the three

verbs جاء 'to come', رأيت 'I saw' and مررت 'I came by' are typical and often used

in Arabic grammar books in order to identify the functionality of a defective

noun.

It is extremely hard to identify the functionality of this defective noun

فتى in the SL sentence by its diacritics only, but its verb can help

in this identification. Therefore its equivalence must be chosen very

43

carefully as the semantic aspect will certainly be lost, if its syntactic position is identified incorrectly.

Also here is another similar noun, which is a proper noun, the name Moses as in the following three examples,

1. جاء موسى.

    Moses came.

2. رأيت موسى.

    I saw **Moses**

3. مررت بموسى.

    I came **by Moses**.

But diacritics here are not used, but one can identify the syntactic position of the noun by analysing the verb. This analysis would show whether the noun here is the subject of the verb or the object of the verb.

Incidentally, another issue can be discussed here with regards to proper names, especially religious people or names of places, are problematic in finding their most appropriate equivalence. An effective strategy here is to do extensive research about them before attempting to give their equivalent. It is clear that **equivalents of proper names** for people or places are problematic at times at the surface level at least. Here are some **names of Prophets** in the SL and TL: إبراهيم Abraham, إسماعيل Ismail; إسحق Isaac, يعقوب Jacob, يوسف Joseph, يونس Jonah, داوود David, طالوت Goliath, جالوت Gabriel, جبرائيل Noah, نوح Job, أيوب Moses, موسى Jesus, عيسى Talot, شمعون Simon. Not only names of people but also some **place names** in the

ST are also problematic: أريحا Jericho, الخليل Hebron, الجليل Galilee, الفرات Euphrates, دجلة Tigris, بحر قزوين Caspian Sea, نهر العاصي The Orontes, طيبة Thebes (in Egypt), إشبيلية Seville, مالقة Malaga, اليابسة Ibiza, غرناطة Granada, الشبونةLisbon, جبل طارق Gibraltar, الدار البيضاء Casablanca, تدمر Palmyra, الجبل الأسود Montenegro, الطرف الأغر Trafalgar. But when the ST is referring to, say, Job, for his tremendous patience; if such connotative meaning is implied, then it must be conveyed. Peter Newmark (1981/1986) says, "In semantic translation, the transferred proper name is mandatory" (p.151).

Newmark also stipulates, "unless… a person's name already has an accepted translation it should not be translated but must be adhered to, unless the name is used as a metaphor" (p.70). The latter concept is clarified further in communicative translation by Newmark when he says, the name can be re-used when it has "the same sense in the TL", which is the case in question here, that is why it is translated here in Examples 1-3. However, sometimes proper names are "treated purely connotatively", and are normally translated by their connotation, because they are used for their connotative meaning, and "may require two or three 'senses' in the translation" (p.151); but it is not the case here.

Going back the main point of discussion the defective nouns, it is the syntactic aspect of the defective nouns that determine as to whether they are acting as subject or object, which can only be known through the analysis of the verb of the clause or sentence. Failure to recognise

45

that aspect of the defective nouns certainly leads to making a major translation error.

2.2. The defective noun الاسم المنقوص that ends with ي alongside its English equivalence

This kind of defective noun in the SL sentence can pose yet another problem in translation. It needs to be understood by analysing first the sentence, and in particular its verb. It is the same way done in the previous paragraph (*para.* 2.1). Here are examples in the SL and their TL equivalence:

1.   جاء القاضي.
The judge came.

2.   رأيت القاضيَ.
I saw **the judge**.

3.   مررت بالقاضي.
I came by **the judge**.

4.   جاء قاضٍ.
A judge came.

5.   رأيت قاضياً.
I saw **a judge**.

6.   مررت بقاضٍ.
I came by **a judge**.

7.   هذه جوارٍ.
These are **maids**.

8.   مررت بجوارٍ.
I came by **maids**.

9.   رأيت جواريَ.
I saw **maids**.

The strategy is first to identify the position of the defective noun in the SL and its different forms as a consequence, in order to find its most appropriate equivalence. It is easy to identify this defective noun when defined by a determiner such as *the* (as in Examples 1-3) since its defective part of the noun stays, but when the defective noun is undefined with an indeterminer such as *a* or *an* as in Examples 4 and 6.

It is worth noting that there are words in Arabic which are orthographically similar but mean two completely different things, such as 'بجوار' which could mean 'by maids' as in Example 8 but can also be misread to mean 'near to'. But the latter meaning makes the SL sentence incomplete semantically.

Another example of such defective nouns is the SL word محامي 'lawyer' because of its contracted form محامٍ again due to its functional position in the sentence such as

جاء محامٍ. 'A lawyer came' and مررت بمحامٍ. 'I came by a lawyer'.

So the student or professional translator needs first to have a keen eye to distinguish the defective noun and its different functionalities in the Arabic sentence. This helps to find its most appropriate TL equivalence, and subsequently convey the exact meaning in the TL sentence. This is the strategy to adopt in order to deal with these defective nouns.

2.3. Another type of defective noun الإسم المعتل and its English equivalence
In Arabic it hard to identify the possessive pronoun of the defective noun that ends with ي *ya'*. The solution is to detect the functional position of that defective noun in the SL sentence. Here are three

examples and their TL equivalence which elaborate this particular point,

1.   جاء صديقي.
    My friend came.
2.   رأيت صديقي.
I saw **my friend**.
3.   مررت بصديقي.
I came **by my friend**.

Note how Examples 1 and 2 have the same defective noun صديق with the same possessives but their *syntactic* functionality is different. That is, they are both *orthographically similar but syntactically different*. The same can be said about the *plural* form of the defective noun when its possessive pronoun is in its first person singular, e.g.

4.   جاء أصدقائي.
My friends came.
5.   رأيت أصدقائي.
I saw **my friends**.
6.   مررت بأصدقائي.
I came **by my friends**.
7.   جاءت أخواتي.
My sisters came.
8.   رأيت أخواتي.
I saw **my sisters**.
9.   مررت بأخواتي.
I came **by my sisters**.

It is clear in Examples 4-6 that the defective Arabic nouns with their possessives are similar orthographically but totally different syntactically. The same comment can be applied to Examples 7-9. Incidentally, it is noticeable that some students make a common mistake of distinguishing between إخوتي 'my brothers' and أخواتي 'my

sisters', as they are orthographically similar to an extent, and the difference is only in adding an *alif* in the middle, especially as many students never bother to add the *hamza* to the initial *alif*.

The task of finding the TL equivalence seems simple only after analysing correctly the syntax or the functionality of this type of defective noun and its possessive; otherwise it would have been problematic for both the student and the professional translator to find its appropriate equivalence.

The defective noun alongside its possessive is not only problematic in its plural form but also in its duality, especially when diacritics are not used which is a common practice in Arabic newspapers. Here are few examples,

10.   جاء صديقاي.

   My two friends came.

11.   رأيت صديقيّ.

   I saw **my two friends**.

12.   مررت بصديقيّ.

   I came by **my two friends**.

Now Example 13 may be easy to analyse syntactically and therefore its English equivalence is easily found. But Examples 14 and 15 require special care. If the diacritic *shadda* which indicates the doubling of the letter ي *ya'* is not used in print.

Here are examples for the other defective noun فتى 'a boy' discussed earlier in paragraph 2.1 in Examples 1-3, with regards to its

49

functionality, whether acting as subject, object, or predicate. Here it is discussed in the following examples in its possessive,

13.　　هذا **فتاي**.
　　　This is **my boy**.

14.　　رأيت **فتاي**.
　　　I saw **my boy**.

15.　　مررت **بفتاي**.
　　　I came **by my boy**.

The defective noun فتى 'a boy' with its possessives makes it appear orthographically similar in all three examples 13-15, but their syntactic functional position is changing. That defective noun acts in the nominal sentence as predicate in Example 13, as object in the verbal sentence in Example 14, and as part of the prepositional phrase in Example 15. Note that the danger here is that the student might analyse the defective noun mistakenly here as if it were in its dual form, and that is certainly inaccurate.

The possessive pronoun of the defective noun makes the job of the analyst of the SL sentence even harder when diacritics are not used as the case is in the majority of non-specialised Arabic grammar books. It is often the case in books about technology or science where their objectives are only to deliver the message correctly and pay no attention to diacritics. The same is done in newspapers nowadays and on the internet and in short messaging service on mobiles, in which diacritics are often totally ignored as the job of adding them is tiresome and time-consuming.

Here are few examples of some defective noun with its possessive pronoun assuming different functional positions in the SL sentence, and how essential the diacritic *shadda* is in order to help the translator or student get the right meaning of the Arabic sentence before providing an appropriate equivalence,

16. جاء محاميّ.
My lawyer came.
17. رأيت محاميّ.
I saw **my lawyer**.
18. مررت بمحاميّ.
      I came by **my lawyer**.

The equivalence in the TL appears simple here but has only become so after the defective noun with its possessive pronoun has been analysed to its basic form syntactically. Finally, it is time to have a quick look at some prepositions in Arabic which are basically redundant and what strategy to adopt when translating them into English.

2.4. Redundant Arabic prepositions and their English equivalence

There are prepositions in Arabic that are redundant and, al-Rājiḥī (1988, p.26) explains, has no meaningful task implied in its function. It may, however, be used in Arabic for stylistic reasons. They are extra but non-functional prepositions and need to be identified syntactically by the analytical eye of the student or professional translator in order to be deleted in English. The strategy is then to have *no English equivalence for such prepositions*. Here are few examples from al-Rājiḥī's book with their TL equivalence,

1.　　ما جاء **من** رجل.
　　No man came.

2.　　ما رأيت **من** رجل.
　　I saw no man.

3.　　"لست عليهم **ب**مصيطر" (*The qur'ān*, 88:22)
　　'You are not there to control them.' (Haleem, p.419)
'You are not [the] one to manage (men's) affairs.' (Yūsuf 'Alī, p.783) [*addition in square brackets is not in original*]
'You are not a dictator over them'. (al-Hilālī and Khan, p.833)

It is clear that the prepositions highlight in bold in Arabic have no equivalence in English in these instances. The reason is that these prepositions are redundant in the SL in the first place. Incidentally, it must be pointed out that the word صيطر is written in al-Rājiḥī's book with a س and not ص as seen in various copies of *The qur'ān*. al-Thaʿālibi in *Fiqh al-Lugha* (p.88) says that these two letters are interchangeable.

4.　　هل **من** مخلصين يفعلون ذلك؟
　　Are there no dedicated people to do that?

5.　　ليسا **ب**مؤمنِين.
　　They both are not truly faithful.

6.　　ليسوا **ب**مؤمنِينَ.
　　They are not truly faithful.

It is rather dangerous not to recognise these extra or redundant prepositions in the SL, and *delete them immediately* in the TL as they are not proper functioning prepositions; their functionality is almost nil in the SL, save for their bombastic style.

2.5. Redundant Arabic semi-prepositions and their English equivalence

There are semi-prepositions which are also redundant (al-Rājiḥī, p.27) but have no function in terms of syntax, therefore they need to be deleted in the TL sentence. Failure to identify these types of preposition would create a problem for the student and the professional translator which they can do without as there are other issues to deal with in the process of translation. Here are two examples to clarify the point about redundant Arabic semi-prepositions and their English equivalence,

1. رُبّ ضارة نافعة.
a.   Harm can (sometimes) be useful. (literal and interlinear translation)
b.   **Many a** harmful thing can be useful. (literal and interlinear translation)
c.   Every cloud has a silver lining. (communicative translation, being a proverb)

Translations (a) and (b) are literal and interlinear but are totally unacceptable, as they hardly makes sense in English. Translation (c), however, though dynamic with its totally different words and TL grammar, is certainly acceptable. It is also idiomatic and carries the same message as that in the ST.

Also, this Arabic semi-preposition رب with no diacritics can be a homonym with two different meanings: 'God' when رب is a noun or 'many a' when رب is a redundant semi-preposition as Hans Wehr

53

translates this preposition (p.320). That is why it needs to be avoided particularly in audiovisual translation.

Fischer follows suite in his translation of رب as in the following example,

2.   "رُبّ رجل كريم قد لقيت".

'**Many a** noble man have I met' (p.179).

Moreover, there are other particles are used like this one below which is used for emphasis.

إنَّ زيداً قائم.

Zayd is **certainly** standing.

Here its English equivalence is not omitted but converted into an adverb 'certainly' to highlight that emphasis in Arabic.

Here are examples which give a total summary of the whole chapter, regarding the use of the particle إن for emphasis,

"قُلْ إنَّ الْهُدَى هُدَى اللـه."   (*The qur'ān*, 3:73)

a.   "[Prophet] tell them, 'True guidance is the guidance of God' " (Haleem, p.39).

b.   "Say, 'True guidance is the Guidance of Allah' " (Yūsuf 'Alī, p.64).

c.   "Say (O Muhammad): '**Verily**! Right guidance is the Guidance of Allah' (al-Hilālī and Khan, p.81). (*my emphasis*)

d.   "Say, Guidance is **truly** the Guidance of God" (*my translation and emphasis*).

It is clear that the word 'إِنَّ' needs to be highlighted in the target text, and it means 'certainly' or 'truly' as in Translation (d). That certainty is revealed in Translation (c) only a little. An interesting addition is seen in Translations (a), (b) and (c) which might be useful but not necessarily required, and that is the adjective 'true' or 'right' in Translation (c).

An exercise on the use of ما in negation and the use of the redundant preposition is this,

"وَمَا رَبُّكَ بِظَلَّامٍ لِّلْعَبِيدِ." (*The qur'ān*, 41:46)

a.   '...your Lord is **never** unjust to His creatures' (Haleem, p.310).

b.   '...**nor** is your Lord ever unjust (in the least) to His Servants' (Yūsuf 'Alī, p.594).

c.   'And your Lord is **not** at all unjust to (His) slaves' (al-Hilālī and Khan, p.649).

d.   'And you Lord is never unjust to His servants' (*my translation*).

Here is another exercise,

" مَّا أَنزَلَ اللَّـه بِهَا مِن سُلْطَانٍ." (*The qur'ān*, 12:40)

a.   'names for which God has sent down **no sanction**' (Haleem, p.148).

b.   'names... for which Allah has sent down **no authority**' (Yūsuf 'Alī, p.273).

c.   'names...for which Allāh has sent down **no authority**' (al-Hilālī and Khan, p.309).

55

This one above is another example for the word ما in negation and also the redundant Arabic preposition من which is deleted in English. Here is another exercise for the redundant preposition in Arabic which is being deleted in English,

"مَا لَهُم بِهِ مِنْ عِلْمٍ وَلَا لِآبَائِهِمْ." (*The qur'ān*, 18:5)

a.   "They have **no** knowledge about this, **nor** did their forefathers" (Haleem, p.183).

b.   "No knowledge have they of such a thing, nor had their fathers" (Yūsuf 'Alī, p.342).

c.   "**No** knowledge have they of such a thing, **nor** had their fathers" (al-Hilālī and Khan, p.385).

Another exercise of a redundant preposition is here,

"قُلْ كَفَى بِاللـه شَهِيدًا بَيْنِي وَبَيْنَكُمْ." (*The qur'ān*, 13:43)

a.   "Say, 'God is sufficient witness between me and you' " (Haleem, p.157).

b.   "Say: 'Enough for a witness between me and you is Allah' " (Yūsuf 'Alī, p.292).

c.   "Say, 'Sufficient as a witness between me and you is Allāh' " (al-Hilālī and Khan, p.327).

d.   "Say, 'God is a sufficient witness between you all and me' " (*my translation*)

Here it is worth noting that the 'you' is in the plural form in Arabic but in English, so it should be compensated by the word 'all'. It is essential to note that in English the fixed expression is 'you and I' as in the example 'Let us go, you and I'; whereas in Arabic the

56

commonly known order is 'أنا وأنت' and not 'أنت وأنا'. This explains the shift in the word order of this Arabic expression بيني وبينكم to 'you and me' and not 'me and you'.

Here is the last exercise which highlights the use of the noun من,

" مَن يَهْدِ اللَّه فَهُوَ الْمُهْتَدِ." (*The qur'ān*, 18:17)

a.   "...**those people** God guides are rightly guided" (Haleem, p.184).

b.   "...**he** whom Allah guides is rightly guided" (Yūsuf 'Alī, p.344).

c.   "...**He** whom Allāh guides, he is the rightly guided" (al-Hilālī and Khan, p.387).

d.   "He whom God guides is the rightly guided one" (*my translation*).

2.6. Functionality of Arabic pronouns and certain nouns along with their English equivalence

Among the words in the SL that are problematic in translation, though they appear simple, are pronouns, demonstrative pronouns أسماء الإشارة, relative pronouns الأسماء الموصولة, interrogatives أسماء الاستفهام, and conditionals أسماء الشرط, compound nouns regarding numbers in particular and finally miscellaneous nouns which have certain functions in the SL. Their equivalence in the TL can be an issue or obstacle.

57

2.6.1. *Arabic Pronouns and their English equivalence*

Arabic pronouns are problematic when it comes to finding their equivalence, as there is the differentiation between singular, dual and plural pronouns as well as between their feminine and masculine forms in the SL. They are various types (see al-Rājiḥī, pp.35-47): separate or detached pronouns, connected (prefixed or suffixed) pronouns and latent pronouns, see the TL equivalence of such grammatical terms in Cachia (pp.57, 75, 43).

Here are few examples of the separate or detached pronouns with their equivalence,

1. أنا عربي.

I am an Arab. [*masculine*]

Incidentally, one cannot say 'Arabic' here, which is a common error when translating that word into English, as the word عربي refers to the nationality and identity and not to the language.

2. أنا عربية.

I am an Arab. [*feminine*]

3. أنت عربي.

You are an Arab. [*masculine*]

4. أنتما مخلصان.

a. **You <u>both</u>** are dedicated. [*masculine*]

b. **You <u>two</u>** are dedicated. [*masculine*]

Translation (a) and (b) are both appropriate.

5. أنتن مجدات.

You <u>all</u> are hardworking. [*feminine*]

6. إياه أقصد.

It is he I refer to.

7.   "إياك نعبد."

a. "**It is You** we worship' (Haleem, p.3).

b. "**You** do we worship" (Yūsuf ʿAlī, p.1).

c. "**You** (alone) we worship" (al-Hilālī and Khan, p.1).

Here the English equivalence of such detached pronouns is straightforward and requires no much effort, because these Arabic nouns are similar in function to those in English. Moreover, in Example 7, translation (a) is most appropriate, as it is communicative and more emphatic than the other two translations (b) and (c).

2.6.2. Pronominal suffixes or connected pronouns ضمائر متصلة with their relevant English equivalence

Pronominal suffixes or connected pronouns (Cachia, p.57) need to be identified in terms of their functional position in the SL, they are connected either to a noun, verb or particle, and can be either in the *nominative, accusative* or *genitive* case (al-Rājiḥī, p.37), so that the student or the professional translator knows whether the pronominal suffix in a sentence is acting as object, subject or predicate,

1.   زارنـي زيد.
Zayd visited **me**.

2.   زارك زيد.
Zayd visited **you**.

3.   زارنا زيد.
Zayd visited **us**.

4.   إنـه مجد.
He is hardworking.

5.   هذا كتابـي.
This is **my** book.

6. مررت بـهم.
I came **by them**.

7. هذا عملـك.
This is **your** work.

8. لولاك ما جئت.
It is **you** who have made me come.

Here in the last example, Example 8, the word لولا acts as a redundant semi-preposition and therefore can be deleted in the TL (English). This example can also be analysed as a conditional sentence to mean '**had it <u>not</u> been for you**, I would <u>not</u> have come' – the negative-negative format. Peter Newmark calls this 'double negatives'. He writes, "All double negatives have a possible 'strong' or 'weak' interpretation"; he then gives an example " 'not unworthy' may mean 'extremely worthy' or 'quite worthy' " (p.168). So in order to avoid confusion here one can keep double negatives in the TL as well, since they are in the SL. On occasions they can also be replaced with one positive when this stylistic feature is not intended in the original. Also, it is worth noting here Fischer's example about conditional clauses:

- "من نام عن حقهم لم أنم."
- 'If anyone overlooks what is due [to] him [*sic*], I shall not overlook it'
(Fischer, p.234).

Here are further examples of pronominal suffixes which need to be analysed in the SL before attempting to produce a target text,

9. عساني أن أفلح.
I may succeed.

10. عساك أن تبلغ المنى.
You may achieve your goal (or your objective).

11. عساها أن توفق.

She may succeed.

12.   إنك أنت خيرهم جميعاً.

You <u>are</u> the best of **them** all.

13.   المؤمن هو الذي يؤمن بالله.

The faithful is **the one** who believes in God.

14.   ظننته هو أحسنهم.

I reckoned (or thought) **he** <u>was</u> the best of **them**.

In Example 14, the ST gives emphasis on 'he', whilst the emphasis in the TT is demonstrated in the form of underlining the verb 'was'.

15.   قد قرب إليه الجيش الذي ظن أنه بعيد.

'The army was close to him when **he thought** it was far' (Fischer, p.219). (*my emphasis*)

In the following example the ST gives emphasis on 'he', and the emphasis in the TT is in the form of underlining the verb 'is' as well,

16.   زيد هو المجد.

Zayd <u>is</u> the hardworking person.

17.   ظننته زيدٌ كريم.

I thought **Zayd** was generous.

In Example 17, one must remember that the two objects to the verb ظن (I guessed/thought or surmised or reckoned) – 'him' mentioned in the ST; here the whole sentence 'Zayd was generous' in the ST acts as second object (al-Rājiḥī, p.42). But in the TT this is connotative and only one object in the form of the second clause is enough to serve this purpose. The same can be said about Examples 18 and 19,

18.   زيدٌ قام.

Zayd stood.

19.   هند قامت.

Hind stood.

Pronominal suffixes are often obvious as in the following,

20.   أحب وطنــي.
I love my country.

Another valid equivalence is I love '**my** *homeland*', or '**my** *fatherland*' if you are from Germany.

21.   نحب وطنـنا.
We love our country.

22.   كن صادقاً.
Be honest.

However, in Example 22 the pronominal suffix is unclear as it is in the imperative mode.

Here are few exercises that summarise points discussed above.

"وَكُنَّا **نَحْنُ** الْوَارِثِينَ." (*The qur'ān*, 28:58)
a. "We are the only heir" (Haleem, p.249).

b "And we are their heirs!" (Yūsuf 'Alī, p.476)

c. "And verily! We have been the inheritors" (al-Hilālī and Khan, p.524).

d. "And *We* have been the only heir" (*my translation*).

The only comment here is the mix with the tenses, in Arabic it is certainly the past which is linked to the present; and its equivalence is definitely the present perfect and not the present in English. Also, the detached pronoun نحن 'we' is used for emphasis indicated with the adverb 'verily' in translation (c); but it is italicised in translation (d) to reflect that emphasis more truthfully.

Here is another exercise,

"كُنتَ أَنتَ الرَّقِيبَ عَلَيْهِمْ." (The qur'ān, 5:117)

a. "You alone have been the watcher over them" (Haleem, p.79).

b. "You were the Watcher over them" (Yūsuf ʿAlī, p.140).

c. "You were the Watcher over them" (al-Hilālī and Khan, p.168).

d. "*You* have been the Watcher over them" (*my translation*)

Again the issue of connecting the past tense with the present tense as it is implied in the ST and needs to be conveyed. Also the emphasis demonstrated in the pronoun أنت which needs to be highlighted in the TT in the form of the italicised 'you'.

A further exercise is this,

"إن تُرَنِ أَنَا أَقَلَّ مِنكَ مَالًا وَوَلَدًا. فَعَسَى رَبِّي أَن يُؤْتِيَنِ خَيْرًا مِن جنتِـك." (The qur'ān, 18:39-40)

a. "Although you see I have less wealth and offspring than you, my Lord may well give me something better than your garden" (Haleem, p.186).

b. "If you do see me less than you in wealth and sons, It may be that my Lord will give me something better than your garden" (Yūsuf ʿAlī, p.348)

c. "If you see me less than you in wealth, and children, It may be that my Lord will give me something better than your garden" (al-Hilālī and Khan, p.390-91).

d. "If you see *me* less than you in wealth and children, then my Lord may give me something better than your garden" (*my translation*).

63

The comment here is about the use of إنْ which means 'if', but more importantly the use of the detached pronoun أنا which needs to be seen in the TT in the form of the italicised 'me' in translation (d).

" إِن كَانَ هَـذَا هُوَ الْحَقَّ مِنْ عِندِكَ." (*The qur'ān*, 8:32)
a. "if this really is the truth from You…" (Haleem, p.112).

b. "if this is indeed the Truth from You…" (Yūsuf 'Alī, p.203).

c. "If this (the Qur'ān) is indeed the truth (revealed) from You…" (al-Hilālī and Khan, p.235).

d. "If this has indeed been the Truth from You…" (*my translation*).

It is clear from the three translations (a), (b) and (c) that the emphasis implied in the pronoun هو is seen in the form of an English adverb 'really' or 'indeed'. A further point is that the past in the ST which implies also the present can only be conveyed in English using the present perfect tense, as we have seen before.

" (وما تُقدِّموا لأنفسِكم من خيرٍ تَجِدُوهُ عندَ اللـه هُوَ خَيْرًا وَأَعْظَمَ أَجْرًا." (*The qur'ān*, 73:20)
a. "(Whatever good you store up for yourselves) you will find with God, better and with a greater reward" (Haleem, p.396).

b. "(And whatever good you send forth for your souls) you shall find it in Allah's Presence - indeed, better and greater, in Reward" (Yūsuf 'Alī, p.743).

c. "(And whatever good you send before you for yourselves,) you will certainly find it with Allāh, better and greater in reward" (al-Hilālī and Khan, p.795).

d. "(And **whatever** good you send forth for yourselves,) you will **certainly** find it in the sight of God, good too and more greatly rewarded" (*my translation*).

One comment here is the detached pronoun هو 'it' which is used for emphasis in the ST, so its equivalence in English need to give that effect by using the adverb 'certainly. Also the pronominal pronoun in تجدوه is an object, and this needs to be identified syntactically before an appropriate equivalence is found. The collocational expression ما... من with the word ما meaning 'whatever' and the redundant preposition من what has no function in the ST, and therefore can certainly be deleted in the TT. Also, it is clear that the pronoun 'you' refers to the plural and not singular 'you' in Arabic, demonstrated in the reflective pronoun 'yourselves'. Further, the Arabic word خير 'good' is repeated for a purpose in the above holy verse; and that is, to imply that what is 'good will be good'. Also, another problematic expression is عند الله in Arabic which has various equivalence in English, because the preposition عند means, according to Ryding, either 'at', 'near', 'for', or 'in one's view' (p.399) but sometimes it means 'with' as in the above translations (a), (b) and (c). In fact, the most appropriate equivalence is 'in the sight of' to mean 'in the view of', which is used in other translations of that expression in Yūsuf 'Alī's version of the holy verse (2:262).

Going back to the use of the detached pronoun in Arabic, here is another exercise:

65

" قُلْ هُوَ اللـه أَحَدٌ." (*The qur'ān*, 112:1)

a. "Say, 'He is God the One' " (Haleem, p.444).

b. "Say: He is Allah, the One and Only" (Yūsuf 'Alī, p.814).

c. "Say (O Muhammad): 'He is Allāh, (the One)' " (al-Hilālī and Khan, p.854).

d. "Say, 'He *is* God, the One and Only' " (*my translation*).

Translation (d) is most appropriate, the reasons are:

- First, the emphasis implied in the pronoun هو used for emphasis, and its equivalence is in italicizing 'is'.

- The English collocation 'the one and only' is most appropriate.

- The use of a comma after the word 'Say' in English is more common than the use of the colon.

- The use of single inverted commas is necessary in English being a direct speech.

- God is the English equivalence being the One known to the target religious audience whether Christians or Jews.

Here is an exercise of the pronominal suffix,

" فَإِنَّهَا لَا تَعْمَى الْأَبْصَارُ وَلَكِنْ تَعْمَى الْقُلُوبُ الَّتِي فِي آلصدور." (*The qur'ān*, 22:46)
a. "It is not people's eyes that are blind, but their hearts within their breasts" (Haleem, p.212).

b. "Truly it is not their eyes that are blind, but their hearts which are in their breasts" (Yūsuf 'Alī, p.402).

c. "Verily, it is not the eyes that grow blind, but it is the hearts which are in the breasts that grow blind" (al-Hilālī and Khan, p.450).

d. "Verily, it is not their eyes that grow blind, but their hearts within their chests" (*my translation*).

Now it is vital to point out that the pronominal suffix in فإنها refers to 'the eyes' which need to be syntactically analysed. The ف is used for emphasis and translated into either 'verily' or 'truly'. Also, semantically the most appropriate English equivalence of the word صدور is 'chests' and not 'breasts', as the latter equivalence refers *only* to the female chest (as in the term 'breastfeeding') whereas the former includes both the male and female.

Here are in this exercise below a detached pronoun and two pronominal suffixes,

" نَحْنُ نَقُصُّ عَلَيْكَ نَبَأَهُم بِالْحَقِّ." (*The qur'ān*, 18:13)
a. "[Prophet], we shall tell you their story as it really was" (Haleem, p.183).

b. "We relate to you their story in truth" (Yūsuf 'Alī, p.343).

c. "We narrate unto you (O Muhammad) their story with truth" (al-Hilālī and Khan, p.386).

d. "*We* tell you their story truthfully" (*my translation*).

It is the pronoun نحن in the ST which is emphasized and needs to italicised the English equivalence 'we' as in translation (d). Both 'truthfully' and the collocation 'in truth' are good equivalence for بالحق as in translations (b) and (d); and they are both more appropriate than 'with truth' in translation (c).

Here is the final exercise in this set of exercises,

"بَلْ إِيَّاهُ تَدْعُونَ." " (*The qurʾān*, 6:41)

a. "No indeed, it is on Him that you would call" (Haleem, p.82).

b. "Nay-on Him would you call" (Yūsuf ʿAlī, p.146).

c. "Nay! To Him Alone you would call" (al-Hilālī and Khan, p.175).

d. "Nay! It is upon Him you would call" (*my translation*).

2.6.2. Demonstrative pronouns أسماء الإشارة *along with their equivalence*

Now having given examples about pronouns in their various cases in the ST

sentence, it is time to see how demonstrative pronouns are transferred in the TT

when they act as subject, predicate or object, and can also be used in the genitive

case (see al-Rājiḥī, pp.51-5). Here are few examples of these demonstrative

pronouns in the ST and their equivalence in the TT.

1.   ذا رجل (أو هذا رجل).
This is a man.

2.   ذي طالبة (أو هذه طالبة).
This is a student. [*feminine*]

3.   أولاء رجال (أو هؤلاء رجال).
These are men.

4.   ذاك زيد.
That is Zayd.

5.   ذلك زيد.
That is Zayd.

6.   أولئك رجال.
Those are men.

7.   أعجبني هذا اللاعب.
I liked **this** player.

8.   مررت بهؤلاء الرجال.

I came by **these** men.

9.   هَأنذا.

Here I am.

10.   هَأنتَ ذا (أو هَأنتِ ذي).

Here you are.

11.   "هَاأنتُمْ هَـؤُلاء جَادَلْتُمْ..." (*The qur'ān*, 4:109)

These demonstrative pronouns are self-explanatory in the above examples along with their equivalence.

Now here are few exercises about the demonstrative pronouns,

"تِلْكَ أُمَّةٌ قَدْ خَلَتْ". (*The qur'ān*, 2:134)

a. "That community passed away" (Haleem, p.15).

b. "That was a people that has passed away" (Yūsuf 'Alī, p.22).

c. "That was a nation who has passed away" (al-Hilālī and Khan, p.26).

d. "That was a nation which had passed away" (*my translation*).

The initial 'that' in all the translations above is clearly a demonstrative pronoun. It is advisable not to use the second 'that' the way Yūsuf 'Alī has done. Also, there are two clauses in the ST and that is not achieved in translation (a). Translation (b) has two issues the word 'people' and the present perfect tense in English which should be avoided. It is the past perfect tense implied in the ST in the use of 'قد' or just the simple past tense.

Here is another exercise,

"ذَلِكَ الْفَضْلُ مِنَ الـله". (*The qur'ān*, 4:70)

a. "**That** is God's favour" (Haleem, p.57).

b. "**Such** is the bounty from Allah" (Yūsuf 'Alī, p.98).

c. "**Such** is the Bounty from Allāh" (al-Hilālī and Khan, p.120).

d." **Such** bounty is from God" (*my translation*).

A rather problematic exercise is this one below,

" هَاأَنتُمْ هَـؤُلَاء جَادَلْتُمْ عَنْهُمْ فِي الْحَيَاةِ الدُّنْيَا." (*The qur'ān*, 4:109)
a. "**There you** [believers] **are**, arguing on their behalf in this life" (Haleem, p.61).

b. "Ah! **These** are the sort of men on whose behalf you may contend in this world" (Yūsuf 'Alī, p.105).

c. "Lo! You are **those** who have argued for them in the life of this world" (al-Hilālī and Khan, p.128).

d. "**Here you are**, arguing for **those** in this worldly life" (*my translation*).

Here it must be pointed out the problematic demonstrative pronoun هؤلاء meaning either 'these' (you the believers) or 'those' (they the betrayers). Now in translation (b) 'these' refers to the betrayers and in translation (c) 'those' refers to 'you'. Obviously, there is a huge difference between the two translation. This coherence issue is settled in translation (d), which clearly shows who is 'those'. Here it is the word هؤلاء is fronted for emphasis on those who are deceivers, sinners, or betrayers. And the pronominal suffix عنهم clearly shows the anaphoric reference to 'those' in the ST, and an interlinear translation would be 'Here you are, **those** you argued for **them** in this worldly

70

life'. This latter translation is grammatically unacceptable, that is why translation (d) is more appropriate.

Another exercise for demonstrative pronouns is the following holy verse,

" فَقَالُواْ هَـٰذَا لِلّهِ بِزَعْمِهِمْ وَهَـٰذَا لِشُرَكَآئِنَا." (The qur'ān, 6:136)

a. "They apportion to God... saying, 'This is for God – so they claim!- 'and this is for our idols.' " (Haleem, p.90).

b. "they say, according to their fancies: 'This is for Allah, and this-for our 'partners' "! (Yūsuf 'Alī, p.161).

c. "they say: 'This is for Allāh according to their claim, and this is for our (Allāh's so-called) partners' " (al-Hilālī and Khan, p.193).

Now here 'this' is straightforward and show no complication. The closer is translation (a) for the use of 'idols', though the surface meaning is 'partners' which is demonstrated in translations (b) and (c).

Finally, here is a further example of demonstrative pronouns,

" أُوْلَـئِكَ هُمُ الْخَاسِرُونَ." (The qur'ān, 2:27)

a. "these are the losers" (Haleem, p.6).

b. "these cause loss (only) to themselves" (Yūsuf 'Alī, p.5).

c. "it is they who are the losers" (al-Hilālī and Khan, p.7).

d. "these are the losers" (my translation).

71

The implied emphasis in the ST is clearly shown in the pronoun هم 'they' and is only felt in translations (c) and (d); but in (c) the omission of the demonstrative pronoun has made it weaker, compared to translation (d). Also, one can give an exegetic translation, i.e. "**these** *are* the ones who are the losers" and that way translation (d) becomes more compact, and compactness and clarity are essential in translation.

Having finished with demonstrative pronouns and how one can translate them in different contexts, it is time to discuss how to find equivalence to relative pronouns.

2.6.3. Relative pronouns الأسماء الموصولة *in the SL and their equivalence*

In the SL these pronouns change depending on the subject or object and can be singular, dual or plural and can also be in the feminine and masculine modes (al-Rājiḥī, p.51), but their equivalence is still the same 'who' regardless of the status of the subject. This point is elaborated in the following examples, that has 'who' in the TL but in the SL the relative pronoun is constantly changing, in accordance with what the subject or object is,

1.　　جاء اللذان نجحا.
The two who had succeeded came. [*dual and masculine*]

2.　　رأيت اللتين نجحتا.
I saw **the two who** had succeeded. [*dual and feminine*]

3. جاء الذي نجح. (أو جاء من نجح.)

The one who had succeeded came.

4. رأيت الذي نجح.

I saw **the one who** had succeeded.

5. مررت بالذي نجح.

I came by **the one who** had succeeded.

6. جاء الذين نجحوا.

The ones who had succeeded came.

7. رأيت اللائي نجحن.

I saw **the ones who** had succeeded. [*plural and feminine*]

8. رأيت من نجحا.

I saw **the two who** had succeeded.

9. مررت بمن نجحن.

I came by **the ones who** had succeeded. [*plural and feminine*]

10. سيفوز أيُّهم مجتهد.

Whoever is a hard worker, will win.

11. سأكافئ أيُّهم مجتهد.

I will reward **whoever** is a hard worker.

12. سنشيد بأيُّهم مجتهد.

We will praise **whoever** is a hard worker.

However, when the relative pronoun is referring to 'things' in the SL, it is ما and in this case the relative pronoun in the TL has a different equivalent – 'what', e.g.

لقد نفد ما عندنا اليوم.

What we have has run out.

Incidentally, there seems to be some confusion with the use of two Arabic words which have two completely different meanings: نفد and نفذ.   Students and indeed few translators make a common mistake using of these two words instead of the other.   So this confusion must be clarified here. Unlike the Arabic word used in the example above which means 'to lack', 'run out' or 'be short of', the Arabic word نفذ

means 'to pierce through something' or 'to make a hole in something'. It is a common Arabic error even by native speakers of Arabic. Another common error, though a minor one and mostly related to pronunciation and to modern Arabic writing, is the incorrect use of the Arabic letter ض as ظ, a good example is the word أيضا or حفاضات which is colloquially mispronounced with the letter ظ. One would say مضبوط and not مظبوط as some people say in colloquial Arabic.

In short, it is clear that there are variations of the relative pronoun 'who' in the SL, but such variations have either 'who' or 'whoever' in the TL. But when the relative pronoun is referring to inanimate objects, or fauna and flora, and in that case the word 'what' or 'which' is the equivalence and at times 'that' – depending how far the relative pronoun in the TL is from its referent.

Here are few exercises which might be helpful to further understand how to find equivalence to relative pronouns.

" وَلَهُ مَن فِي السَّمَاوَاتِ وَالْأَرْضِ وَمَنْ عِندَهُ لَا يَسْتَكْبِرُونَ عَنْ عِبَادَتِهِ." (The qur'ān, 21:19)
a. "Everyone in the heavens and earth belongs to Him, and those **that** are with Him are never too proud to worship Him, nor do they grow weary;" (Haleem, p.204).

b. "To Him belong all (creatures) in the heavens and on earth: even those **who** are in His (very) Presence are not too proud to serve Him, nor are they (ever) weary (of His service): [sic]" (Yūsuf 'Alī, p.384).

c. "To Him belongs **whosoever** is in the heavens and on earth. And those **who** are near Him (i.e. the angels) are not too proud to worship

Him, nor are they weary (of His worship)" (al-Hilālī and Khan, p.431).

d. "To Him belong all those **who** are in the heavens and on earth, and even those **who** are in His Presence are not too arrogant to worship Him" (*my translation*).

It is essential to delve deeper into the meaning of the ST before attempting to produce the TT. All translations above are variations on the same theme, but to pay more attention the SL syntax is to stick to translation (d). Note that sometimes the choice of one word makes a different at the lexical and semantic level, e.g. the adjective 'arrogant' in translation (d), and 'to be arrogant' has a negative effect which is not found in the adjective 'proud', and 'to be proud' which has a positive effect. The TL former corresponds in its negativity to the SL verb يستكبرون.

"مَا عِندَكُمْ يَنفَدُ وَمَا عِندَ اللّـهِ بَاقٍ." (*The qur'ān*, 16:96)
a. "**What** you have runs out but **what** God has endures" (Haleem, p.172).

b. "**What** is with you must vanish: **what** is with Allah will endure" (Yūsuf 'Alī, p.322).

c. "**Whatever** is with you, will be exhausted, and **whatever** is with Allāh (of good deeds) will remain" (al-Hilālī and Khan, p.362).

d. "**All** you have will run out, but **all** God has will endure" (*my translation*).

Now the use of ما and its equivalence are exhausted in the first chapter of this book; and all translations (a-d) are therefore acceptable.

75

However, the contrast or juxtaposition clearly highlighted in using the comma and the interjection 'but' in translation (d) and the use of tenses present and future may make this translation stand out.

Another exercise that is related to relative pronouns in Arabic and their English equivalence is,

" أَفَمَن يَعْلَمُ أَنَّمَا أُنزِلَ إِلَيْكَ مِن رَبِّكَ الْحَقُّ كَمَنْ هُوَ أَعْمَى." (*The qur'ān*, 13:19)

a. "Can someone **who** knows that the revelation from your Lord is the Truth be equal to someone **who** is blind [to it]?" (Haleem, p.155).

b. "Is then one **who** does know that that which has been revealed unto you from your Lord is the Truth, like one **who** is blind?" (Yūsuf 'Alī, p.288).

c. "Shall he then **who** knows that what has been revealed unto you (O Muhammad) from your Lord is the truth be like him **who** is blind?" (al-Hilālī and Khan, p.323).

d. "Can the person, **who** knows what your Lord reveals to you is the Truth, be equal to the one **who** is ignorant?" (*my translation*).

Now in translation (b) the use of two 'thats' makes the syntax rather awkward, though the sense is still understood. In translation (d) the Arabic word أعمى cannot be translated here as 'blind'; the reason is that the juxtaposition is clear between the person who is informed and knowledgeable to that who is ignorant and not blind. However, translation (a) hits the bull's eye when it has the addition 'to it' which clears that ambiguity.

Here is another exercise using relative pronouns.

" ثُمَّ لَنَنزِعَنَّ مِن كُلِّ شِيعَةٍ أَيُّهُمْ أَشَدُّ عَلَى الرَّحْمَنِ عِتِيًّا." (*The qur'ān*, 19:69)

a. "We shall seize out of each group those **who** were most disobedient towards the Lord of Mercy" (Haleem, p.194).

b. "Then shall We certainly drag out from every sect all those **who** were worst in obstinate rebellion against (Allah) Most Gracious" (Yūsuf ʿAlī, p.365).

c. "Then indeed We shall drag out from every sect all those **who** were worst in obstinate rebellion against the Most Gracious (Allāh)" (al-Hilālī and Khan, p.410).

d. "Then We will remove from each and every sect those **who** is most recalcitrant to the Most Merciful" (*my translation*).

Obviously, the relative pronoun 'who' is seen to in all translations above. Unlike the other translations here, translation (d) shows how important the choice of equivalent words to the Arabic word عتيا 'recalcitrant' is. Also, the use of 'will' instead of 'shall' must not be ignored, when 'shall' is usually used with the pronoun 'we' in the future tense; this is to refer to the certainty of the action. Finally, the English expression 'each and every' is used in translation (d) to refer to every single sect or group.

Here is another exercise about relative pronouns to show how their equivalence is found in practical terms,

"هُوَ الَّذِي جَعَلَ لَكُمُ اللَّيْلَ لِتَسْكُنُواْ فِيهِ وَالنَّهَارَ مُبْصِرًا." (*The qurʾān*, 10:67)
a. "It is He **who** made the night so that you can rest in it and the daylight so that you can see" (Haleem, p.133).

b. "He it is **that** has made you the Night that you may rest therein, and the Day to make things visible (to you)" (Yūsuf ʿAlī, p.244).

77

c. "He it is **Who** has appointed for you the night that you may rest therein, and the day to make things visible (to you)" (al-Hilālī and Khan, p.280).

d. "He is the One **Who** has made the night for you to rest therein, and the day to see things" (*my translation*).

A further exercise is this,

"أَلَمْ يَأْتِهِمْ نَبَأُ الَّذِينَ مِن قَبْلِهِمْ." (*The qur'ān*, 9:70)
a. "Have they never heard the stories about their predecessors" (Haleem, p.122).

b. "Has not the story reached them of those before them?" (Yūsuf 'Alī, p.222).

c. "Has not the story reached them of those before them?" (al-Hilālī and Khan, p.255).

d. "Have they not heard the story about those **who** were before them?" (*my translation*).

A final exercise is the following,

"وَاتْلُ عَلَيْهِمْ نَبَأَ الَّذِي آتَيْنَاهُ آيَاتِنَا." (*The qur'ān*, 7:175)
a. "[Prophet], tell them the story of the man to **whom** We gave Our messages:" (Haleem, p.107).

b. "Relate to them the story of the man **whom** We sent Our Signs" (Yūsuf 'Alī, p.194).

c. "And recite (O Muhammad) to them the story of him to **whom** We gave Our Ayāt (proofs, evidences, verses, lessons, signs, revelations etc.)" (al-Hilālī and Khan, p.226).

d. "And relate to them the story of the man to **whom** We revealed Our verses (messages)" (*my translation*).

Now having covered some aspects of relative pronouns in Arabic and how they are translated into English within various contexts. It is time to discuss verbal nouns and their English equivalence.

2.6.4. Verbal nouns أسماء الأفعال and their English equivalence

Verbal nouns in the SL are usually used as commands (in the imperative), or in the present or past tense (al-Rājiḥī, pp.56-8), they are nouns acting as verbs, but their equivalence is usually an utterance, as in the following examples:

1. صه يا علي. (بمعنى أصمت)
Shush, Ali! (Meaning, Be quiet!)

2. آمين (بمعنى استجب)
Amen! (Meaning, Please ask my prayer!)

3. حيّ على الصلاة (بمعنى أقبل)
Come to prayer.

4. هيّا. (بمعنى أسرع)
Hurry! (Meaning, Go quickly!)

5. هلمّ. (بمعنى اقترب)
Closer! (Meaning, Come closer.)

6. عليك الصدق. (بمعنى إلزم)
Be honest.

7. إليك عني. (بمعنى ابتعد)
Away from me! (Keep away!)

8. أمامك. (بمعنى تقدّم)
Ahead! (Meaning, Go ahead!)

9. وراءك. (بمعنى تأخر)
Back!
OR: **Behind**! (Meaning, Stay behind!)

10. مكانك. (بمعنى اثبت)

Steady! (Meaning, Stay where you are.)

OR: **Freeze!**

11.   حذارٍ من الكلبِ. (بمعنى إحذر)

Beware of the dog! (Be careful of the dog!)

12.   رويدك. (بمعنى تمهل) على رِسْلِك.

Easy!

OR: **Slow!**

13.   شتان. (بمعنى افترق)

Huge difference!

Another similar example is,

شتان الجدُّ والإهمالُ. (Fischer, 2000)

There is **huge** (or massive) **difference between** working hard and negligence.

Fischer uses the equivalent 'how unlike', but in his example he uses 'how different': شتان الطامع واليائس 'how different are those who still have hope from those who have given up hope!' (p.140)   It is clear that such translation is exegetic; a more appropriate translation would be 'how different is the greedy from the desperate'; however, one cannot assess Fischer's translation as the book is mainly focussed on Arabic syntax and it is not a book on translation. Although the word 'between' is not used in the SL (Arabic), it must be inserted in the TL in order to correspond to the TL grammar.

14.   هيهاتَ للمهمل الفلاح. (بمعنى بَعُد)

The complacent person (or the negligent person) is **far from** succeeding.

15.   أفٍ. (بمعنى أتضجر)

Faugh!

OR: **Ugh!** (Meaning, to grumble or whine.)

To sum, the equivalence of these verbal nouns in the SL is an utterance, a preposition, phrase or phrasal verb in the TL. It all depends on the meaning of the verbal noun in the SL first – in Example 14, the equivalence is in the form of a prepositional or phrasal verb, 'to be far from'. Further, in most cases verbal nouns in the SL are used for exclamation; and their equivalence has become problematic, because its form in the TL varies between an utterance, a preposition, phrasal verb and phrase. The student or professional translator needs to understand fully the sense of the verbal noun, before attempting to find its equivalence.

Finally, here are exercises about verbal nouns and their English equivalence:

" يَا أَيُّهَا الَّذِينَ آمَنُواْ عَلَيْكُمْ أَنفُسَكُمْ لاَ يَضُرُّكُم مَّن ضَلَّ إِذَا اهْتَدَيْتُمْ."

(*The qur'ān*, 5:105)

a. "You who believe, **you are responsible for your own souls**; if anyone else goes astray it will not harm you so long as you follow the guidance" (Haleem, p.78).

b. "O you who believe! **Guard your own souls**: if you follow (right) guidance, no hurt can come to you from those who stray" (Yūsuf 'Alī, p.137).

c. "O you who believe! **Take care of your ownselves**. If you follow the (right) guidance [and enjoin what is right (Islāmic Monotheism and all that Islām orders one to do) and forbid what is wrong (polytheism, disbelief and all that Islām has forbidden)] no hurt can come to you from those who are in error" (al-Hilālī and Khan, p.165).

d. "O you who believe! **Care for your own souls**, and when you follow the (right) guidance, the misguided can never hurt you" (*my translation*).

Another exercise is here to see how Arabic verbal nouns are translated into English.

"قُلْ هَلُمَّ شُهَدَاءكُمُ." (*The qur'ān*, 6:150)
a. "Say, 'Bring your witnesses…' " (Haleem, p.92).

b. "Say: 'Bring forward your witnesses…' " (Yūsuf 'Alī, p.164).

c. "Say: 'Bring forward your witnesses, …' " (al-Hilālī and Khan, p.196).

"هَلُمَّ إِلَيْنَا." (*The qur'ān*, 33:18).
a. "Come and join us" (Haleem, p.267).

b. "Come along to us" (Yūsuf 'Alī, p.510).

c. "Come here towards us" (al-Hilālī and Khan, p.562).

Translation (b) is closest of this verbal noun هلم but the implied message is clearer in translation (a) in the context. Here is another exercise that has yet another verbal noun.

"هَيْهَاتَ هَيْهَاتَ لِمَا تُوعَدُونَ." (*The qur'ān*, 23:36)
a. "What you are promised is very far-fetched" (Haleem, p.216).

b. "Far, very far is that which you are promised" (Yūsuf 'Alī, p.410).

c. "Far, very far is that which you are promised" (al-Hilālī and Khan, p.458).

d. "Too far (to achieve) is what you have been promised" (*my translation*).

It is important to note that هيهات being repeated twice implies that such promises are never to be achieved, its equivalence 'too far' gives that exact meaning, for the negativity implied in that Arabic ST. Also, attention should be paid to tenses (present simple and present perfect tenses and not simple present throughout the whole verse.

Here is the final exercise that shows how the Arabic verbal noun is translated into English.

"فَلاَ تَقُل لَّهُمَآ أُفٍّ وَلاَ تَنْهَرْهُمَا." (*The qur'ān*, 17:23)

a. "say no word that shows impatience with them, and do not be harsh with them" (Haleem, p.176).

b. "say not to them a word of contempt, nor repel them" (Yūsuf ʿAlī, p.330).

c. "say not to them a word of disrespect, nor shout at them" (al-Hilālī and Khan, p.371).

d. "Never express a word of grumble to them, nor reproach them" (*my translation*).

Another translation, though quite literal, is "do not say to them 'Faugh!' nor reproach them".

Now having finished with Arabic verbal nouns and their English equivalence, it is time to see how interrogatives in Arabic are translated into English.

2.6.5. *Interrogatives* أسماء الاستفهام *and their TL equivalence*

Interrogatives in the SL are translated in a simple way, with one-to-one equivalence. Here are various interrogatives with their counterparts in the TL,

1.   أيُ رجلٍ جاء؟

Which man came?

2.   أيُ كتابٍ قرأت؟

Which book you read?

3.   مَن جاء؟

Who came?

4.   مَن رأيت اليوم؟

Who did you see today?

5.   أبو مَن هذا؟

Whose father is this?

6.   ما هذا؟

What is this?

7.   ما فعلتَ اليوم؟

What did you do today?

8.   لِمَ فعلتَ هذا؟

Why did you do this?

9.   بِمَ تحفر البئر؟

With what do you drill the well?

OR: **What** do you drill the well **with**?

The difference between the two translations here is merely in the style, with the first translation being more formal. And the same can be said of the following example about the use of preposition at the start of the question or at the end of it, as that preposition is used with that verb in both the SL and the TL. It is worth noting here that prepositions are always attached to the interrogative in the SL, Arabic, and cannot be shifted to the end of the question the way they can in the TL.

10.   عَمَّ تسأل؟

What are you asking **about**?

Here are further interrogatives in the SL which have straightforward equivalence

in the TL:

11.   ماذا في يدك؟

What is in your hand?

12.   أين ذهب زيد؟

Where did Zayd go?

13.   متى جاء عليّ؟

When did Ali come?

14.   متى السفر؟

When do you travel?

15.   أيان تسافر؟

When will you travel?

With the interrogative 'when' in the SL that has more than one equivalence, it

can be slightly problematic as in Example 15, which refers more to the future and

that needs to be shown in the TL. So interrogatives are only problematic, when

they are polysemous in the SL but their equivalence in the TL is the same, that is

when the interrogative has more than one equivalence in the SL, as in the case of

the interrogative 'how' where its equivalence can be either كيف or كم, this is clear

in examples 16-24 below,

16.   كيف أنت؟

How are you?

17.   كيف جئت؟

How did you arrive?

It is vital to point out that countable and uncountable nouns in the TL have a certain grammatical rule, the former requires 'much' to refer to the amount or quantity as in examples 18 and 24 below, and the latter requires 'many' as in examples 19-23 below,

18. كم مالك؟

How **much** money do you have?

19. كم طالباً حضر؟

How **many** students were present?

20. كم ساعة قرأت؟

How **many** hours did you read?

21. كم ميلاً سرت؟

How **many** miles did you walk?

22. كم ضربة ضربته؟

How **many** punches did you hit him?

23. كم كتاباً قرأت؟

How **many** books did you read?

24. بكم قرشٍ اشتريته؟

How **much** did you buy it **for**?

Again, as in examples 9 and 10 above, the preposition in Example 24 comes immediately before the interrogative word 'how', whilst in the TL it must be put at the end. To sum up, the TL equivalence of any SL interrogative is more or less straightforward and should not be problematic.

Here are some exercises to see how Arabic interrogatives are dealt with in order to find their English equivalence.

"عَمَّ يَتَسَاءلُونَ." (*The qur'ān*, 78:1)

a. "**What** do they question…?" (Haleem, p.405).

b. "Concerning **what** are they disputing?" (Yūsuf 'Alī, p.758)

c. "**What** are they asking (one another) about?" (al-Hilālī and Khan, p.809).

It is clear that all English translations above are straightforward with regards to the interrogative form in Arabic and how its equivalent in English. Incidentally, the only issue is the use of tenses either continuous or simple present; the present continuous tense in English is certainly most appropriate in the above exercise, as it is more natural in English to have it in this context that to have the simple present tense.

Here is another exercise where the interrogative is used in Arabic and needs an appropriate equivalence in English.

" قُل لِّمَن مَّا فِي السَّمَاوَاتِ وَالأَرْضِ قُل لِلَّهِ." (*The qur'ān*, 6:12)
a. "Say, 'To **whom** belongs **all that** is in the heavens and earth?' " (Haleem, p.81).

b. "Say, 'To **whom** belongs **all that** is in the heavens and on earth?' " (Yūsuf 'Alī, p.142).

c. "Say (O Muhammad): 'To **whom** belongs **all that** is in the heavens and the earth?' " (al-Hilālī and Khan, p.170).

All three translations show how the interrogative 'whom' is used in English as an equivalent to the Arabic one. Further, note the use of ما which is discussed earlier in this book. It is vital to point out here that translation (b) is the most appropriate here because it has followed the

87

TL grammar with the use of two different prepositions: one for 'the heavens' and the other for 'earth'.

Here is a more complex exercise with two Arabic interrogatives and their English equivalence.

" أَفَلَا يَنظُرُونَ إِلَى الْإِبِلِ كَيْفَ خُلِقَتْ." (*The qur'ān*, 88:17)

a. "Do the disbelievers not see how rain clouds are formed" (Haleem, p.419) [Haleem explains that rain clouds is the best equivalence for إبل; now this matches Maulana's translation of the same holy verse: "See they not the clouds, how they are created"].

b. "Do they not look at the Camels, how they are made?" (Yūsuf 'Alī, p.783).

c. "Do they not look at the camels, how they are created?" (al-Hilālī and Khan, p.832).

d. "Why do they not see **how** camels are created?" (*my translation*).

As for the interrogatives here they are clear and their equivalence in English is also straightforward. Furthermore, as there is a discrepancy among the first three translations (a), (b) and (c) here with regards to the word إبل. Although one can see the context as Haleem is suggesting about the word إبل which could mean 'cloud', but it is the verb خلقت 'to create'. Perhaps the reference here is to the process of reproduction, rather to the formation of clouds; this could be one interpretation. Incidentally, the use of 'the' before 'camels' violates the TL grammar in translations (b) and (c); as the implication is that it is referring to camels in general. Also, it is the use of the Arabic letter ف in أفلا تنظرون, which requires the use of the interrogative 'why' and not simply use the simple form of question 'do they not look' or 'do the believers not see'. This particular element or characteristic is clearer in the following much more complex exercise. This one also uses two different interrogatives in Arabic, let us see how their equivalence looks like.

" قُلْ مَن رَّبُّ السَّمَاوَاتِ وَالأَرْضِ قُلِ اللّـهُ قُلْ أَفَاتَّخَذْتُم مِّن دُونِهِ أَوْلِيَاء لاَ يَمْلِكُونَ لأَنفُسِهِمْ نَفْعًا وَلاَ ضَرًّا.ًا" (*The qur'ān*, 13:16).

a. "Say [Prophet], '**Who** is Lord of the heavens and the earth?' Say, 'God.' Say, '**Why** do you take protectors other than Him, **who** can neither benefit nor harm even themselves?' (Haleem, p.154).

b. "Say: '**Who** is the Lord and Sustainer of the heavens and the earth?' Say: "(It is) Allah.' Say: '**Do** you then take (or worship) protectors other than Him, such as have no power either for good or for harm to themselves?' " (Yūsuf 'Alī, pp.287-88).

c. "Say (O Muhammad): '**Who** is the Lord of the heavens and the earth?' Say: '(It is) Allāh.' Say: '**Have** you then taken (for worship) *Auliyā* (protectors) other than Him, such as have no power either for benefit or for harm to themselves?' " (al-Hilālī and Khan, p.322).

Also, the interrogative 'why' is most appropriate in this translation; it is the equivalence to ف in أفاتخذتم. So every detail counts in the SL and the TL. It is clear that the choice of the interrogative counts. In the other two translations (b) and (c), the second question 'do you then take' or 'have you then taken' is not as effective as the inquisitive 'why' in the first translation above by Haleem. Translation (a) is also most interesting as it uses the word 'who' in English twice, with two different functions, the second time is obviously not as interrogative but as relative pronoun.

89

But, unlike the ف used in the above two exercises, the use of ف in the following exercise is totally different as it implies either the English conjunction 'and' or 'so'.

"فَبِأَيِّ حَدِيثٍ بَعْدَهُ يُؤْمِنُون." (*The qur'ān*, 7:185)

a. **"What** [other revelation] will they believe in if they do not believe in this?" (Haleem, p.107)

b. **"In what** Message after this will they then believe?" (Yūsuf 'Alī, p.195)

c. **"In what** Message after this will they then believe?" (al-Hilālī and Khan, p.228)

The equivalence in English in the above exercise is also clear with regards to the use of the interrogative. Here is another exercise which has two questions.

"يَسْأَلُونَكَ عَنِ السَّاعَةِ أَيَّانَ مُرْسَاهَا. فِيمَ أَنتَ مِن ذِكْرَاهَا." (*The qur'ān*, 79:42-43)

a. "They ask you [Prophet] about the Hour, saying, '**When** will it arrive?', but **how** can you tell [them] that?" (Haleem, p.408)

b. "They ask you about the Hour – '**When** will be its appointed time?' **Wherein** are you (concerned) with the declaration thereof?" (Yūsuf 'Alī, p.763)

c. "They ask you (O Muhammad) about the Hour – **when** will be its appointed time? You have no knowledge to say anything about it" (al-Hilālī and Khan, p.814).

Given the analysis done on the interrogative before, it is clear which of the three professional translators is using them which is not. Translation (a) here has certainly succeeded in its syntactic analysis of the ST, and the TT is definitely most appropriate.

Finally, here is the final exercise to finish off this part about interrogatives and their English equivalence.

" وَيَقُولُونَ مَتَى هَـٰذَا الْوَعْدُ إِن كُنتُمْ صَادِقِينَ." (*The qur'ān*, 10:48)

a. "They ask, '**When** will this promise be fulfilled, if **what** you say is true?' " (Haleem, p.132)

b. "They say: '**When** will this promise come to pass – if you speak the truth?' " (Yūsuf 'Alī, p.214)

c. "And they say: '**When** will be this promise (the torment or the Day of Resurrection), if you speak the truth?' " (al-Hilālī and Khan, p.277)

Again there is close similarity in the interrogative form among all translations here, but it is worth noting that translation (a) is most appropriate; however, it must be noted that 'what' is the relative pronoun there and not an interrogative.

Having talked about interrogatives and their equivalence in English in this part, it is time to move conditionals.

2.6.6. *Conditionals* أسماء الشرط *and their equivalence*
Conditionals are used in conditional sentences in the SL and their TL equivalence has similar function. Here are few examples along with their equivalence to demonstrate this point here,

1. إِنْ زيد جاء فأكرمه.
If Zayd comes, treat him in a hospitable manner.
2. إِمّا تـرَ زيداً فأكرمه.

91

When you see Zayd, treat him in a hospitable manner.

3.   أيُّ رجلٍ يعملْ خيراً يجدْ جزاءه.

Any man, who does a good deed, gets his reward.

4.   مَن يذاكرْ ينجحْ.

Whoever revises his studies (well), will succeed.

Here it is clear that the 'whoever' is referring to students in the SL, that is why the phrase 'his studies' is added in the TL, in order to clarify the meaning accurately.   Addition here is vital in order to help convey the message fully. James Dickins refers to this feature in one's translation as a necessary tool at times and calls it 'exegetic translation' as opposed to 'gist translation' which gives the gist of the text (pp.9-10,24).

5.   مَن تصادقْ أصادقه.

Whoever you make friends with, will also be my friend.

6.   مهما تعمل يعلمه الـلـه.

God know **whatever** you do.

7.   متى تأتِ أكرمْك.

Whenever you come, I will treat you in a hospitable manner.

Incidentally, the particle كلما here can also be used. It is worth noting that there is a common error by translators, they repeat the particle twice in the same sentence; this happens due to the fact that in English one says 'the more... the more' as in this SL example (Arabic) by Fischer (2002, p.235): ' كان كلما أكثرَ كان أجودَ كلاماً [sic] (obviously a printing error regarding the word order, the sentence should read   كلما كان أكثرَ كلاماً كان أجودَ). And its TL equivalence is, '**The more** he spoke, **the better** he got.' So, unlike in English, in Arabic كلما is never repeated in the same sentence.

8.   أيانَ تأتِ أكرِمْك.

Whenever you come (in the future), I will treat you in a hospitable manner.

9.   أين يذهبْ يحترمْه الناس.

Wherever he goes, people show respect to him.

10.   أنّى تأتِه تأتِ رجلاً كريماً.

Whenever you go to him, you find him hospitable.

Also in Example 11 on a higher level of analysis and production of translation, which focuses on the meaning and not just merely on the transfer of words from one language to another, the interesting point to raise here is that in the SL the verb used in both clauses is the same, but in the TL two different verbs are used, otherwise the translation would have been 'awkward' structure and style. It is weird to say in English, 'whenever you go to him, you go to a generous man'; this translation would have been too literal as well.

11.   حيثما يذهبْ يجدْ صديقاً.

Wherever he goes, he makes friends.

12.   إذا جاء زيد فأكرمه.

If Zayd comes, treat him in a hospitable manner.

It is clear that these conditionals in the SL are no different in their function from those in the TL, but can be problematic when the sense is not well understood.

Here are few exercises that help to understand how to use conditionals in Arabic along with their English equivalence.

" وَإن تَعُودُواْ نَعُدْ." (*The qur'ān*, 8:19)

a. "**If** you return, so shall We" (Haleem, p.111).

b. "**if** you return (to the attack), so shall We" (Yūsuf 'Alī, p.201).

93

c. "and **if** you return (to the attack), so shall We return" (al-Hilālī and Khan, p.233).

Another exercise is the following.

"مَن يَعْمَلْ سُوءًا يُجْزَ بِهِ." (*The qur'ān*, 4:123)
a. "anyone who does wrong will be requited for it" (Haleem, p.62).

b. "whoever works evil will be requited accordingly" (Yūsuf 'Alī, p.107).

c. "whosoever works evil, will have the recompense thereof" (al-Hilālī and Khan, p.130).

d. "whoever does an evil deed, will be recompensed for it" (*my translation*).

All translations (a-d) have used the conditional forms, as they are in the STs. Another exercise that has a conditional form or structure is the following,

"أَيْنَمَا تَكُونُواْ يُدْرِككُّمُ الْمَوْتُ." (*The qur'ān*, 4:78)
a. "Death will overtake you **no matter where you may be**" (Haleem, p.58).

b. "**Wherever you are**, death will find you out" (Yūsuf 'Alī, p.99)

c. "**Wheresoever you may be**, death will overtake you" (al-Hilālī and Khan, p.121).

d. "**Wherever you are**, death will find you" (*my translation*).

Translation (a) has fronted the second part of the conditional sentence unnecessarily. Translation (b) the preposition 'out' is redundant. In

94

translation (c) the verb 'to overtake' seems unusual, whereas translation (d) is simple but serves the purpose of the SL.

A further exercise about conditionals in Arabic and their equivalence in English is the following,

" إلاَّ تَفْعَلُوهُ تَكُن فِتْنَةٌ فِي الأَرْض وفَسَادٌ كَبِير." (*The qur'ān*, 8:73)

a. "**If you do not do the same**, there will be persecution in the land and great corruption" (Haleem, p.115).

b. "**unless you do this**, (protect each other), there would be tumult and oppression on earth and great mischief" (Yūsuf 'Alī, p.209).

c. "(and) **if you** (Muslims of the whole world collectively) **do not do so** [i.e. become allies, as one united block under one *Khalifah* (a chief Muslim ruler for the whole Muslim world) to make victorious Allāh's religion of Islāmic Monotheism], there will be *Fitnah* (wars, battles, polytheism) and oppression on the earth" (al-Hilālī and Khan, p.241).

d. "**If you do not act in the same way** (protect each other), there will be sedition in the land and grave corruption" (*my translation*).

All these four translation fulfil the conditional form of the sentence in both Arabic and English. In addition, the word الأرض is not necessarily 'earth', as there is no juxtaposition between the heavens and earth, but rather referring to a certain place, that is why the phrase 'in the land' is more appropriate. Also, the choice of words is the difference among all these translations, and the use of words such as 'sedition' or 'persecution' or the loan word 'Fitnah' merely transliterated and then explained. Translation (c) is certainly exegetic, and is helpful only for those who are after paraphrasing method when translation. But it must be noted that, unlike the adjective 'great' with its positive effect which is not the one intended in the ST, the adjective 'grave' gives the same effect intended, by conveying the same negativity felt in the ST.

Here is another exercise which shows how the Arabic conditional sentence is conveyed in its English equivalence.

" وَمَا يَفْعَلُواْ مِنْ خَيْرٍ فَلَن يُكْفَرُوْهُ." (The qur'ān, 3:115)
a. "and they will not be denied [the reward] for **whatever good deeds they do**" (Haleem, p.43).

b. "**Of the good that they do**, nothing will be rejected of them" (Yūsuf 'Alī, p.71).

c. "**And whatever good they do**, nothing will be rejected of them" (al-Hilālī and Khan, p.90).

The last exercise about the conditional sentence in Arabic and its English equivalence is this,

" إِمَّا يَبْلُغَنَّ عِندَكَ الْكِبَرَ أَحَدُهُمَا أَوْ كِلاَهُمَا فَلاَ تَقُل لَّهُمَآ أُفٍّ." (The qur'ān, 17:23)
a. "**If** either or both of them reach old age with you, **say no word** that shows impatience with them" (Haleem, p.176).

b. "Whether one or both of them attain old age in your life, **say not** to them a word of contempt" (Yūsuf 'Alī, p.330).
c. "**If** one of them or both of them attain old age in your life, **say not** to them a word of disrespect" (al-Hilālī and Khan, p.371).
d. "**If** either of them or they both reach old age during your lifetime, **never express** a word of grumble to them, nor reproach them" (*my translation*).

So the conditional sentence in Arabic may have its English

equivalence with the use of 'if' or not, depending on the context as seen above in translation (b). Having now covered the conditional SL sentence and its English equivalence it is time to see what is the English equivalence of compound nouns for certain numbers.

2.6.7. Compound nouns for certain numbers and their English equivalence

There are certain compound nouns in the SL mainly numbers from 11 to 19 whose equivalence is not necessarily under the same category syntactically, as in the following:

1. جاء أحدَ عشرَ رجلاً.
Eleven men came.

2. جاء اثنا عشرَ رجلاً.
Twelve men came.

3. مررت باثنتي عشرةَ بنتاً.
I came by **twelve** girls.

4. رأيت أربعة عشرَ رجلاً.
I saw **fourteen** men.

5. مررت بخمسَ عشرةَ بنتاً.
I came by **fifteen** girls.

Interestingly is to see the translation of the number 'billion' as 'بليار' (See Ryding, p.353) as in the example by Ryder, 'بليوني دولار' with its equivalence 'two billion dollars'; or her example 'بنحو ثلاثة بلايين دولار' (Ryding, p.395). However, 'مليار' is more common in Arabic and should be referred to more – i.e. ملياري دولار' or
'بنحو ثلاثة مليارات'.

It is clear that there is huge difference in the SL, but no difference at all in the TL with regard to the usage of these numbers for masculine

97

and feminine. This needs to be taken care of swhen producing their equivalence. But these so-called 'compound nouns in the SL are not limited to these numbers but also some adverbial phrases for time and place that are considered as compound nouns in the SL, and therefore are problematic in the TL, as in the following examples:

6.   فلان يأتينا صباحَ مساءَ.

Mr. So-and-So visits us **in the morning and evening** (or daily).

7.   فلان ينهج في حياته بينَ بينَ.

Mr. So-and-So's lifestyle is just **ok** (or **really 50-50**).

8.   فلان جاري بيتَ بيتَ.

Mr. So-and-So is my neighbour **next door**.

In short, it is vital to point out that these compound nouns for certain numbers in the SL do not correspond to those in the TL in category; what is known as compound nouns in the TL are completely different and have different functions altogether, but we are not here to explain this grammatical feature in the TL as the basis of this chapter is to discuss the structure and functionality of the SL, not the TL.

Here are few exercises about how compound nouns for certain numbers in Arabic are seen in their English equivalence.

" إِنِّي رَأَيْتُ أَحَدَ عَشَرَ كَوْكَبًا." (*The qur'ān*, 12:4)

a. "I have dreamt of **eleven** stars" (Haleem, p.145).

b. "I did see **eleven** stars" (Yūsuf 'Alī, p.268).

c. "I saw (in a dream) **eleven** stars" (al-Hilālī and Khan, p.304).

d. "I did dream of **eleven** planets" (*my translation*).

It is important to point out that such numbers are compound nouns in Arabic but not so in English. These compound nouns for certain numbers in some cases correspond to the masculine/feminine noun which has been modified.

Another interesting point in question, though incidental here in this discussion, is the noun that comes after these numbers in the above holy verse, which is the noun كوكب that can never be a 'star' but rather a 'planet'. Now it is common knowledge that planets are كواكب and stars are نجوم; and the difference between them is massive. In astronomy, planets like the moon reflect light while stars are the source of light like the sun. And the ST talks about planets and not stars.

Another exercise about compound nouns for certain numbers is the following,

" فَانفَجَرَتْ مِنْهُ اثْنَتَا عَشْرَةَ عَيْناً." (The qur'ān, 2:60)
a. "**Twelve** springs gushed out" (Haleem, p.9).

b. "Then gushed forth therefrom **twelve** springs" (Yūsuf 'Alī, p.10).

c. "Then gushed forth therefrom **twelve** springs" (al-Hilālī and Khan, p.13).

d. "From that (rock) twelve springs gushed out" (*my translation*).

This exercise shows that in the ST the word 'spring' is feminine that is why the compound noun for the number 'twelve' is also feminine,

99

whereas in the earlier exercise the word 'planet' is masculine in Arabic with its compound noun for the number 'eleven' is also masculine. However, in the TT (English) such masculine/feminine distinction is not essential, as these numbers are 'neutral' in English.

The final exercise also shows how the Arabic compound noun for certain numbers is translated into English, but this time with the number 'nineteen'.

"عَلَيْهَا تِسْعَةَ عَشَرَ." (*The qur'ān*, 74:30)
a. "There are **nineteen** in charge of it" (Haleem, p.396).

b. "Over it are **Nineteen**" (Yūsuf 'Alī, p.745).

c. "Over it are **nineteen** (angels as guardians and keepers of Hell)" (al-Hilālī and Khan, p.797).

d. "It (the Fire) is run by **nineteen** (angels)" (*my translation*).

The Arabic number 'nineteen' is a compound noun for the word 'angels' who are masculine, and whose compound noun must be different, i.e. feminine. But such details about the femininity or masculinity of these Arabic compound nouns for certain numbers are unnecessary to be there in the English equivalence.

2.6.8. *Miscellaneous nouns* أسماء متفرقة

The final feature to be discussed here is the use of some nouns in the SL that may appear to be not nouns in the TL but rather adverbs of place or time

1. ‏لقد فعل ذلك من **قبل**.

He did that **before**.

It is worth noting that the sentence in English "he did that **before**" can be back-translated into Arabic, ‏سبق أن فعل ذلك.

2. ‏مضى **أمس**.

Yesterday is gone.

3. ‏زرت صديقي **أمس**.

I visited my friend **yesterday**.

4. ‏عجبت من **أمس**.

I was surprised by **yesterday**.

5. ‏عرفنا السعادة **إذ** كنا صغاراً.

We knew happiness **only when** we were young (or kids/children).

6. ‏إنه يعمل **الآن**.

He is working **now**.

The sentence in Example 6 can be translated in another way, 'it is working **now**'; the reason is for this confusion is the pronoun in the SL is not clear, whether it is 'someone who is not working now' or 'an object/thing is not working now'.

7. ‏اجلس **حيث** صديقك جالس.

Sit **next to where** your friend is sitting.

Here few exercises that help in understanding how Arabic adverbs of time or place are translated into English.

‏"سَنَسْتَدْرِجُهُم مِّنْ **حَيْثُ** لاَ يَعْلَمُونَ." (*The qur'ān*, 7:182)

a. "But We lead on those... step by step, without them realizing it" (Haleem, p.107).

b. "Those... We shall gradually visit with punishment, **in ways** they perceive not" (Yūsuf ʿAlī, p.195).

c. "We shall gradually seize them with punishment **in ways** they perceive not" (al-Hilālī and Khan, p.227).

d. "We shall lead them gradually to their punishment **when** they are (totally) unaware" (*my translation*).

So, it is easy to find English equivalence to such adverb of time in the ST. Here

is another exercise with an adverb of time is this,

"الآنَ جِئْتَ بِالْحَقِّ." (*The qur'ān*, 2:71)

a. "**Now** have you brought the truth" (Haleem, p.10).

b. "**Now** have you brought the truth" (Yūsuf ʿAlī, p.12).

c. "**Now** you have brought the truth" (al-Hilālī and Khan, p.15).

Another exercise which shows what the Arabic adverb of time and its English equivalence are, is the following:

"وَاذْكُرُواْ إِذْ أَنتُمْ قَلِيلٌ." (*The qur'ān*, 8:26)

a. "Remember **when** you were few" (Haleem, p.112).

b. "Call to mind **when** you were a small (band)" (Yūsuf ʿAlī, p.202).

c. "And remember **when** you were few" (al-Hilālī and Khan, p.234).

The last exercise that shows adverbs of time in the ST and their TT equivalence is this one,

"لِلَّهِ الْأَمْرُ مِن قَبْلُ وَمِن بَعْدُ." (*The qur'ān*, 30:4)

a. "God is in command, **first and last**" (Haleem, p.257).

b. "With Allah is the Decision, **in the past and in the future**" (Yūsuf ʿAlī, p.491).

c. "The decision of the matter, **before and after** (these events) is only with Allāh, (before the defeat of the Romans by the Persians, and after the defeat of the Persians by the Romans)" (al-Hilālī and Khan, p.540).

d. "God is in command **before and after** events" (*my translation*).

It is evident how adverbs of time in the ST are translated in the TT.

Now, to sum up, it is essential to identify the status of word in the SL before one can attempt to find its equivalence in the TL; so analysing the syntax accurately in the SL is the key to finding its most appropriate equivalence. We have seen that in the five forms of the verb, defective nouns with certain endings, defective verbs in the present and past tenses, redundant prepositions and semi-prepositions, and finally in pronouns and certain nouns in the SL. This syntactic analysis of the functionality of these various words is done first for the purpose of finding their appropriate equivalence.

2.7. Duality and gender in Arabic with their English equivalence

After discussing these five forms of the verb, the discussion has moved to defective nouns with certain endings in the SL and how their equivalence is found. Also, defective verbs in the present and past tenses and how they can be analysed before attempting to find their equivalence are tackled under the above sub-heading. Then we have seen how to identify redundant prepositions and semi-prepositions in the SL and what to do with them when searching for their

103

equivalence. And finally there is an analysis of the functionality of pronouns and certain nouns and how their equivalence is worked out. Now it is time to move to duality and gender as issues encountered when analysing the ST and finding its most appropriate equivalence in English.

> The verb in the SL (Arabic) changes more than that in the TL (English) due to the duality of the subject as well as its masculinity or femininity in the unit, whether it is a phrase or sentence.

2.7.1. Duality

It is really a major problem when translating from Arabic into English. There are common errors relating to it. But first let us see what one of the translation theorists think of this issue.

Mona Baker (1992) refers to duality in some languages such as Arabic that is not used in other languages like English. Here Baker points out,

> English speakers are not particularly interested in establishing whether there are two or more than two persons or objects. It may sometimes be necessary or desirable in certain contexts to specify plurality or duality in languages which do not normally specify such information because they do not have a category of number or a dual form. (p.89)

But Baker warns,

> However, as with any grammatical category, a translator working from a language with a category of number into one without such a category must be careful not to over-specify this type of information in the target text. Unless the context

specifically demands it, regular reference to information normally left unspecified in a given language will only make the translation awkward and unnatural because it will not reflect normal ways of reporting experience in the target language. (p.90)

However, there is this fear of over-specificity when finding an equivalence in English which may make the translation 'awkward and unnatural', but duality in particular must be strictly respected in the TL syntax rather respecting the SL when it comes to duality it must be strictly followed in the TL equivalence, even though it is almost non-existent in English. This method is essential to convey the exact message across in the TL. Awkwardness and unnaturalness occur when the translator or student shows no confidence in their TL expression. Communicative translation is to be used in order to remove that awkwardness and unnaturalness felt in being too specific in one's translation. But the syntactic element of duality must be adhered to.

Here is an error made by Karin Ryding in her book on classical Arabic grammar, 'تحمل بتوأمين' with its TL equivalence, 'She is pregnant with twins' (p.332). Now the word 'توأم' means 'two babies' in Arabic; and 'توأمان' can mean 'four babies'. So the more appropriate equivalence to Ryding's example is, 'she is pregnant with two twins'.

2.7.2. Gender

The issue of **gender** in Arabic must not be ignored in English translation. Baker states,

105

> **Gender** is a grammatical distinction according to which a noun or pronoun is classified as either masculine or feminine in some languages. The distinction applies to nouns which refer to animate beings as well as those which refer to inanimate objects. (p.90) [*emphasis in the original*]

Linguistically, gender is considered by Alan Cruse (2000) as

> a classification system for nouns, which affects such grammatical matters as agreement and pronominal reference... It is usual to make a distinction between **natural gender** and **grammatical gender**. English is usually said to exhibit natural gender... since the appropriate noun (*he, she, it*) can be predicted with a high degree of success purely on the basis of the sex (male, female, or neuter) of the referent. (pp.272-73) [*emphasis in the original*]

However, gender is not often discussed in detail with regards to Arabic and its equivalence in English. Bakers fails to point out that inanimate objects in the SL (Arabic) when in plural, their corresponding pronouns or pro-forms when co-referencing as well as anaphoric and cataphoric referencing, the third feminine singular pronoun, the feminine one is used, along with its other grammatical issues such as "agreement and pronominal reference". *In Other Words*, Mona Baker (1992) explains, "**Anaphoric reference** involves using a word or phrase to refer back to another word or phrase that occurred earlier in the text" (p.178). **Cataphoric reference**, however, involves using a word or phrase to refer forward to another word or phrase that is going to occur later in the text.

To elaborate this point further, one can rely on Ryding's two examples though used in a different context,

- 'في منشوراتها **هذه**.'
'in **these** of **its** publications' (p.114).

106

It is crucial to know that the feminine singular pronoun of the animate plural or its pro-form is rightly highlighted by Ryding in the following example,

- 'وكثير من الناس لا **تأكل** أغذية إلا من مصادر نباتية.'

'Many **people** only **eat** (f.sg.) food from plant sources' (p.128). [*my emphasis*; *f.sg. = feminine singular*]

But in Arabic there are more varieties which create a major problem in finding their TL equivalence due to gender-related matters (masculine and feminine ones). Ryding when discussing numbers fails to point out that some nouns in Arabic are both masculine and feminine, when she says, 'في أحد مستشفيات جدة' with its TL equivalence 'in one of the hospitals of Jidda' (p.331). A quick and simple search in the archive of the widely distributed Arabic newspaper *al-Sharq al-Awsat* shows that this Arabic phrase can also be 'في إحدى مستشفيات جدة' and here there will be translation loss. This simple search shows 1203 entries for 'هذه المستشفى' (*feminine*) and 1192 entries for 'هذا المستشفى' (*masculine*).

Another example is the masculine/feminine word 'بلد' ('هذا البلد' and 'هذه البلد'). Both the masculine and feminine forms are acceptable. Here are examples in the feminine form:

- فتقدم إلي رجل من أصحاب **هذه البلد.**

(*One thousand and one nights, p.575* Arabic version retrieved from *www.alwaraq.net*)

- A man from the local community of this town has asked to marry me.

An interesting note here is that the title of this book is also officially translated communicatively as *The Arabian Nights: Tales of 1,001 Nights* by Penguin Publishing House or *1001 Arabian Nights* by the translator Sir Richard Francis Burton.

Similar examples about this masculine/feminine word are,

- ولا سررت بعودي إلى **هذه البلد** إلا من أجله. (al-Thaʿālibī's *Yatīmat al-Dahr*, p.78)
It was only for him that I was pleased to come back to **this town**.

- وبآخر هذا الجبل المذكور، في آخر البسيط البستاني الغربي من **هذه البلد**... (Ibn Jubayr, *Riḥlat Ibn Jubayr*, p.104)
And at the bottom of this aforementioned mountain, at the far end of the west orchard-like plateau of **this town**...

Such a word is problematic because of its gender, particularly when you have classical references referring to it as both masculine and feminine. In *The qurʾān* it is in the masculine form,

'وَإِذْ قَالَ إِبْرَاهِيمُ رَبِّ اجْعَلْ هَـذَا الْبَلَدَ آمِنًا' (*The qurʾān*, 14:35)

a. "Remember when Abraham said, 'Lord, make **this town** safe!' " (Haleem, p.160)
b. "Remember Abraham said: 'O my Lord! Make **this city** one of peace and security' " (Yūsuf ʿAlī, p.298).
c. "And (remember) when Ibrāhīm (Abraham) said: 'O my Lord! Make **this city** (Makkah) one of peace and security' " (al-Hilālī and Khan, p.333)
Now it is not the fact that whether it is a town or city, but rather the demonstrative noun which is under discussion. As to which

108

translation of the above holy verse is most appropriate the proper noun is 'domesticated' in Haleem's and Yūsuf 'Alī's versions, that is making it closer to the target reader by using 'Abraham' and not its transliteration as in translation (c) (that is, al-Hilālī and Khan's version). Another interesting equivalence here is the word آمِنًا which is translated as 'safe' or 'peace and security'. Here the most appropriate equivalence is to use the term 'safe and sound' or 'safe and secure'. The verb 'remember' is an addition in the translation which might be justified here. So the proposed version to this holy verse can be, "And when Abraham said: 'Lord! Make this town safe and secure' ".

Also, the same comment about words which are both masculine and feminine can apply to the word 'حال' which can be written as 'حالة' too, but the latter is in its feminine form. Ryding gives an example about a certain form of verbs,

- 'هم في حال صحة متدهورة.'
a. 'They are in a **deteriorating** *state* of health' (p.112) [*emphasis in original but my italics*]
b. Their state of health is deteriorating.

But the above example fails to notice the 'unnaturalness' of using 'حال' ('state') in this instance, and it would be more appropriate to say 'هم في حالة صحية متدهورة'. It is true that 'حال' is a dual gender noun (Ryding, p.125), so do the words above.

Chapter Three: Arabic word acting as verb and its English equivalence

The focus here is on the SL, Arabic, and how to analyse it at word level before finding its TL equivalence. First, when the word acts as verb with the five forms which correspond to the subject.

3.1. The five forms of verb الأفعال الخمسة and their English equivalence

When the subject of the verb is singular in Arabic, its English equivalence is simple and straightforward, and requires no major structural changes. In English the verb in its simple and continuous aspects changes into three different forms when its subject is either *he*, *she* or *it* as well as when its subject is in plural.

1.   ذهب محمد إلى المدينة صباحاً.

Muhammad **went** downtown in the morning. (simple aspect)

2.   رأيت شجراتٍ مثمرةً في أماكنَ كثيرةٍ.

I **saw** fruitful trees in many places. (simple aspect)

3.   يقرأ محمد كتاباً.

Muhammad **is reading** a book. (continuous aspect)

4.   يقرأ محمد في البيت كتاب النحو.

Muhammad **is reading** a grammar book at home. (continuous aspect)

The simple aspect of the past tense in Arabic has its English equivalence in the same aspect (simple past in Arabic = simple past in English). But it is clear from Examples 3 and 4 that they both have to be in the continuous aspect in English, the reason is that such a statement in Arabic refers to the action being done now and it is <u>not</u> *habitual* but rather *temporary*. A further note on Example 2 is the

111

adjective مثمرة 'fruitful' is in the singular feminine form and not in plural, since 'trees' is an inanimate noun, though sometimes that noun can be figuratively pluralised as in cartoon films or children's books.

In English there are singularity and plurality only, but in Arabic there is also duality and gender, which is discussed earlier. In the SL (Arabic) some particles are attached to the end of the verb when the subject is masculine or feminine as well as when in its dual and plural forms and these are attached prefixes and suffixes in the SL in order to convey the meaning, as Ryding (p.441) describes them. Let us see how the SL and its TL equivalence work in the following examples alongside their English equivalence,

5. يقرأ الطالبان كتابين.
The two students are reading two books. (continuous aspect)

6. تقرأ الطالبتان كتابين.
The two students are reading two books. (continuous aspect)

7. المحتاجون يطلبون العون من القادرين.
The needy ask for help from the well-off. (simple aspect, as it is factual information)

8. المحتاجات يطلبن المساعدة من القادرات.
The needy ask for help from the well-off. (simple aspect, as it is factual information)

Also in Examples 5 and 6 the continuous aspect in the TL is necessary as there is no connotative habituality in the SL, and no adverbs are used to indicate habituality or factuality, that way it is in English. However, in Examples 7 and 8 the factual element is clear in Arabic.

Therefore, the simple aspect of the tense must be used in the English translation.

A more problematic example of the verb (along with the aspect of tenses, though this is not the topic under discussion here) is this holy verse,

9.   "فإن لم **تفعلوا ولن تفعلوا** فاتقوا النار التي وقودها الناس والحجارة." (*The qur'ān*, 2:24)

a. 'If **you cannot do** this – and **you never will** – then **beware** of the Fire prepared for the disbelievers, whose fuel is men and stones' (Haleem, p.6).

b. 'And if **you cannot** – and of a surety **you cannot** – then **fear** the Fire whose fuel is Men and Stones' (Yūsuf 'Alī, p.4).

c. 'But if **you do it not**, and **you can never do** it, then **fear** the Fire (Hell) whose fuel is men and stones' (al-Hilālī and Khan, p.6).

d. 'But if **you did not do** it, and **you will never do**, then fear the Fire whose fuel is people and stones' (*my translation*).

It is clear that the dual subject in the SL (Arabic) in Examples 5 and 6 has not affected the verb as this is a verbal sentence where the verb in the Arabic sentence comes first (verb + subject + objects or rest of the sentence).   But in the nominal sentence in Examples 7-9 the verb clearly shows its plurality, and plurality is also clear in its ending. This plurality, however, cannot be seen in English in Example 9 – in the use of pronoun 'you' which can refer to both singular and plural in Arabic but not so in English.

Furthermore, in Example 9 one might wonder which translation is closest to the Arabic syntactically. In fact there are two verbs in the first SL conditional clause 'فإن لم تفعلوا ولن تفعلوا', here there is the past and the present tense which have not been conveyed properly in these three translation of the holy verse. The first verb which is in negation is in the past tense, whereas the second verb is certainly in the present tense, i.e. 'But if **you did not do** this before, and **you will never do**, then fear...'. Here it is vital to emphasis the tenses here which are obvious at the surface level at least. Also another issue is the choice of words for الناس which is 'people' and not just 'men', as the word 'men' is more limiting than 'people' which includes both men and women.

3.2. The present aspect of defective verbs الفعل المضارع المعتل الآخر

It is not enough to know the present aspect of the verb in the SL, but one needs to know how certain types of verbs, namely the defective verbs, change in negation. Here are few examples in the SL and their TL equivalence,

1.   هو يسعى إلى الخير.
He **endeavours** to do good deeds.

2.   إنه لن يرضى بما تعرض عليه.
He is **not going to be satisfied** with what you have offered him.

114

The defective SL verbs سعى 'to endeavour' and رضي 'to satisfy' are defective, and can be contracted due to its functionality in the SL sentence; therefore, the translation or students needs to identify that change in the verb in order to find its most appropriate equivalence in the TL. The simple present tense in Arabic has kept the defective verb in its full form with no contraction, and this makes its TL equivalence more straightforward.   This point is elaborated in Example 1, but in Example 2 though the Arabic sentence has the simple aspect of the present, the negation gives it a near future element, that is why its TL equivalence has the phrase 'going to' to imply the future.   The reason is the particle لن in Arabic implies the future and needs the verbal TL phrase 'is going to'. Further, the verb رضي in Arabic is used in an *active* sentence but converted into a *passive* one in the TL 'to be satisfied'. This conversion is dues to the fact that in the TL grammar this verb must be *passive*. So the TL equivalence must follow its TL grammar.

Furthermore, here is another example of the verb رضي alongside its TL equivalence given by Ryding (p.106), though she is discussing it from a different perspective - how the active participle acts as predicate adjective in Arabic,

-      'قال المدرب إنه راض.'

'The coach said that he **was satisfied**.' [*emphasis in original*]

What is interesting here is that the *nominal* SL clause is converted into a *verbal* clause, and has changed its *active* form into a *passive* one. This proves that even the adjective of the defective verb رضي require even a change from nominal to verbal clause, and from active to

115

passive. Note that the past tense in the SL has the simple aspect and the same is done in the TL.

Here are some more examples of defective verbs along with their TL equivalence,

3.   يدعو الناس إلى الخير.

He **prompts** people to do good deeds.

4.   يحبّ أن يعفوَ عن المسيء.

He likes to **forgive** the wrongdoer.

5.   هو يأتيك بالخبر اليقين.

He will surely **provide** you with the truth.

A quick syntactic analysis shows that the three defective verbs are not contracted and are all in the simple present tense, so their TL equivalence is straightforward. But when the defective SL verbs are in negation, their forms are changed following certain grammatical rule. The translator or student needs to be aware of that.

Here is an example with the defective verb يأتي 'to come',

6.   لن يأتيَ اليومَ.

a. He **won't come** today.

b. He **is not going to come** today.

Now Example 6 might appear easy, but it is not due the use of the particle لن which indicates the present and future, that is why its TL equivalence has the future tense. Both translations (a) and (b) are perfectly acceptable. Translation (a), however, is more emphatic but is colloquial due to the use of contracted form of 'will not'. Note that contracted forms are only used in colloquial and spoken English and not in academic writing.

The defective verb يأتي becomes problematic when the sentence is in negation and it is in the past tense, because it appears in its short form. Here is an example,

7.   لم يأتِ أمس.
He **did not come** yesterday.

Note that the particle لم is for the past tense whilst the particle لن is used for the present and future tenses.

Here are another two defective verbs whose forms are contracted in negation, and they are both in the present tense,

8.   لا تخشَ غيرَ اللـه.
Fear no one but God.
9.   لا تدعُ إلا إلى الخير.
Only propagate to do good deeds.

The two words تخش and تدع above can be misread by students and translator, as they are orthographical similar to another two words which mean 'to rattle' and 'to let' respectively. But the diacritics here make a difference as they help the translator and student identify the right meaning of the SL words, and this would help find their appropriate TL equivalence. So it is crucial to analyse the structure of the sentence correctly based on the correct analysis of the defective verb here.

To sum up, here are few examples or actually exercises from the holy Book with
the defective verbs in negation,

"وَلَا تَقْفُ مَا لَيْسَ لَكَ بِهِ عِلْمٌ." (*The qur'ān*, 17:36)
a. '**Do not follow** blindly what you do not know to be true' (Haleem, p.177).

b. 'And **pursue not** that of which you have no knowledge' (Yūsuf 'Alī, p.331).

c. 'And **follow not** (O man...) that of which you have no knowledge' (al-Hilālī
and Khan, p.373).

Notice how the defective verb تقفو 'to follow' or 'to pursue' has been contracted
in the imperative form with the negation as well can be mistakenly read تقف 'to
stand', if diacritics are not included.   Note that, unlike the particle لَن, the
negation particle لا indicates only the present and not the future.

"لَن نَّدْعُوَ مِن دُونِهِ إِلَهًا." (*The qur'ān*, 18:14)
a. 'We **shall never call upon** any god other than Him' (Haleem, p.184).

b. '**Never shall we call upon** any god other than Him' (Yūsuf 'Alī, p.343).

c. '... **never shall we call upon** any *ilāh* (god) other than Him' (al-Hilālī and
Khan, p.386).

Notice the particle لن with its future characteristic which has made Haleem use
the English auxiliary verb 'shall'.

It is also clear how the contraction of the defective verb can be problematic.

"وَلاَ تَمْشِ فِي الأَرْضِ مَرَحًا." (*The qur'ān*, 17:37)

a. '**Do not strut** arrogantly about the earth' (Haleem, p.177).

b. '**Nor walk** on the earth with insolence' (Yūsuf 'Alī, p.332).

c. 'And **walk not** on the earth with conceit and arrogance' (al-Hilālī and Khan, p.373).

d. 'And do walk no on the earth with haughtiness and arrogance' (*my translation*).

Incidentally, the English equivalence 'strut' used by Haleem, though implicitly accurate in the word مرحا according to *Lisān al-'Arab*, is inappropriate. It is the haughtiness, loftiness and pompousness which are implied in that holy verse. Haleem has been unsuccessful in the verb choice here, 'walk' would have been a better English equivalence. A final contracted form of a defective form here is the following example,

"وَلَا تَنسَ نَصِيبَكَ مِنَ الدُّنْيَا." (*The qur'ān*, 28:77)

a. '...but **do not neglect** your rightful share in this world' (Haleem, p.250)

b. '...**nor forget** your portion in this world' (Yūsuf 'Alī, p.478-79).

c. '...and **forget not** your portion of lawful enjoyment in this world' (al-Hilālī and Khan, p.526).

d. '... and **do not forget** to take your rightful share in this world' (*my translation*).

119

3.3. The past tense of the Arabic verb and its English equivalence

There are two cases to discuss about the past tense of the Arabic verb here: one is when the structure of the SL sentence is simple, i.e. consisting of just one clause, and two is the complex structure of the SL sentence, that is when it has more than one clause. Also what would be their English equivalence?

3.3.1. In a simple structure of the sentence

When the past tense of the Arabic verb refers to its duality or feminine form, the student or student needs to note that the English verb stayed the same in all three forms (masculine, feminine and dual) as in the following examples,

1.   فهم الطالب.
The student **understood**.
2.   فهمت الطالبة.
The student **understood**.
3.   الطالبان فهما.
The <u>two</u> students **understood**.

Verbs in the SL do change as discussed earlier due to the status of the subject, when it is in its *singular, dual,* or *plural* form or when the Arabic verb refers to a *masculine* or *feminine*. Here are further examples to that effect,

4.   فهمتُ الدرس.
I **understood** the lesson.
5.   فهمتَ الدرس.
You **understood** the lesson. [*masculine*]

6.   فهمتِ الدرس.
She **understood** the lesson.

It is clear that only the diacritics help in one's comprehension of the SL sentences above. In the dual form it is essential in English to use the word 'both', as in the following example,

7.   فهمتما الدرس.
You <u>both</u> **understood** the lesson.

The word 'both' is vital here, otherwise the subject 'you' would be referring to the singular 'you', the dual 'you' or the plural 'you', though the English verb keeps the same form. Indeed, it keeps its form with all pronouns even in the plural form. Here are a couple of examples,

8.   فهمنا الدرس.
We **understood** the lesson.

9.   فهمتم الدرس.
You <u>all</u> **understood** the lesson. [*masculine*]

10.   فهمتن الدرس.
You <u>all</u> **understood** the lesson. [*feminine*]

It is absolutely clear in Example 7 that the subject is in the dual form in the SL and is the same in the TL, but the feminine aspect is not clearly defined in the TL, the way it is in the SL – so there is translation loss. Again, there is no difference in Examples 9 and 10 between the masculine and feminine forms of the English verb – which is yet another translation loss here.

121

3.3.2. In a complex structure of the sentence

It is when there is a complex structure of the sentence with the nominal being primary and the verbal as secondary, but using the same subject in the SL. This is a special case in the SL (Arabic) when the subject is used twice in the same sentence within which there are two clauses, a nominal primary sentence and a verbal secondary one, but the latter is acting as predicate to the subject of the nominal sentence. Such a complex structure is certainly problematic and needs to be analysed properly in order to point out how to re-encode it in the TL. Here and in the same sentence, e.g.

1.   الطالبات فهمن الدرس.
The students were **the ones** who understood the lesson. [*feminine*]

2.   الطلاب فهموا الدرس.
 The students were **the ones** who understood the lesson. [*masculine*]

3.   الأولاد رمَوْا الكرة.
The kids were **the ones** who <u>threw</u> the ball.

4.   هم دعَوْا إلى الخير.
They were **the ones** who <u>propagated</u> to do good deeds.

It is clear that unless the signposted to indicate the feminine or masculine form, the student or the professional translator is not to know – another translation loss appears here. But this obstacle is easily solved in audiovisual translation, as it will be clear from the image on screen. It is worthwhile reminding here that examples 3 and 4 use defective verbs (underlined above) as well which makes the task even harder to analyse, in order to get the correct equivalent.

Now in English the imperative form of the verb is the same for both the singular and plural modes, but it is not the case in Arabic where the imperative form changes according to the subject who is being addressed. The following examples elaborate this point,

1.   ذاكرْ تنجح.

Study and you will succeed.

2.   ذاكرْن تنجحْن.

Study and you will <u>all</u> succeed. [*feminine*]

3.   ذاكروا تنجحوا.

Study and you will <u>all</u> succeed. [*masculine*]

It is essential to have the word 'all' in Examples 2 and 3 to differentiate between the singular 'you' and the plural one. Also, one needs to note that the dual 'you' if it were here in one of the examples above then the word 'both' needs to take the place of 'all'.

3.5. Verbs in the present tense with the feminine 'n' نون النسوة or the emphatic 'n' نون التوكيد and their English equivalence

It is common in the SL to have the letter ن added to the verb in order to mean something in particular, either to indicate the *feminine* mode of the verb or for *emphasis*, since both have the double stress shown in their diacritics. It is critical to analyse the verb with this attachment ن in order to see which mode is used in the SL, so that its equivalence in the TL is selected carefully.

In the following example it is clear that the ن refers to the feminine mode highlighted in the word 'female students' in the SL, and

123

obviously not so in the TL, but it still makes the analysis of the Arabic verb easier
to handle,

1.   الطالبات يكتبْنَ.

The female students are the ones who are writing. [*feminine*]

But that task is not as easy with the emphatic ن 'n' in the SL, except when the
diacritic ّ is added to the letter ب or when examining the referent, as in the
following examples which all refer to males, save for Example 4 which refers to
females,

1.   لتنجحانّ أيها المجدان.

You, <u>two</u> hardworking students, are **certainly** to succeed.

2.   والله ليُفلحَنّ المجدُ.

I swear [by God], the hard worker is **certainly** to succeed.

3.   لتنجحنّ أيها المجدون.

You, hard workers, are **certainly** to succeed.

4.   لتنجَحِنّ أيتها المجدة.

You, female hard worker, are **certainly** to succeed.

The emphatic 'n' ن is there in the SL and needs to be re-encoded in the end
product in the TL – in the translation. So the use of the adverb 'certainly' can do
the job.   A further note needs to be added to Example 2, the phase 'by God' is
not often used in English, but is implied and connotative.

Chapter Four: Superseding auxiliary verbs النواسخ in the nominal SL sentence and their TL equivalence

The superseding auxiliary verbs are only used to start a nominal SL sentence, and they are going to be listed below.

4.1. كان = verb 'to be' Acting as,

4.1.1. Proper verb to mean 'happen':

1.   تلبدت السماء بالغيوم واشتدت الريح فكان المطرُ.
The sky was cloudy and the wind was strong, so **it rained**.
OR: The sky became overcast and the storm intensified, so **it rained**.

There is no difference between the two translations above, save for the choice of verbs. In translation it is often unnecessary to follow the same pattern as that in the SL sentence. In the first translation, however, the interesting point is the use of verbs in both the SL and TL. All the verbs in the SL sentence are main verbs to mean: 'heavily clouded', 'intensified' and 'rained'. Interestingly in the first translation the verb 'to be' is used twice in the first two TL clauses and whilst the verb 'to rain' is used in the third TL clause, because the verb 'to be' in the TL is a proper verb and not an auxiliary.

The verb in the first SL clause is completely different from that in the TL equivalence – using in the TL the verb 'to be' but in the SL 'became overcast' or 'heavily clouded' is the literal translation – the latter verb rarely used in the TL, as it is awkward to say 'the sky was

125

heavily clouded'; but 'became overcast' might be more appropriate translation. The same comment can be said about the second clause regarding its verb – i.e. the use of the verb 'to be' in the TL but in the SL the main verb means literally 'intensified', but a verb that does not collocate with 'the wind' but rather with the word 'storm'.

4.1.2. Auxiliary to the nominal SL sentence:

2.   كان زيد قائماً.

Zayd **was** standing.

In Example 2, the nominal SL sentence is transferred into a verbal one in the TL.

3.   أكون سعيداً حين يكون أخي سعيداً.

I **am** happy, only when my brother **is**.

The ellipsis is necessary in the TL, as it is connotative; so there is no need to repeat the word 'happy', the way it is repeated in the SL.

4.   كن مستعداً.

Be ready.

In Example 4 there is the imperative being used in both the nominal SL sentence and its TL equivalence.

4.1.3. Present participle or gerund:

5.   أحبه لكونه شجاعاً.

I love him **for being** brave (or courageous).

6.   زيدٌ كائنٌ أخاك.

Zayd, **being** your brother.

It is clear in Example 6 that the TL equivalence is not necessarily a sentence but merely a phrase or an utterance – as the use of 'being' may make the TL sentence a fragment.

4.1.4. In a collocation:

7. سأعاقب المهمل كائناً من كان.

I will punish the negligent person **whoever he is**.

8. سأدفع ثمن هذا الشيء كائناً ما كان.

I will pay for this thing **whatever it is**.

4.1.5. Redundant verb for exclamation:

9. ما كان أطيبَ خلقَه.

How lovely **were** his manners (or, was his character)!

The word 'ما' here is used for exclamation. Although the verb 'to be' is used redundantly in the nominal SL sentence, it is essential in the TL equivalence.

4.1.6. In a conditional form:

10. ما كان من إنسانٍ إلا وله أجل.

Each and every man has a time appointed for his death.

It is obvious here that the verb 'to be' is totally unnecessary in the SL sentence, that is why it has no place in the TL equivalence. In fact the conjunction و in the SL sentence is redundant but necessary in this case, whereas it does not exist in the TL equivalence. There is a need to use exegetic translation here for two reasons one is that the word 'death' connotative in the SL sentence but so obvious in the TL equivalence if it is to be overlooked. The other problematic issue often discussed is the use of 'man' to mean 'mankind' in English, but from a feminist point of view that is really a dilemma to say the least. Another collocation is 'each and every' which is more effective, as the translated text becomes more meaningful and effective when it is full of corresponding collocations and is clear from the ambiguity implicitly mentioned in the word 'time' in Arabic.

4.1.7. In negation in the present tense:

11.　　　لم أكُ أفعل ذلك.

I was not doing that.

Negation rules in the SL are really problematic as they are not often used in spoken Arabic and therefore many students and professional translators tend to make mistakes in them. Example 11 above is the perfect example.

4.1.8. Being omitted from SL sentence:

12.　　　أما أنت كريماً فأنت محبوب. (بمعنى، أنت محبوب لأن كنت كريماً.)

Since you **have been** generous, people love you (or you are popular).

This is yet another dilemma the student or the professional translator encounter, the verb 'to be' is omitted from the first SL clause, but must be there in the first TL clause.

128

4.1.9. Being omitted alongside its subject or predicate:

It is also a big issue when verbs or pronouns are omitted in the SL for certain grammatical or stylistic reason, as students and professional translators may not have a good command of the SL, Arabic in this instance, and therefore could misunderstand the original SL text.

13. كل إنسان محاسب على عمله؛ إن (كان) خيراً فخير وإن (كان) شراً فشر.

Each and every man **is** accountable for his action (or deed), whether it is good or evil.

It is not only the omission that is problematic but also the repetition in the SL sentence. It is vital to point out that the repetition in the last two clauses in the SL sentence is essential but it is not required in the TL equivalence, it is connotative and therefore a literal equivalence is totally undesirable – i.e. 'when good **it is** good, and when evil **it is** evil'.

14. أقرأ كل يوم ولو (كان) صحيفةً.

Every day I read anything, even a newspaper.

So omission in the TL equivalence is also desirable; otherwise the TL style will be awkward, translating the latter clause literally as 'even if that thing is a newspaper'.

15. كل إنسان محاسب على عمله إن (كان في عمله) خيرٌ فخيرٌ وإن (كان في عمله) شرٌّ فشرٌّ.

Each and every man is accountable for his own action, whether that action is good or evil.

Each and every man is accountable for his action (or deed), when (his deed is) good it is good, and when (his deed is) evil it is evil.

129

In Example 15 it is a desirable method to omit a number of words as in the case of the first translation compared to the second. It is often wrongly assumed that one should do literal translation so as to be as close as possible to the SL text, but being too close creates a crooked an bad style in the TL text, so the translator needs to be aware of that danger – not to be too close to the original text for fear of producing a strange looking text in the TL.

4.2. ظل = Be still or continue to do

Here is an example,

16.   ظل زيد قائماً.
Zayd **is still** standing.

4.3. أصبح = to become (but usually implies 'morning time')

Here is an example,

17.   أصبح الطفل رجلاً.

>   The child **has become** a man.
>   The child **is now** a man.

4.4. أضحى = to become (but usually implies 'late morning time')

Here are a couple of examples,

18.   أضحى العامل مستغرقاً في عمله.
The worker is **now quite** involved in his work.
19.   أضحى العلم ضرورياً.
The flag has **now become** necessary.

OR: The flag **becomes** necessary.

4.4.1. As proper verb, e.g.

20. ظل نائماً حتى أضحى

He stayed asleep till (or until it was) **late morning**.

Note that 'until' can be used here. Moreover, here is an example by Fischer (223) worth discussing: 'ساروا حتى طلعت الشمس.' with its TL equivalence, 'They travelled **until** the sun came up.' The meaning here in Example 20 is that he slept till he entered as it were the late morning period.

4.5. أمسى = to become or end up (but usually implies 'evening time')

21. أمسى المجهول معلوماً.

The unknown eventually **becomes** known.

22. أمسي قد انقطع الحبل بيني وبينه.

'I shall end up such that the bond between him and me will have been severed' (Fischer, p.221).

In Example 21 the addition of 'eventually' gives the added effect required in the TL sentence which is implicit in the nominal SL sentence. Another more appropriate and commonly used equivalence for this addition is 'at the end of the day', which is certainly more appropriate and gives in a way the literal meaning of this superseding auxiliary verb – i.e. its implicit SL meaning of 'evening time'.

4.6. بات = to stay (but usually implies 'all night long')

This superseding verb can be used either as auxiliary or proper verb in the SL and the student or professional translator needs to be aware of that during the process of their translation.

4.6.1. As an auxiliary, e.g.

23.　　بات الطالب ساهراً.
The students stayed up all night.

It must be point out here that it is not auxiliary in the TL equivalence but a fully fledged verb 'to stay up'. This is a pitfall that might be overlooked by students or professional translators.

4.6.2. As a proper verb, e.g.

24.　　بات الغريب في بيتنا.
The stranger **stayed** in our house **overnight**.
OR: We **have put up** the stranger in our house.

It is significant to not that the SL sentence is verbal and not nominal. Also, the word 'overnight' is connotative in the SL sentence that is why it is added. However, the period of his 'stay' might be sometimes longer than 'overnight', like for over a week or more. But that is implicit in the TL equivalence, unless it is declared in the SL sentence which is not the case here in Example 23.

4.7. صار = to become (implying 'to transform')

٢٥. صار العبد حراً.

The slave **has become** free.

OR: The slave **is now** free.

It is worth noting that the TL word 'become' is not necessarily the exact equivalence to the SL word صار. The verb 'to be' and the adverb 'now' can be an appropriate equivalence for that SL word.

4.7.1. Other similar auxiliary verbs with similar function and meaning to the verb صار = 'to become'

آض = *to become*

٢٦. آض الغلام رجلاً.

The kid **has become** a man.

عاد = *to become or turn into*

٢٧.   عادت القريةُ مدينةً.

The village **has now turned into** a town.

The implicit 'now' in the SL sentence is not connotative in the TL equivalence, and therefore needs to be used explicitly.

رجع = *to come back to*

٢٨.   رجع الضال مهدياً.

The misguided one **came back to** his senses.

OR: The misguided **has now been** rightly guided.

The collocation 'to come back to his senses' is most appropriate in the first TL equivalence. However, the second translation features the play on words 'guided' and 'misguided'.

133

استحال ا = *to become, change into, turn into*

29. استحالت النار رماداً.

The fire **is now** ashes.

The fire **has turned into** ashes.

Such a wonderful SL verb is hardly used by students and professional translators when translating from English into Arabic; it is noticeable that they often use the verb 'تحول' instead, it is not wrong of course, but enriching their translation with a variety of vocabulary is one of the tools that helps in the process of translation.

ارتد = *to become, change into*

30. ارتد المريض صحيحاً.

The patient **is now** well (or healthy).

OR: The patient has now fully recovered.

This superseding auxiliary verb in Example 30 can be confused with another verb which is a proper verb as in the example below,

31. ارتد بصر الأعمى.

The blind man **has regained** his sight.

تحول = *to become or transform into*

    (*cf.* example 29 in the paragraph 4.7.1)

32. تحول القمح خبزاً.

The grain **has become** bread.

OR: The grain **has been transformed into** bread.

The latter translation of Example 32 is not ideal for audiovisual translation as there are so many words (7 words) whilst the former translation has less words (5 words), and shortening is one of the techniques adopted due the spatial and temporal restrictions. For further discussion on audiovisual translation, see Ahmad Khuddro's "Subtitling

Triangle: Technique and Practice", *Translating voices for audiovisuals*.

غدا = *to become (implying 'tomorrow')*

33. غدا العمل مرهقاً.

The work **has become** exhausting (or trying).

34. غدا عمله مربحاً.

His work **has become** lucrative (or profitable).

The implicit word 'tomorrow' in the SL sentence is also connotative in the TL

equivalence, as seen in examples 33 and 34. The synonyms inserted in between

brackets are useful to enrich one's vocabulary. Thesauri are the best dictionaries

to use when translating, as they offer students and professional translators with a

number of synonyms for each lexical word in the TL. *Roget's'* is one of the best

English thesauri to use, in Arabic there are لسان العرب *Lisān al-'Arab* by Ibn

ManZūr and تاج العروس *Tāj al-'Arūs* by Murtaḍā al-Zubaydī (b.1144AH-1204)

to get monolingual synonyms.

4.8. ليس = not to be

There are words which have the same function as ليس and 'not to be' as their TL

equivalence. The SL words are ما، لا، لات، إن.

35. ليس زيد قائماً.

Zayd **is not** standing.

36. ليس إنسانٌ إلا وله أجل.

There **is no** man who has no time appointed for his death.

In Example 36, the golden rule of negative-negative formula is applied to imply the positive formula.

There are words which have the same function as ليس and 'not to be' as their TL equivalence. The SL words are, ما، لا، لات، إن

The use of ما

1.　　　ما زيد قائماً.

Zayd **is not** standing.

Fronting the predicate after ما

2.　　　ما في البيت أحد.

No one is **at home**.

Redundant ما and إن

3.　　　ما إنْ زيد قائم.

Zayd **is not** standing.

Redundant ما and إلا

4.　　　ما محمد إلا رسول.

Mohammed is **no more than** a Messenger.

No fronting the predicate before the subject when ما is used to function as ليس

5.　　　ما زيد قارئا كتاباً.

Zayd **is not reading** a book.

The word 'book' is here functioning as the object of reading.

No fronting the predicate before the subject when ما is used to function as ليس

6.　　　ما للشر أنت ساعياً. أو: ما للشر أنت ساعٍ.

You **are not** seeking to do evil.

If there is a conjunction after the predicate of ما

7.　　　ما زيدٌ قائماً بل جالس. أو: ما زيدٌ قائماً لكن جالس.

Zayd **is not** standing **but** sitting.

OR: Zayd is sitting, **not** standing.

Redundant preposition connected to the predicate of ما

8. ما زيدٌ بقائم.

Zayd **is not** standing.

لا functioning as ليس 'not to be'

9. لا خيرٌ ضائعاً. أو: لا خيرٌ ضائعٌ.

No good action is wasted.

OR: **No** deed is done in vain.

10. لا خيرٌ إلا مثمرٌ.

No good action is **but** useful (beneficial).

11. لا مؤمنٌ ظالماً أحداً.

No believer **is** to treat anyone unjustly.

In Example 11 here the word 'anyone' is obviously the object of the verb 'treat'.

12. لا عندك خيرٌ ضائعاً. أو: لا عندك خيرٌ ضائعٌ.

No good action you do **is** wasted (done in vain).

إنْ functioning as ليس 'not to be'

13. إنْ الخيرُ ضائعاً.

Good action **is not** wasted (done in vain).

لاتَ functioning as ليس 'not to be'

14. ندم الآن ولاتَ حينَ مندم. أو: تندم الآن ولاتَ حينُ مندم.

You regret now, but there **is no** time for regret.

15. لقد فروا ولاتَ ساعةَ فرار.

لقد فروا ولاتَ أوانَ فرار.

They fled and it **was not the hour** for fleeing.

OR: They fled and it **was not the time** for fleeing.

Here are good exercises for ما، ولات (the latter is discussion earlier, see the discussion of the particle ما earlier in Section I) when they have the same function as ليس; all with their TL equivalence.

- "فَنَادَوْا وَلَاتَ حِينَ مَنَاصٍ " (*The qur'ān*, 38:3)

a. "They all cried out, **once it was too late**, for escape" (Haleem, p.290).

b. "In the end they cried (for mercy) – when **there was no longer time** for being saved" (Yūsuf ʿAlī, p.556).

c. "And they cried out when **there was no longer time** for escape" (al-Hilālī and Khan, p.609).

Here translation (c) is most appropriate syntactically and semantically. Now the following exercises are arranged accordingly to their level of complexity, the simplest first:

- "مَا هُنَّ أُمَّهَاتِهِمْ" (*The qur'ān*, 58:2)
"they are **not** their mothers" (Haleem, p.362).

- "مَا أَنتُمْ إِلاَّ بَشَرٌ مِّثْلُنَا" (*The qur'ān*, 36:15)
a. "You are only men like ourselves" (Haleem, p.280) [*this verse is numbered incorrectly in Haleem's version as verse no. 16*].
b. "You are only men like ourselves" (Yūsuf ʿAlī, p.537).
c. "You are only human beings like ourselves" (al-Hilālī and Khan, p.589).

Again, translation (c) is most appropriate, due to the fact that the word بشر has its most appropriate equivalence, though in the context the intended were 'men' and not all human beings.

- "وَمَا أَنَا إِلَّا نَذِيرٌ مُّبِينٌ" (*The qur'ān*, 46:9)
a. "I only warn you plainly" (Haleem, p.327).
b. "I am but a Warner open and clear" (Yūsuf ʿAlī, p.625).

c. "and I am but a plain warner" (al-Hilālī and Khan, p.682).

d. "and I am just a genuinely foreboding harbinger" (*my translation*).

- "وَمَا أَمْرُنَا إِلَّا وَاحِدَةٌ كَلَمْحٍ بِالبَصَر" (*The qur'ān*, 54:50)

a. "when we ordain something it happens at once, in the blink of an eye" (Haleem, p.352).

b. "And Our Command is but a single (act) – like the twinkling of an eye" (Yūsuf 'Alī, p.669).

c. "And our Commandment is but one as the twinkling of an eye" (al-Hilālī and Khan, p.727).

d. "And Our Command is done in a single act, in the blink of an eye" (*my translation*).

- "وَمَا رَبُّكَ بِغَافِلٍ عَمَّا يَعْمَلُونَ" (*The qur'ān*, 6:132)

a. "your Lord is **not** unaware of anything they do" (Haleem, p.90).

b. "for your Lord is **not** unmindful of anything they do" (Yūsuf 'Alī, p.161).

c. "And your Lord is **not** unaware of what they do" (al-Hilālī and Khan, p.192).

It is worth noting that translation (c) above is most appropriate of all the translations.

4.9. زال (لا) = to be still (implying 'continuity')

37. ما زال زيد قائماً.

Zayd **was still** standing.

38. لا زال بيتك مقصوداً.

Your house **was still** visited constantly.
OR: Your house **was still** targeted.

The difference between the two translations in Example 38 is based on the context, which is not the point of discussion here, but it is related to situationality as discussed by de Beaugrande (1981/7th ed. 1994, pp.163-81).

4.10. انفك (ما) = to be still (implying 'continuity')

39.   ما انفك زيد مشغولاً.
 Zayd **is still** busy.
OR: Zayd **is still tied up with** work.

The second translation is more appropriate as the TL verb 'be tied up' is closer to the meaning of the SL verb 'ما انفك', although the TL equivalence of the whole nominal SL sentence is a verbal and not nominal one.

4.11. فتئ (ما) = to be still (implying 'continuity')

40.   ما فتئ الطالب يذاكر.
The student **is still** revising.
OR: The student **is revising** assiduously (or persistently).
OR: The student **has not stopped** revising **at all**.

It is clear that all these translations can be considered appropriate with little additions of adverbs such as 'assiduously' or 'persistently', so that they give the same meaning and effect. The third translation seems to have the most appropriate TL verb, and implies continuity as well through its negative-negative formula.

4.12. برح (ما) = to be still (implying 'continuity')

41.   ما برح الحارس واقفاً.

The guard **is still** standing.

The implicit meaning is that he is still standing and 'has not left his post'.

4.13. دام (ما) = to be so long as (implying 'for a certain period of time')

42.   ينجح الطالب ما دام مجداً.

The student succeeds so long as he is hard-working.

But when ما implies negation, then the superseding verb ما دام will no longer be an auxiliary but a proper verb, e.g.

43.   ما دام شيء.

Nothing **lasts** forever.

Here are exercises about Superseding auxiliary verbs (النواسخ) in the nominal SL sentence and their TL equivalence

" وَلَمْ يَكُ مِنَ الْمُشْرِكِينَ " (*The qur'ān*, 16:120)

a. "He was not an idolater" (Haleem, p.174).

b. "and he joined not gods with Allah" (Yūsuf 'Alī, p.325).

c. "and he was not one of those who were *Al-Mushrikūn* (polytheists, idolaters, disbelievers in the Oneness of Allāh, and those who joined partners with Allāh)" (al-Hilālī and Khan, p.365).

141

"وَلَمْ أَكُ بَغِيًّا" (*The qur'ān*, 19:20) "

a. "I have not **been** unchaste" (Haleem, p.192).

b. "and I **am** not unchaste?" (Yūsuf 'Alī, p.359).

c. "nor **am** I unchaste?" (al-Hilālī and Khan, p.404).

One more exercise is this.

"فَأَلْقُوهُ عَلَى وَجْهِ أَبِي يَأْتِ بَصِيرًا." (*The qur'ān*, 12:93)

a. "and lay it over my father's face: he will recover his sight" (Haleem, p.151)

b. "and cast it over the face of my father: he will **come** to see (clearly)" (Yūsuf 'Alī, p.281).

c. "and cast it over the face of my father, he will **become** clear-sighted" (al-Hilālī and Khan, p.317).

Here is a further exercise.

" أَلَيْسَ اللـه بِعَزِيزٍ ذِي انتِقَامٍ." (*The qur'ān*, 39:37).

a. "**Is God not** mighty and capable of retribution?" (Haleem, p.297)

b. "**Is not** Allah Exalted in Power, (able to enforce His Will), Lord of Retribution?" (Yūsuf 'Alī, p.570)

c. "**Is not** Allāh All-Mighty, Possessor of Retribution?" (al-Hilālī and Khan, p.623)

d. "**Is God not** most powerful and capable of retribution?"

Translations (b) and (c) violate English grammar, by placing 'not' before the subject.

Here is another exercise.

" قَالُواْ تَاللـه تَفْتَأُ تَذْكُرُ يُوسُفَ حتى تكون..." (*The qur'ān*, 12:85)

a. "They said, 'By God! You will… if you **do not stop** thinking of Joseph…' "
(Haleem, p.151).

b. "They said: 'By Allah! **(never)** will you **cease** to remember Joseph until you
reach…" (Yūsuf ʿAlī, p.280).

c. "They said: 'By Allāh! You will **never cease** remembering Yūsuf (Joseph) until
you become…' " (al-Hilālī and Khan, p.315).

d. "They said, 'By God! **Stop** mentioning Joseph **incessantly** otherwise you
will…' " (*my translation*).

A further exercise is this one,

"وَأَوْصَانِي بِالصَّلَاةِ وَالزَّكَاةِ مَا دُمْتُ حَيًّا." (*The qurʾān*, 19:31)

a. "He commanded me to pray, to give alms **as long as** I live" (Haleem, p.192).

b. "and [He] has enjoined on me Prayer and Charity **as long as** I live" (Yūsuf
ʿAlī, p.361).

c. "and [He] has enjoined on me Salāt (prayer), and Zakāt, **as long as** I live" (al-
Hilālī and Khan, p.405).

Translation (a) needs the conjunction 'and' instead of the comma, and to drop
the infinitive particle 'to', i.e. 'to pray and give alms'; the reason is that TL
grammar requires such obvious procedure. Translation (b) is most appropriate,
whereas translation (c) needs after the loan word 'Zakāt' a word to explain it, as
it is foreign to English readers, the way that translation has done with the loan
word Salāt which has been explained or actually translated.

"كُونُواْ قَوَّامِينَ بِالْقِسْطِ." (*The qurʾān*, 4:135)

a. "uphold justice" (Haleem, p.63).

143

b. "Stand out firmly for justice" (Yūsuf 'Alī, p.109).

c. "Stand out firmly for justice" (al-Hilālī and Khan, p.132).

d. "**Be** upholders of justice" (*my translation*).

"وَكَانَ حَقًّا عَلَيْنَا نَصْرُ الْمُؤْمِنِينَ." (*The qur'ān*, 30:47)

a. "We make it Our duty to help the believers" (Haleem, p.260).

b. "and it **was** due from Us to aid those who believed" (Yūsuf 'Alī, p.497).

c. "and (as for) the believers, it **was** incumbent upon Us to help (them)" (al-Hilālī and Khan, p.546).

d. "and it **was** incumbent upon Us to assist the believers" (*my translation*).

One more exercise is this,

"فَسُبْحَانَ اللـهِ حِينَ تُمْسُونَ وَحِينَ تُصْبِحُونَ." (*The qur'ān*, 30:17)

a. "So celebrate God's glory **in the evening, in the morning**" (Haleem, p.258)

b. "So (give) glory to Allah, when you **reach eventide** and when you **rise in the morning**" (Yūsuf 'Alī, p.492).

c. "So glorify Allāh [above all that (evil) they associate with Him (O believers)], when you **come up to the evening** [i.e. offer the (*Maghrib*) sunset and ('*Ishā*) night prayers], and when you **enter the morning** [i.e. offer the (*Fajr*) morning prayer]" (al-Hilālī and Khan, p.542).

d. "So you glorify God **in the evening, in the morning**" (*my translation*).

Another exercise is the following,

" وَإِن كَانَ ذُو عُسْرَةٍ فَنَظِرَةٌ إِلَى مَيْسَرَةٍ." (The qur'ān, 2:280)

a. "If the debtor **is in difficulty**, then delay things until matters become easier for him" (Haleem, p.32).

b. "If the debtor **is in a difficulty**, grant him time till it is easy for him to repay" (Yūsuf 'Alī, p.51).

c. "And if the debtor **is in a hard time** (has no money), then grant him time till it is easy for him to repay" (al-Hilālī and Khan, p.65).

d. "If he [the debtor] **is in distress**, then be easy on him" (*my translation*).

More interesting exercises are the following,

" وَلَمْ تَكُن لَّهُ فِئَةٌ يَنصُرُونَهُ مِن دُونِ اللهِ وَمَا كَانَ مُنتَصِرًا." (The qur'ān, 18:43)

a. "He **had no** forces to help him other than God – he could not even help himself" (Haleem, p.186).

b. "**Nor had** he numbers to help him against Allah, nor was he able to deliver himself" (Yūsuf 'Alī, p.348).

c. "And he **had no** group of men to help him against Allāh, **nor could** he defend (or save) himself" (al-Hilālī and Khan, p.391).

Another exercise is this one,

" وَمَا كَانَ لَنَا أَن نَّأْتِيَكُم بِسُلْطَانٍ إِلَّا بِإِذْنِ اللهِ." (The qur'ān, 14:11)

a. "We **cannot** bring you any proof unless God permits it" (Haleem, p.159).

b. "It **is not** for us to bring you an authority except as Allah permits" (Yūsuf 'Alī, p.295).

c. "It **is not** ours to bring you an authority (proof) except by the Permission of Allāh" (al-Hilālī and Khan, p.329).

d. "We **could only** bring you an authority, God permitting" (*my translation*).

The only difference between translations (a-c) and translation (d) is that the latter gives the positive form of the SL sentence, instead of the negative-negative form in the ST.

" وَأَخَذَ الَّذِينَ ظَلَمُوا الصَّيْحَةُ فَأَصْبَحُوا فِي دِيَارِهِمْ جَاثِمِينَ." (*The qur'ān*, 11:67)

a. "The blast struck the evildoers and they lay dead in their homes" (Haleem, p.141).

b. "The (mighty) Blast overtook the wrong-doers, and they lay prostrate in their homes **before the morning**" (Yūsuf ʿAlī, p.259).

c. "And *As-Saihah* (torment – awful cry) overtook the wrong-doers, so they lay (dead), prostrate in their homes" (al-Hilālī and Khan, p.296).

d. "And the cry struck those who were unjust, and **by the morning** they lay face down in their own homes" (*my translation*).

" أَلَمْ تَكُنْ آيَاتِي تُتْلَى عَلَيْكُمْ فَكُنتُم بِهَا تُكَذِّبُونَ." (*The qur'ān*, 23:105)

a. "**Were** my messages **not** recited over and over to you and still you **rejected** them?" (Haleem, p.219)

b. "**Were not** My Signs rehearsed to you, and you **did** but treat them as falsehood?" (Yūsuf ʿAlī, p.416)

c. "**Were not** My Verses (this Qur'ān) recited to you, and then you **used to** deny them?" (al-Hilālī and Khan, p.465)

d. "**Had My Verses not been** recited to you, but you **considered** them untrue?" (*my translation*)

" وَمَا كُنتَ بِجَانِبِ الْغَرْبِيِّ إِذْ قَضَيْنَا إِلَى مُوسَى الْأَمْرَ وَمَا كُنتَ مِنَ الشَّاهِدِينَ." (*The qur'ān*, 28:44)

a. "You [Muhammad] **were not** present on the western side of the mountain when We gave Our command to Moses: you **were not** there" (Haleem, p.248).

b. "You **were not** on the Western side when We decreed the Commission to Moses, **nor were** you a witness (of those events)" (Yūsuf 'Alī, p.474).

c. "And you (O Muhammad) **were not** on the western side (of the Mount), when We made clear to *Mūsā* (Moses) the commandment, and you **were not** among the witnesses" (al-Hilālī and Khan, p.521).

"أَوَلَيْسَ الـلـه بِأَعْلَمَ بِمَا فِي صُدُورِ الْعَالَمِينَ." (The qur'ān, 29:10)

a. "**Does** God **not** know best what is in everyone's hearts?" (Haleem, p.252)

b. "**Does not** Allah know best all that is in the hearts of all Creation?" (Yūsuf 'Alī, p.482)

c. "**Is not** Allāh Best Aware of what is in the breasts of the *'Alamīn* (mankind and jinn)" (al-Hilālī and Khan, p.530).

It is really problematic lexically regarding the TL culture/social-specific equivalence for the word صدور - earlier in the book discussed (p.49), whether to translate the word صدر as 'chest' or 'breast' – but here it is referring to the 'hearts' as in translations (a) and (b).

A further exercise is this,

"لَقَدْ كَانَ لَكُمْ فِي رَسُولِ الـلـه أُسْوَةٌ حَسَنَةٌ لِّمَن كَانَ يَرْجُو الـلـه وَالْيَوْمَ (The qur'ān, 33:21)
الْآخِرَ وَذَكَرَ الـلـه كَثِيرًا."

a. "The Messenger of God **is** an excellent model for those of you who **put** your hope in God and the Last Day and remember Him often" (Haleem, p.268).

b. "You **have** indeed in the Messenger of Allah a beautiful pattern (of conduct) for any one whose hope **is** in Allah and the Final Day, and who engages much in the Praise of Allah" (Yūsuf 'Alī, p.511).

c. "Indeed in the Messenger of Allāh (Muhammad) you **have** a good example to follow for him who **hopes** for (the Meeting with) Allāh and the Last Day, and remembers Allāh much" (al-Hilālī and Khan, p.562).

It is clear here that the present tense is used in all the translations, though the ST is using the past tense. The style is rather rare, to translate the past tense in the ST into the present tense in the TT.

Chapter Five: SL verbs of appropinquation, beginning and beseeching (أفعال المقاربة والشروع والرجاء) functioning as auxiliary and their English equivalence

5.1. SL verbs of approximation, along with their equivalence

It is important to note that approximation SL verbs acts in the same way as that of the verb 'to be', in that it supersedes the nominal sentence and its predicate is a verbal clause (al-Rājiḥī, p.138). Their equivalence may be in the form of a phrasal verb 'to be about to' or can be introduced as an adverb to give the sense of approximation.

5.1.1. كاد = To be about to or almost

1.   كاد زيد يصل.

Zayd **was about to** arrive.

OR: Zayd **has almost arrived**.

2.   كاد النعام يطير.

'The ostrich can almost fly' (Fischer, p.221).

The first translation of Example 1 uses 'to be about to', while the second uses the adverb 'almost' and both versions give the same meaning and effect as that in the nominal SL sentence above. Also the tense in the SL sentence is in the past and needs to be so in the TL equivalence. The same comment applies to the following example,

5.1.2. أوشك = To be about to

Here is an example,

3.   أوشك زيد أن يصل.

Zayd **was about** to arrive.

OR: Zayd **has almost arrived.**

In examples 3 and 4 the present tense is used in the nominal SL sentence and must be used in the TL equivalence.

4.   .يوشك زيد أن يصل
Zayd **is about to** arrive.

5.   .يكاد زيد يصل
Zayd **is about to** arrive.

5.2. SL verbs of initiation and their equivalence:

Initiation verbs have similar function syntactically as the verb 'to be', in that they need their subject and predicate; but their predicate must be a verb sentence. Their TL equivalence is 'to start to', 'to set out to' or 'to begin'.

5.2.1. شرع = To start to
6.   .شرع زيدٌ يقرأ
Zayd **started to** read.

5.2.2. هبّ = To start or to rush to

7.   .هبت الفتاة تساعد في إعداد الطعام
The girl **rushed to** help prepare food.

5.2.3. هلهل = to start to become

8.   .هلهل الولد قميصه
The boy **let** his shirt **become** shabby.

5.2.4. جعل = to make someone do or to begin

9.   جعل الطفلة تضحك.

He **made** the little girl laugh.

جعلت أحذرهم.

'I began to warn them' (Fischer's TL equivalence, see p.221).

5.2.5. طفق = To start to do or to do something suddenly

10.   طفق الولد يبني بيتاً من الورق.

The boy **set out to** build a house of cards.

11.   طفق القوم يرجعون.

'**Suddenly** the people returned' Fischer's TL equivalence, p.221).

5.2.6. أخذ = To start to do or to begin

12.   أخذ الصبي يطلب الحلوى.

The kid **started to** demand for sweets.

13.   أخذ يعاتبه.

'He **began** to blame him' (Fischer's TL equivalence, p.221).

5.2.7. اخلولقت = To start or To be about to

14.   اخلولقت السحابة أن تمطر.

The cloud **starts to** rain.

15.   اخلولق الشتاء أن يحل.

Winter **starts to** come.

16.   اخلولق الكرب أن ينفرج.

Grief **is about to** be driven away.

5.3. SL verbs of beseeching and their equivalence

The predicate of the nominal SL sentence is a verbal sentence with its verb 'may

hopefully' or 'will/shall hopefully', e.g.

5.3.1. عسى = To hope to happen

17.   عسى زيد أن يوفق. أو: عسى زيد يوفق.

Zayd **may hopefully** succeed.

OR: Zayd **will hopefully** succeed.

18.   عسى الله أن يشفيك.

May God help you recover from your illness.

It is important to add the phrase 'from your illness' as it is not connotative in the TL equivalence, the way it is in the SL sentence.

Here are few exercises to see SL Verbs of appropinquation, beginning and beseeching (أفعال المقاربة والشروع والرجاء) functioning as auxiliary and their English equivalence.

"عَسَى رَبُّكُمْ أَن يَرْحَمَكُمْ." (*The qur'ān*, 17:8)

a. "Your Lord **may** yet have mercy on you" (Haleem, p.175).

b. "It **may be** that you Lord may (yet) show Mercy unto you" (Yūsuf 'Alī, p.328).

c. "[And We said in the Taurāt (Torah)]: 'It **may be** that you Lord may show mercy unto you' " (al-Hilālī and Khan, p.369).

"فَعَسَى الله أَن يَأْتِيَ بِالْفَتْحِ." (*The qur'ān*, 5:52)

a. "But God **may well** bring about a triumph" (Haleem, p.73).

b. "**Perhaps** Allah will give (you) victory" (Yūsuf 'Alī, p.128).

c. "**Perhaps** Allāh **may** bring a victory" (al-Hilālī and Khan, p.153).

d. "So God **may** help (you) attain victory" (*my translation*).

Translation (c) is overemphatic on the probability, using two words 'perhaps' and 'may'; so there is redundancy there. It is worth noting that the word فتح can also mean 'a conquest'; its plural فتوحات is 'conquests'.

" وَمَا كَادُواْ يَفْعَلُونَ." (*The qur'ān*, 2:71)

a. "though they **almost** failed to do so" (Haleem, p.10).

b. "but not with good-will" (Yūsuf 'Alī, p.12)

c. "though they **were near to** not doing it" (al-Hilālī and Khan, p.15).

Now translation (b) follows the sense more than the wording of the ST.

" يَكَادُ زَيْتُهَا يُضِيءُ." (*The qur'ān*, 24:35)

a. "whose oil **almost** gives light" (Haleem, p.223).

b. "whose oil is **well-nigh** luminous" (Yūsuf 'Alī, p.424).

c. "whose oil would **almost** glow forth (of itself)" (al-Hilālī and Khan, p.472).

The final exercise here is this,

" وَطَفِقَا يَخْصِفَانِ عَلَيْهِمَا مِن وَرَقِ الْجَنَّةِ." (*The qur'ān*, 7:22)

a. "they **began to** put together leaves from the Garden to cover themselves" (Haleem, p.95).

b. "and they **began to** sew together the leaves of the Garden over their bodies" (Yūsuf 'Alī, p.170).

c. "and they **began to** cover themselves with the leaves of Paradise" (al-Hilālī and Khan, p.202).

153

PART II: Equivalence at sentence level

Chapter Six: Nominal SL sentence and its TL equivalence

There are two types of sentences in the SL, nominal and verbal sentences; but it is not the case in the TL which has only one type, the verbal sentence. This means that the student and professional translator need to be aware of this significant difference between the two languages in order to decide the appropriate TL equivalence for these two TL types of sentences. It is the nominal sentence in the SL which needs extra attention as it is not there in the TL, this sentence consists of the subject and the predicate, and at time the predicate can be in the form of a verbal clause or fronted and transposed before the subject. This means that more than one clause can be used in one sentence as we are going to see in the following examples. Such variations of the nominal sentence are problematic and need to be analysed syntactically before their equivalence can be correctly identified or chosen.

6.1. The subject in the nominal SL sentence and its corresponding equivalence in the TL

It is a job in itself to identify the subject in the SL, as it is one of the two main elements that form a nominal sentence in the SL. Failure to do so will result in producing an incorrect equivalence. Here are examples that elaborate this point,

157

1.   لا إله إلا اللـه خيرُ ما يقول مؤمن.

'No god but God' is the best thing the Faithful would say.

This sentence in the SL is a complex nominal one, which has three clauses and this is clear in its equivalence in the TL.

2.   الصيفَ ضيعتِ اللبن مثلُ قديم.

'You have missed your chance' is an old proverb.

Here in Example 2 the proverb itself is a verbal sentence in the SL acting as subject but can be also translated in the TL as nominal sentence – 'it's too late' – for it carries the same meaning and effect as those in the SL. These two translations of the above proverb is based on language and culture, as proverbs are by default pregnant with meaning and culture. Moreover, the literal translation of the proverb - "in the summer she missed the milk' – is far from obvious at different levels – its syntactic and semantic level. Perhaps implementing one of the seven standards of text linguistics on this sentence might work, namely intertextuality – that is to have a previous text within the current text. The cultural and textual analysis actually works well with proverbs, because they are rich in culture, and the syntactic analysis at the levels of word and sentence are not enough to help in finding the appropriate equivalence. One needs to probe deeper mainly into the cultural dimension.

Going back to the syntactic analysis, the main point of the discussion in this chapter, Example 3 below - not unlike Example 2 - is yet another complex nominal sentence in the SL; and based on such

158

analysis of the SL here, one can find the appropriate equivalence. This example is a verse from the holy *Qur'ān*,

3. ("وأن تصوموا خيرٌ لكم" (بمعنى وصيامكم خيرٌ لكم).

'**Fasting** is better for you.'

Although a similar equivalence to this example is 'to fast is better for you', which is a kind of parallelism – that is, to have the infinitive acting as subject. This brings to mind the commonly quoted sentence in English 'to err is human' which is similar in terms of structure. In Example 3, the subject in this nominal sentence is a verb in the infinitive form acting as subject which can be translated as gerund in the TL. Now the SL nominal sentence 'هم نيام' is translated by Fischer 'They are sleeping', (*Op.cit.*, 189) but when translating one must stick more closely to the SL structure where possible, and as it is a nominal SL sentence then its TL equivalence is 'They are asleep'. The same syntactic analysis can be done to Example 4:

4. أن تذاكرَ أنفعُ لك.

Studying is good for you (or useful to you).

5. هل من رجلٍ في البيت؟

Is there **a man** in the house?

In the analysis of the above example, Example 5, the subject is 'man' and the predicate is 'in the house'; also, there is the redundant preposition which needs to be omitted before finding the sentence equivalence. Failure to analyse the sentence syntactically means that one will find difficulty in finding its appropriate equivalence. It is clear that the syntactic analysis is essential at the sentence level, which is the first step towards training students and professional translators, unless the sentence is pregnant with culture as in the case of the proverb in Example 2 above.

6. بحسبك رزق الله.

What you earn will hopefully suffice (with God blessing).

This is such a structurally complex sentence; the words highlighted in Example 6 indicate the subject and predicate. It is vital to note that a redundant preposition is attached to the subject and needs to be omitted when producing the equivalence. Obviously the first word with the omission of the preposition acts as subject based on the above syntactic analysis and the following word is the predicate. This method helps in breaking down the sentence to its essentials. Moreover, the phrase 'with God blessing' is connotative in the TL, therefore its inclusion is optional. The implication in the SL is, 'May God help you not to ask others for help, because He make you earn enough' (see al-Rājiḥī, pp.85-6); such a structurally complex sentence semantically makes it difficult to analyse in simple terms.

7. كيف بك عند احتدام الأمر؟

What would you do when things get going?

The focus is on the two words highlighted in the SL here: The interrogative is the fronted or transposed predicate, (This term is translated either 'predicate placed in front or transposed', see Cachia, p.60) followed by the redundant preposition; and the pronominal suffice is acting as subject. Such analysis is essential to understand the sense of the sentence before attempting to find its appropriate equivalence. To prove how effective the syntactic analysis is when translating, here is yet another example of a nominal sentence,

8. رُبّ امرأةٍ أعظمُ من رجل.

A woman may be greater than a man.

In the way the computer works when reading a sentence in English in terms of grammar, by locating the noun acting as subject, then the verb and the rest of the sentence, one needs to omit the first word immediately here as it is a redundant preposition and the following word 'a woman' is the subject followed immediately by the predicate in this instance. Here is another instance of a nominal sentence in the SL,

9. ما جشعٌ بنافع.

Greed (or, Covetousness) is no good.

In Example 9, the first word helps with the negation only and has no other function in this nominal sentence (al-Rājiḥī, p.88), the second word is the subject 'greed' or 'covetousness' acting as subject, and the final word has a redundant preposition attached which is to be omitted as it has no function as we have seen earlier in the discussion on translating redundant prepositions and finally 'good' or 'useful' which is the predicate.

Such analysis has helped to understand the SL, and its equivalence is found accordingly, it is in fact not only to know the lexical meaning of each word, but also to know its syntactical relation with other words in order to know the exact structure of the whole sentence.

Identifying the subject of a nominal sentence is just as problematic as that of identifying the predicate.

10.   في الصدق نجاة.

Honesty is the best way out.

Unlike Example 9, in Example 10 the preposition is fundamental to the structure of the sentence and has a function, it acts in combination with the noun 'honesty' as subject – i.e. the prepositional phrase acting as subject - and the final word is the predicate here. The same can be said about the prepositional phrase in the following example,

11.   أمام البيت رجل.

There is in front of the house a man.
OR: In front of the house there is a man.

But it will be more confusing when the prepositional phrase acts as predicate, as in the example blow,

12.   نصرٌ للمؤمنين.

Victory is achieved for the Faithful.

It is obvious that Example 12 is more complex and requires more attention in order to produce the TL sentence as it can be interpreted as the implication is that it is hoped that 'victory is achieved' for them and not by them as students and professional translators might assume. Here we pray that 'the Faithful are victorious'. One can see the incorrect analysis of this nominal sentence can lead to an incorrect or inaccurate translation.

Another important element that needs to be present in the TL with regard to translating a nominal sentence is the use of verb 'to be'. it might appear in examples 11 and 12 that no verb is required in the TL as it is not there in the SL, but it is essential to have one in the TL, which is the verb 'to be', otherwise the TL sentence is incorrect.

Another issue in the translation of nominal SL sentences is the use of the verbal sentence within it acting as predicate and the subject is just a noun, here is an example,

13.   صديقٌ نفعَك وفاؤه.
There is a friend whose allegiance (or loyalty) is useful (or beneficial) to you.

It is clear that the verbal sentence which acts as predicate is used in the SL as a secondary clause that serves the purpose. Now these examples of the nominal sentence in the SL prove that such a sentence is problematic in the TL, as the prepositional phrase or the verbal sentence within the nominal sentence can both act as subject or predicate in the SL and that fact needs to be conveyed truthfully in the TL. It is helpful to add the verbal structure 'there is' or 'there are' or something similar in order to produce a good TL sentence, otherwise the translation has no correct structure, and the TL sentence will be just a phrase and not a sentence. However, having said that it must be pointed out that the product must correspond to the TL grammar and not necessarily to the SL grammar; but the syntactic analysis of the SL is still essential in order to understand the sense of the sentence before attempting to translate it.

In Example 14 below, the same can be said about how the prepositional phrase acts as predicate. But it is vital to know that the word 'generous' is merely an adjective here in the SL, and not to be confused when its noun is defined with a definite particle 'the'. Here the noun is not defined and both the noun and its adjective are acting as subject. This is yet another pitfall which students and professional translators might encounter and need to be aware of.

14.   رجل كريم في البيت.

There is a generous man in the house.

OR: A generous man is in the house.

So as soon as one realises that he/she is dealing with a nominal sentence, the first task is to identify the subject and the predicate, as they vary in the SL, as they sometimes can be in the form of a prepositional phrase or just a noun with an extra non-functional preposition or a verbal sentence acting as predicate as we have seen earlier. Here are two more examples of nominal sentences with their verbal sentences acting as predicate in the SL,

15.   رُجَيْلٌ (تصغير رجل) يتحدث.

There is a small man who is talking.

OR: A small man is talking.

Here the SL diminutive noun 'small man' has no direct equivalent; as in the case of 'novel'- 'novelette'.

16.   رَجُلا علم يتناقشان.

There are two scholars who are involved in a discussion.

OR: Two scholars are involved in a discussion.

As in the case in Example 14 in which the subject consists of two words (adjective and noun), here in Example 16 is a complex dual noun acting as subject, consisting of two words. And the verbal sentence acts as predicate in the SL, in the TL it is produced as a secondary clause to the main clause – 'there are two scholars'. Often students fail to recognise this type of structure in the SL. At times as in the above examples 15 and 16 as there are in the TL two clauses, they can be made into just one clause, 'A small man is talking' and 'Two scholars are involved in a discussion'. This is better in style in the TL.

More complex nominal SL sentences require careful handling, as in the following where the subject is in the second part of the conditional sentence,

17.   إن يكن منك إخلاص فإخلاصٌ لك.
Your **loyalty** is for your own benefit (in the end).

It is true that the clause 'if you are loyal', it is connotative in the TL, that is why it is omitted in the translation – which can be considered a gist translation. But also exegetic translation (Dickins, pp.9-10) is sometimes useful when the phrase 'in the end' is added in order to serve the purpose in the TL.

18.   لولا إهمال لأفلح.
Had it not been for negligence, he would have succeeded.

It is problematic enough when the subject in the SL is present, but when it is originally connotative and therefore unnecessary, it can be connotative in the TL and can be omitted, as in the following examples,

19.   أين عليّ؟ - مسافرٌ.

Where is Ali? – **Travelling** (or, **on the move**).

20.   كيف الحال؟ - حسنٌ.

How are you? - **Good**.

The subject in the nominal SL sentence can be omitted or delayed on purpose as a form of compliment or criticism, in this case the task of the student or professional translator gets harder, as he/she needs to identify the subject first and decides what the predicate is, as the latter can be fronted. Here is an example,

21.   نعم القائدُ خالدٌ.

He is a good leader, Khalid is!

OR: What a good leader Khalid is.

What a complex structure that is of the nominal SL sentence, it is clear the verbal clause acts as fronted predicate and the subject is delayed in the SL, that is why when translating such a nominal sentence, the syntactic analysis is essential. It is also vital when one makes a pledge, or swear to do something, this kind of style may omit the subject and the prepositional phrase acts as predicate. Here the student and professional translator needs to be sure of which is which, see the following example,

22.   بحياتي لأحافظن على العهد.

I swear (by my life) to keep my promise.

The phrase 'by my life' is connotative in the TL and that is why it is omitted; whilst the connotative element in the SL is in the words 'I swear'. This is a golden rule in translation between Arabic and English with regards to this form of expression.

The nominal SL sentence gets more complicated when the subject is omitted for specificity, as in Example 23,

23.   أحب الفاكهة لا سيّما العنبُ.
I love fruit, **particularly grapes.**

Here the SL predicate - 'grapes' - is there but the subject - 'the fruit' - is not. The connotative meaning is, 'The fruit I like is specifically grapes'; and the exegetic translation is 'I love fruit, and the fruit I love most is grapes'. This syntactic analysis is the way forward to producing a good more appropriate translation of this nominal sentence.

6.2. Where are the SL predicate and its corresponding TL equivalence?

Having looked at the subject in the nominal SL sentence and how its corresponding equivalence can be found, it is time to see how to analyse the predicate and decide what its corresponding or appropriate equivalence is.

167

6.2.1. The predicate in the nominal SL sentence with just one noun, and its equivalence

This predicate can also be a gerund or an adjective as in the following two examples,

1.   زيد مجتهد.

Zayd is **hard working** (or, **assiduous**).

2.   المنظر رائع.

     The view is **wonderful**.

Notice that the verb 'to be' is added in the TL, otherwise the TL sentence would not make sense in the eyes of the TL recipient, as discussed earlier in Example 11 and 12 (see *para*.6.1. above).

6.2.2. The predicate in the nominal SL sentence and its equivalence

It is also problematic when the predicate is the nominal SL sentence is yet another nominal or verbal sentence. Here are few examples,

3.   زيدٌ خلقهُ كريمٌ.

     Zayd is **of a generous character**.

     OR: Zayd **has noble manners**.

It is clear analysing the SL sentence has helped tremendously in the process of translation. It is now obvious nominal sentences are by no means nominal in the TL and must be verbal. And when the predicate is a verbal sentence then the student and professional translator have no choice but to re-produce two verbal clauses in the TL or re-structure them to make one single verbal TL sentence that *makes sense,*

4.   عليّ يتحدث الفرنسية.
       Ali speaks French.

In the nominal SL sentence above, the subject is 'Ali' but the predicate is a whole verbal clause. Notice how the whole SL sentence, which consists of two clauses, is re-produced in the TL in one clause only.

5.   الكتابُ أقرأُه.
The book is **the one I am reading**.
OR: I am reading the book.

It is noticeable that in the second translation of Example 5, the TL equivalence is a verbal sentence, but the emphasis has shifted, so perhaps the first translation is better to give the same *effect* and *meaning* as the original SL sentence.

6.2.3. Nominal SL sentence, whose predicate must be a clause, and its equivalence

There are a number of cases where the predicate must be a clause, and need to be understood that way by the student or professional translator in order to know how to produce an appropriate equivalence. In these cases, the subject stipulates that its predicate is a clause, be it conditional or having a 'pronoun of the fact' ضمير الشأن

(see Cachia, p.57 and Fischer, p.179), or be it the person who is being praised or criticized, or specified from which group of people, or even in the phrase 'How many'; in such cases the predicate must be a clause (al-Rājihī, pp.95-7).

Status pronoun acting as subject with a predicate clause and its TL equivalence

When the pronoun is acting as subject with a predicate clause Here is an example,

6.　　　"قل هو الله أحد."
'Say, He is God the One'

It is vital to indicate that 'He' is the subject of the above nominal SL sentence that must have a sentential predicate, but in the equivalence the verbal clause 'God is the One' is connotative in the translation and therefore not required.

Predicate in a conditional SL sentence and its corresponding equivalence

Here is an example,
7.　　　من يذاكر ينجح.
If **one** studies, he/she will succeed.
OR: The one, who studies, will succeed.

It is clear that the second translation is more appropriate, even though it does not have the same syntactic structure as that in the SL. This proves that the SL structure may not be followed in the TL structure; but the same *meaning* and *effect* in the TL need be achieved. The issue here is for the student or professional translator is to understand the meaning and effect of the SL as the first step towards producing an appropriate equivalence.

A predicate Clause in the form of praise or criticism and its equivalence
It is worth mentioning here that though the predicate in the SL sentence is a verbal clause, it is not so in the TL sentence, but the meaning and effect is still there in the TL.

8. خالد نعم القائد.
Khalid is **a good leader indeed!**
(*cf.* example 31 in paragraph 6.2.4.)

Subject in the nominal SL sentence specified with a verbal clause but in the TL with just one verbal sentence.

Here is an example,
9.   نحن – العربَ – نكرم الضيف.
We – **the Arabs**- show hospitality to our guests.

It is clear that in Example 8 the nominal sentence is not necessarily translated as nominal but just verbal one because it gives the same effect and meaning as that in the SL. In the TL sentence specification is just indicated in the subject and its parenthetical phrase 'the Arabs'.

171

Predicative كأيّن *acting as subject, its clause predicate and their equivalence*

Here is an example,

10.   كأيّن من مريض شفاه اللـه. (بمعنى، كم من مريض شفاه اللـه).
How many patients are **cured by God's power!**

Here it is vital to recognize that the verbal SL sentence in Example 10 acts as predicate, this helps in the syntactic analysis of the nominal SL sentence and certainly enables students or professional translators find the most appropriate equivalence. The subject is clearly 'how many patients', but even that is not even easy to understand, that is why the explanation in between the brackets is added.

6.2.4. Tautology or repetition of the subject for rhetoric, including intensiveness or hyperbole (Cachia, p.15)

Another form of the nominal SL sentence is, and this stipulates the predicate to be a clause as in the following example,

11.   "الحاقة ما الحاقة"
'The Inevitable Hour! **What is the Inevitable Hour?'**
          (Haleem, p.387)

The clause 'what is the Inevitable Hour?' acts as predicate in the nominal SL sentence, whose equivalence gives the same meaning and effect, as Professor Haleem's translation shows.

6.2.5. Repetition of the subject in the form of demonstrative pronoun, its predicate clause and their equivalence

Here is an example,

12.   النجاحُ ذلك أمل كل طالب.
Success, **that is the hope** of every student.

6.3. Predicate as prepositional phrase.

Here is an example,

13.   الطالب في الفصل.
The student is **in class**.

But at times the predicate in the nominal SL sentence is fronted and its equivalence needs to have the same meaning and effect as in the following example,

14.   أمامَ البيت شجرة.
In front of the house there is a tree.

Adverbs of time are also used in the SL, acting as predicate, their equivalence may not be an object in the verbal TL sentence as in the following two examples,

15.   الصومُ يومَ الخميس.
Fasting is **on Thursday**.

16.   الهلالُ الليلةَ. (بمعنى، رؤية الهلال الليلة)
The crescent will be seen **tonight**.

173

It is not clear that the TL equivalence of a nominal SL sentence may not be as easy as it appears to be, and it is only when the syntactic analysis is done that the appropriate effective and meaningful equivalence is found.

6.3.1. Predicate with ف

Here is an example,

17. طالب يذاكر فناجح.

The student who studies will **succeed** (or **pass**).

Although the SL predicate is a noun (highlighted above), its equivalence is merely the verb 'succeed'. The SL predicate can sometimes be an adjective, and its equivalence can be of a similar category, i.e. the TL equivalence of the SL predicates is also an adjective as in the following example,

18. أما عليٌّ فكريم وأمّا أخوه فشجاع.

Ali is **generous**, whilst his brother is **courageous**.

6.3.2. Multiple predicates in the nominal SL sentence and their equivalence

In Examples 19 and 20, it is clear the multiple adjective acting as predicates in the SL sentence and how their equivalence may not be of a similar category but rather an TL phrase that has a noun with a couple of adjectives or a prepositional phrase as in Example 20,

19.   زيدٌ عربيٌّ شجاعٌ كريمٌ.

Zayd is **a courageous and generous Arab.**

20.   التعليم أدبي هندسي تجاري.

   Education is in **literature, engineering and commerce.**

6.3.3. Omission of SL predicate and its equivalence

As we have seen above, the task of the student or professional translator is

extremely hard to find the equivalence of a predicate when it exists, but even

harder when it is implied, e.g.

21.   من في البيت؟ - عليّ. (بمعنى عليّ في البيت)

Who is at home? – **Ali.** (i.e. Ali is **at home.**)

It is important to note that unlike the word 'house', the word 'home' only refers

to family home; whilst the 'house' refers to any building that may not have an

emotional or familial value.

22.   خرجت فإذا صديقي. (أي صديقي موجود، إذا الفجائية).

I went out and **suddenly** my friend was there. (or, … suddenly saw my friend.)

It is worth noting that the clause 'at home' in Example 21 is connotative both in

the SL sentence and the TL equivalence; whereas in Example 22 the clause 'was

there' is only connotative in the SL sentence, due to the use of the word

'suddenly' in the SL.   That clause is not connotative in the TL equivalence.   The

same comment applies to Example 23 below,

23.   لولا العقل لضاع الإنسان. (بمعنى لولا العقل موجود).

175

If the mind had not **been there**, man would have gone astray.

It is clear that the clause 'had been there' is connotative *only* in the SL sentence, due to the use of conditional لولا with its omitted predicate. But it is not so in Example 24, since the predicate 'skilful' *exists* in the SL and is not connotative as in Example 23,

24. لولا اللاعبون **ماهرون** ما فاز الفريق.
Had the players not been **skilful**, the team would not have won.

Remember that the negative-negative form in the TL sentence gives the positive form seen in the SL sentence above.

As discussed earlier when making a pledge or swearing, the predicate is omitted in the SL sentence and some omission is also made in the TL equivalence. See the following set of examples,

25. لعَمرُك لينجحنّ المجد.
Upon your life, the hardworking person will succeed.
26. لحياة أبي لأكافحن.
Upon my father's life, I will fight.
27. لأيمن اللـه لأنصرن المظلوم.
I swear (by God), I will back the unjustly treated person (or the oppressed).

In examples 25, 26 and 27 the omission of 'I swear' is connotative in both the SL and TL versions. Also in Example 27 the phrase 'by God' is connotative that is why it is put in between brackets.

The predicate in the nominal SL sentence is omitted when the subject comes before the conditional particle إن and the predicate is implied in the second part of the conditional sentence highlighted in Example 28,

28.   الطالبُ إن يذاكرْ فهو ناجح.

The student, if he studies (well), will **succeed**.

6.3.4. Fronted or delayed predicate in the nominal SL sentence and its equivalence

It is common to have the predicate delayed or fronted in the nominal SL sentence, this technique might confuse the student or professional translator when analysing that sentence syntactically, and might result in producing an incorrect TL equivalence.

Fronting predicate in the SL sentence and its equivalence

Here is an example of a normal nominal SL sentence with no fronting or delayed predicate,

29.   زيد قادم.

        Zayd is **coming**.

But when the predicate is fronted in the SL sentence, it becomes a major problem in the TL sentence, see Example 30,

30.   قادم زيد.

    The one coming (here) is Zayd.

This example is problematic, because the student or professional translator *must* add 'the one' and even the word 'here' in order to make the TL sentence meaningful, so exegetic translation is used to

177

achieve that aim, otherwise the student or professional translator will fail to produce a good TL equivalence. Now the fronted predicate in examples 31 is also problematic but the use of exclamation in the TL sentence solves this problem,

31.   نعم القائد خالد.
     How an excellent leader Khalid is!

Compare with 'خالد نعم القائد.' with its TL equivalence, Khalid, what an excellent leader he is!' Here the predicate is a verbal sentence but see how the TL equivalence has changed in word order.

Dutifully fronted predicate for interrogative, conditional and exclamation and its equivalence

Here is an example,

32.   من (مبتدأ) **فعل هذا** (خبر).
Who (subject) **did this** (predicate)?

It is clear in the SL sentence there are two clause a nominal one and a secondary verbal clause which acts as predicate in the SL but its equivalence is certainly a verbal TL sentence which consists of one verbal clause only. Here is where the confusion may occur in the mind of the student or professional translator. But the syntactic analysis helps because there are two subjects in the SL sentence: the subject 'who' which requires a predicate and the implicit subject of the verbal sentence; that is why its equivalence could have been problematic had it not been for the syntactic analysis of the nominal SL sentence.

The same can be said about Example 33,

33.   مَن (مبتدأ) يُذاكِر (خبر) ينجح.
The one (subject) **who studies** (predicate) will succeed.

34.   ما (مبتدأ) أكرم العربيّ (خبر).
How generous is the Arab!
OR: The Arab is **extremely generous**.

In the second translation of Example 34, the TL adverb 'extremely' is created to

equate with the word 'ما'; whereas the first translation has used exclamation to

give the same meaning and effect. There is no preference between the two

translations as both give the same meaning but perhaps the first is more effective.

Exclamation is also effective in the following,

35.   كم (مبتدأ) مجدّ وفقه الـله (خبر).
How many hard working people are **successful** (granted by God).

The TL phrase 'granted by God' is connotative, that is why its use is optional.

6.3.5. Predicate is a verbal sentence in the ST
Here is an example,

36.   زيد يلعب.
Zayd, **he is playing**.

179

It must be noted that the pronoun in the TL equivalence is implicit in the SL sentence, but needs to be explicit in the TL.

6.3.6. Subject and predicate in the nominal SL sentence defined and their equivalence

During the syntactic analysis of the nominal SL sentence one usually finds either the subject or predicate undefined; however, when both the subject and predicate are defined in both the SL sentence, their equivalence is straightforward, no matter which one is fronted or delayed,

37.   أخي صديقي.
My brother is **my friend**.
38.   صديقي أخي.
My friend is **my brother**.

6.3.7. Subject strictly defined by predicate, or limited to predicate

No fronting of the predicate when the subject is strictly defined by the predicate or only limited by the predicate in the nominal SL sentence (al-Rājihī, p.107), then its equivalence shows that there is that kind of restriction, this is to give the same meaning and effect as that in the original SL sentence,

39.   إنما محمد رسول.
Muhammad is **certainly** a Messenger.
40.   ما محمد إلا رسول.
'Muhammad is **no more than** a Messenger.'

6.3.8. Predicate with the ف

41.   الذي يذاكر فناجح.

The one who studies will **succeed**.

(*cf.* example 17 in the paragraph 6.3.3.)

Here the TL equivalence of predicate is not of the same category, it is a verb

whilst in the SL it is an adjective, and it means literally 'successful'.

6.3.9. Predicate separated with a pronoun

The predicate in the nominal SL sentence can be separated with a pronoun; its

equivalence is straightforward but it needs to have the verb 'to be' italicised to

give the same effect,

42.   الله هو الكريم.

God *is* the most generous.

6.3.10. Fronting the predicate in interrogative and its equivalence

When fronting the predicate in the nominal SL sentence is possible, it is

important to be aware of it. And the predicate is an interrogative, e.g.

43.   أين بيتك؟

Where is your house?

44.   متى السفر؟

When is your travel?

Here it is easy to find the TL equivalence as this is similar to one

of the seven standards of textuality – i.e. informativity (See de

Beaugrande, pp.139-61) and the theme and rheme relation (Mona Baker, pp.121-22) - theme has the old information and rheme the new information - considering 'where' and 'when' as the unexpected information to be given in the answers to these above questions in examples 43 and 44.

6.3.11. Predicate limited to subject in the nominal SL sentence and their equivalence (*cf.* Examples 39 and 40 in the paragraph 6.3.7.)

As in the paragraph 6.3.7.), the predicate is restricted to the subject in the nominal SL sentence

45. ما ناجح إلا المجد.

Only hard working people are **successful**.

OR: All are to **fail except** for hardworking people.

The limitation is implied in the TL in the use of 'only' in the first translation and the form 'all… except' in the second. The second translation, however, uses the same negative form as that in the SL sentence, which can therefore be considered as more 'faithful' translation, and perhaps more effective.

46. إنما في البيت عليّ.

In the house Ali **certainly** is.

The adverb 'certainly' gives the sense of limitation in the TL equivalence.

6.3.12. Subject undefined in the nominal SL sentence and its sentential or semi-sentential predicate

Here are few examples,

47.   في الفصل طالب.
In class a student is.

48.   عندك كتاب.
You have a book.

49.   نفعكَ إخلاصُه صديقٌ.
His loyalty, your friend's, has been of benefit to you.

In Example 49, however, there is a translation loss, because the word 'a friend' in the SL sentence is not absolutely clear in the TL equivalence. But this cannot be helped; otherwise the style of the TL equivalence would be awkward.

6.3.13. The subject in the ST implicitly refers to a pronoun which acts as the predicate

Here is an example,

50.   في البيت (خبر) أهله (مبتدأ).
In the house (predicate) his family (subject) is.

The word أهل can also mean 'parents'. In this case the TL sentence will be 'In the house his parents are'. Now here are few exercises to show the nominal SL sentence and its TL equivalence.

" وَلَعَبْدٌ مُّؤْمِنٌ خَيْرٌ مِّن مُّشْرِكٍ." (*The qur'ān*, 2:221)

a. "**a believing slave is certainly better** than an idolater" (Haleem, p.25).

b. "**a man slave who believes is better** than an unbeliever" (Yūsuf ʿAlī, p.38).

c. "**a believing slave is better** than a (free) *Mushrik* (idolater)" (al-Hilālī and Khan, p.48).

Here translation (a) is most appropriate syntactically as well as semantically. Translation (b) is not as accurate here, when the word 'an unbeliever' is used as an equivalent to مشرك which is a general one, whereas 'idolater' in translations (a) and (c) is semantically closer. In addition, translation (c) also uses the loan word '*Mushrik*' and then its English equivalence 'idolater', this enriches the translation but the addition of the adjective 'free' is not required as the sense does require it here.

Another exercise about the nominal sentence in the SL with its English equivalence.

" هَلْ مِنْ خَالِقٍ غَيْرُ اللـهِ يَرْزُقُكُم مِنَ السَّماءِ وَالأَرْضِ؟" (*The qurʾān*, 35:3)
a. "**Is there any creator other than God** to give you sustenance from the heavens and earth?" (Haleem, p.277)
b. "**Is there a creator, other than Allah**, to give you Sustenance from heaven or earth?" (Yūsuf ʿAlī, p.529)
c. "**Is there any creator other than Allāh** who provides for you from the sky (rain) and the earth?" (al-Hilālī and Khan, p.581-82)
Translations (a) and (b) have given the English equivalence in one single long nominal sentence, whereas the ST has a secondary verbal clause. But the use of the infinitive 'to give you' serves the purpose

and the whole sentence is certainly cohesive semantically. However, translation

(c) is most appropriate syntactically with the use of the verbal clause 'who

provides for you...'. In addition, though incidental comment is about the

choice of words. The word السماء has a number of synonyms in English, the skill

of the translator or student is in being careful to choice the most appropriate to

the SL meaning. Though, 'heaven' and 'the heavens' are appropriate but they are

not precise in conveying the meaning: 'heaven' can mean 'paradise' and its plural

form can only be used when the SL uses the word السماوات, neither of these two

meanings are relevant in this context. The best English equivalence for such

word is 'sky' used in translation (c), but the translator has tried to be more

specific putting 'rain' in between brackets which has limited the meaning of the

word 'sky' as not only rain is useful but also the sun which is beneficial to earth

or the land for farming for instance.

"وَكَأَيِّن مِّن نَّبِيٍّ قَاتَلَ مَعَهُ رِبِّيُّونَ كَثِيرٌ." (*The qur'ān*, 3:146)

a. "**Many prophets have fought**, with large bands of godly men alongside
them..." (Haleem, p.45).

b. "How many of the Prophets fought (in Allāh's way), and with them (fought)
large bands of godly men?" (Yūsuf 'Alī, p.75)

c. "**And many a Prophet** (i.e. many from amongst the Prophets) fought (in
Allāh's Cause) and along with him (fought) large bands of religious learned
men" (al-Hilālī and Khan, p.95).

d. "**And many a Prophet fought** and alongside him many believers in the Lord
fought!" (*my translation*).

185

The nominal sentence in the SL has a verbal predicate, but its equivalence as seen in the above four translations requires no similar structure, as the TT needs to correspond the TL grammar. Incidentally, the word in Arabic ربيون has two equivalents here: 'godly men' and 'religious learned men'. The SL word رب is often translated as 'Lord', compared to الله and 'God'.

Here is another exercise with a similar syntactic structure.

"وَكَأَيِّن مِّن آيَةٍ فِي السَّمَاوَاتِ وَالأَرْضِ يَمُرُّونَ عَلَيْهَا وَهُمْ عَنْهَا مُعْرِضُونَ." (The qur'ān, 12:105)

a. "and there are many signs in the heavens and the earth that they pass by and give no heed to" (Haleem, p.152).

b. "And how many a sign in the heavens and the earth do they pass pay? Yet they turn (their faces) away from them" (Yūsuf 'Alī, p.283).

c. "And how many a sign in the heavens and the earth they pass by, while they are averse therefrom" (al-Hilālī and Khan, p.318).

d. "And many a sign in the heavens and on earth do they come across but still shirk from!"

It is clear that at the syntactic level translations (c) and (d) are closest. Incidentally, a semantic comment on the word choice forces itself here, as it is highly relevant and certainly interesting. The equivalent of the word آية is polysemous in the SL to mean 'a proof' or 'a verse', 'a sign' and 'a message'. In previous translations discussed in this book of this Arabic word, its equivalent seems to vary (see pp.57, 104). The translator needs to determine which depending on the context and starts the process of eliminating the least relevant equivalent to that Arabic word. As the SL example above mentions 'the heavens and earth' then the equivalent 'verse' should be eliminated from the list of synonyms of the SL word آية.

Here is a further exercise of nominal SL sentence with its English equivalence.

" وَمَا أَصَابَكُم مِّن مُّصِيبَةٍ فَبِمَا كَسَبَتْ أَيْدِيكُمْ." (The qur'ān, 42:30)

a. "**Whatever misfortune befalls you [people], it is because** of what your own hands have done" (Haleem, p.313).

b. "**Whatever misfortune happens to you, is because** of the things your hands have wrought" (Yūsuf 'Alī, p.600).

c. "**And whatever of misfortune befalls you, it is because** of what your hands have earned" (al-Hilālī and Khan, p.657).

d. "**Whatever misfortune you are afflicted by, is just of your own doing** (done by your own hands)" (*my translation*).

In translations (a) and (c) the subject is repeated with the use of the pronoun 'it' and it is not so in translations (b) and (d). It is vital that the SL structure – i.e. the nominal sentence here - is observed in the TL, only when the TL grammar allows that as in translation (d). But this is done on condition that the TT should not suffer and becomes an awkward or awful product.

" وَهُوَ الْغَفُورُ الْوَدُودُ (14) ذُو الْعَرْشِ الْمَجِيدُ (15) فَعَّالٌ لِّمَا يُرِيدُ.(16)" (The qur'ān, 85:14-16)

a. "but **He is the Most Forgiving, the Most Loving. The Glorious Lord of the Throne, He does whatever He will**" (Haleem, p.416).

b. "And **He is the Oft-Forgiving, Full of Loving-Kindness, Lord of the Throne of Glory, Doer** (without let) of all that He intends" (Yūsuf 'Alī, p.777).

187

c. "And He is the Oft-Forgiving, full of love (towards the pious who are real true believers of Islāmic Monotheism), Owner of the throne, the Glorious, (He is the) Doer of whatsoever He intends (or wills)" (al-Hilālī and Khan, p.828).

d. "And **He is the Most Loving-Forgiving.(14) He has the Glorious Throne.(15) He is the Doer of all that He wants** (16)" (*my translation*)

It is essential to see how the three nominal SL sentences are beautifully divided with the numbering in the TL. They need to be processed in the translator's mind correctly before their equivalence is produced. Therefore, their three SL subjects ('He' to be used thrice for each verse) and three SL predicates ('the Most Loving-Forgiving', 'the glorious throne' and 'the doer of...wants') need to be identified before providing their most appropriate equivalence. It must be pointed out that 'the most forgiving' is the predicate of the first one, and not 'the most loving', as translations (a) and (b) suggest. Also here is another possible version of translation (d): 'And He is the Most Loving-Forgiving, has the Glorious Throne and the Doer of all that He wants". Now this last version is acceptable as it is to be closer to the ST, as it drops the repetition of the subject 'He' thrice, but then the whole TT is not divided into separate verses, the way it is done in the ST. Therefore, translation (d) is most appropriate.

Here is another exercise of nominal SL sentence with its equivalence.

" وَالَّذِينَ كَفَرواْ وَكَذَّبُواْ بِآيَاتِنَا أُولَـئِكَ أَصْحَابُ النَّارِ." (*The qur'ān*, 2:39)

a. "**those who disbelieve and deny Our messages shall be in the inhabitants of the Fire**" (Haleem, p.7).

188

b. "But **those who reject Faith and belie Our Signs**, they **shall be companions of the Fire**" (Yūsuf 'Alī, p.7).

c. "But **those who disbelieve and belie Our *Ayāt*** (proofs, evidences, verses, lessons, signs, revelations, etc.) – such **are the dwellers of the Fire**" (al-Hilālī and Khan, p.9)

d. "But **those who disbelieve and belie Our Signs, are the dwellers of Fire**" (*my translation*).

Translations (b) and (c) use two subjects ('those' and 'they', 'those' and 'such' respectively), therefore are less appropriate syntactically than the other two translations (a) and (d). Furthermore, the SL word النار requires no determiner ('the') as it is written in capital. Also, unlike other translations (a), (c) and (d), Translation (b) uses incorrectly the TL word 'companions' for the SL word أصحاب; a much more appropriate TL equivalent is 'the inhabitants' or 'dwellers'.

The penultimate exercise in this group of exercises for the nominal SL sentence and its TL equivalence is this,

"لَهُمْ فِي الدُّنْيَا خِزْيٌ وَلَهُمْ فِي الْآخِرَةِ عَذَابٌ عَظِيمٌ." (*The qur'ān*, 2:114)

a. "there is disgrace for them in this world and painful punishment in the Hereafter" (Haleem, p.14).

●

b. "For them **there is nothing but disgrace** in this world, and in the world to come, **an exceeding torment**" (Yūsuf 'Alī, p.19).

c. "For them **there is disgrace** in this world, and **they will have a great torment** in the Hereafter" (al-Hilālī and Khan, p.22).

d. "They are disgraced in this world, and severe torture in the Hereafter" (*my translation*).

189

Arabic/English syntax in translation

Here we have two nominal clauses in one sentence, in this holy verse; this is the initial syntactic analysis of the ST. There are few points to talk about in this exercise at the syntactic level. In translations (a) and (b), there is a nominal clause followed by another one; whereas translation (c) uses a nominal clause followed by a verbal one. Translation (d) uses the passive form or structure in both clauses. It is the choice of words in all translations (a-d). For the SL word الآخرة its equivalent is certainly 'the Hereafter' and not 'the world to come'; also, the problematic TL phase at the lexical level (relating to the word choice) is the equivalence of عذاب عظيم. Why problematic in translations (b) and (c)? Because they both use in the phrase a countable noun: 'a great torment' or 'an exceeding torment', when it is uncountable, referring to an abstract noun 'punishment', 'torment' or 'torture'. It should be considered uncountable, the way it is with the uncountable noun 'disgrace' which is an abstract noun beautifully used in the first three translations (a-c). The other error in translations (a-c) is the use of the adjectives 'painful' or 'exceeding' or 'great' for 'punishment' or 'torment'. It is essential when collocating adjectives with nouns to use the most appropriate ones. For translation (a) the adjective 'painful' certainly collocates well with 'punishment' but then all types of punishment are 'painful'; and this punishment is nothing special. So the same effect as that in the ST is lost in translation (a). Translations (b) and (c) fail to use the appropriate adjective, because the adjectives 'exceeding' and 'great' has a positive effect. One can 'exceed the limit' which it is true has a negative effect but reaching the limit is not a negative thing. Also 'great' in English

190

is often associated with a positive message and not a negative one. So, translation (d) with its adjective 'grave' is most appropriate.

A final exercise in this group is this,

" وَمِنَ النَّاسِ مَن يَتَّخِذُ مِن دُونِ اللـه أندَاداً." (The qur'ān, 2:165)

a. "Even though **there are some** who choose to worship others besides God as rivals to Him" (Haleem, p.18).

b. "Yet **there are men** who take (for worship) others besides Allah, as equal (with Allah)" (Yūsuf 'Alī, p.27).

c. "And **of mankind are some** who take (for worship) others besides Allāh as rivals (to Allāh)" (al-Hilālī and Khan, p.33).

d. "And **there are some people** who consider (for worship) others besides God as rivals" (*my translation*).

Now having finished with some superseding auxiliaries in the nominal SL sentence and their appropriate equivalence, it is time to introduce other types of auxiliaries in the nominal SL sentence and how their equivalence is found.

Chapter Seven: Other superseding words functioning auxiliaries إِنَّ and its sisters in nominal SL sentence and their English equivalence

It is vital to know the purpose of using the superseding auxiliaries إِنَّ and its sisters, they are used for emphasis, emendation and redressing, to draw similarities, or to express a wish or hope. Their predicates must be a nominal or verbal clause (Al-Rājiḥī, 142).

7.1. إِنَّ or أَنَّ = certainly/actually/definitely

Here are a couple of examples alongside their TL equivalence,

1. إِنَّ زيداً قائمٌ.
   Zayd is **certainly** standing.
2. إِنَّ زيداً خلقُه كريم.
Zayd, he *is* of noble manners.
OR: Zayd is **certainly** of good character.

So this auxiliary in examples 1 and 2 is for emphasis; and the predicate in Example 2 is a nominal clause, but its equivalence needs not be a clause as the case is in the SL sentence. It is essential to follow the TL grammar in the translation and not simply 'walk on a tight-rope with fettered legs' (Dryden criticizes Ben Johnson who adopts metaphrase, as cited in Jeremy Munday, p.25). So the syntactic analysis of the SL sentence is not to follow the SL grammar blindly, but to do that intelligently as seen the above two examples. But sometimes a similar structure can be followed in the TL as in the following example,

3.   إنّ المؤمن يتوكل على الـلـه.

The believer is **certainly** the one who has trust in God.

The superseding auxiliary verb used in Example 3 is for emphasis, and that effect must be seen in the TL sentence. The point is to give the same meaning and effect. The following examples have the same emphasis. It is important to note that whether it is إنّ or أنّ the effect is the same,

4.   إنّ زيداً في البيت.

Zayd is **certainly** at home.

5.   إنّ الكتاب أمامك.

The book is **certainly** in front of you.

6.   إنّ ما عملتَه مثمرٌ.

What you have done is **certainly** productive.

7.   إنّ ما عملتُ مثمرٌ.

What I have done is **certainly** productive.

It is important to note that had it not been for the diacritics it would have been difficult to understand the syntactic structure in examples 6 and 7.

8.   إنّ عملك مثمرٌ.

Your work is **certainly** productive.

9.   أقدّر الذي في عمله أنه مجد.

I appreciate the one who **actually** takes his work seriously.

It is clear in Example 9 that the TL syntactic structure is totally different, but it has the same meaning and effect as those in the SL sentence.

10.   أقدّر طالباً عندي أنه مجد.

I appreciate one of the students I have for being **really** hard working.

11.   أقدّر الطالب **إنه** مجد.

I appreciate the student **as he is** **really** hardworking.

Here the superseding auxiliary SL word is used in a causative case (al-Rāji**ḥ**ī, p.148). That is why that effect is conveyed in the bold TL words.

12.   قال علي **إن** زيداً كريم.

Ali said, **(that)** Zayd was **certainly** generous.

13.   زيد **إنه** مجد.

Zayd, he is **really** hardworking.

14.   يسعدني توفيقك. أو: يسعدني **أنك** موفّق.

I am glad about your **real** success.

I am glad, **(that)** you are **really** successful.

15.   عرفت **أن** زيداً مسافر.

I knew **that** Zayd was travelling.

16.   فرحت **بأن** زيداً ناجح.

I was happy **that** Zayd had **actually** succeeded.

17.   من صفاته **أنه** يساعد المحتاج. أو: من صفاته مساعدة المحتاج.

One of his merits is **that** he **actually** helps the needy.

OR: One of his merits is **actually** helping the needy.

18.   لولا **أنك** مجد ما نجحت.

Have you not been hardworking, you would not have **definitely** succeeded.

If you have not been hardworking, you would not have **definitely** succeeded.

19.   الثابت **أنه** فعل ذلك.

It was true **that** he **certainly** did that.

20.   تعجبني أخلاقه إلا **أنه** كثير النسيان.

I like his ethics, **but** he is **certainly** forgetful.

21.   لو **أنه** ذاكر لنجح.

Had he **actually** studied, he would have succeeded.

OR: If he had **actually** studied, he would have succeeded.

22.   حقاً **أنه** كريم.

Truly, he is **definitely** generous.

195

23.   خرجت **فإذا إن** صديقي واقف.

I went out and **suddenly** my friend was **actually** standing.

24.   خرجت **فإذا أن** صديقي بالباب.

I went out and **suddenly** my friend was **actually** at the door.

One can say 'at the door' or **near** the door', as in Fischer's example ' لاقيته لدى

الباب' and 'I met him **at** the door' (Fischer, p.165).

25.   من يذاكر **فإنه** ناجح.

The one who studies will **certainly** succeed.

Examples 12-25 are all emphatic in their style and that element has been

conveyed in the best way possible in the TL to give the same effect.

26.   أوقن **أنِ** الصبرُ مفتاح الفرج.

I believe **that** patience is the key to happy ending.

27.   ونادى المسلمون **أنْ** نصرَ الـله جيوشهم.

Muslims called **that** God made their armies achieve victory.

7.2. ليت = to wish

Now there is one superseding auxiliary word that expresses a wish.

28.   **ليتما** زيدٌ ناجح. أو: **ليتما** زيداً ناجح.

I wish Zayd **was** successful.

It is crucial to note that the TL equivalence follows the TL grammar with regards

to the use of the verb 'to wish'.

7.3. كأنْ or كأنّ = Just like/ as if/ as though

This superseding auxiliary SL word is used to express some kind of similarity. So the TL equivalence needs to have the same meaning and effect. Here are few examples along with their TL equivalence,

29.   يثور كأنْ (أو كأنه) حيوان هائج.

He gets angry (or agitated) **just like** a ferocious animal.

30.   الجو بارد كأنْ قد أتى الشتاء.

It is cold **as if** winter has come.

31.   الجو حار كأنْ لم ينته الصيف.

It is hot **as if** summer has not ended.

32.   كأنْ بدراً مشرقاً هذا الوجهُ.

Like a shining full moon this face is.

7.4. لكنْ or لكنّ = But/however/yet

This superseding auxiliary word is used in the nominal SL sentence and its purpose is to give a kind of redressing or emendation. It has the same function as 'but', 'however' or 'yet' in English.

33.   زيد مجدّ لكنْ أخوه مهمل.

Zayd is hardworking **but** his brother is complacent (or negligent).

7.5. ل attached to subject or predicate in nominal SL sentence and its equivalence

Sometimes ل is added to the subject or predicate of the nominal SL sentence for even more emphasis (al-Rājiḥī, p.157). This particle is not translatable but one needs to show that emphasis in the TL. Here are more examples with their TL equivalence,

34.   لزيد مجد.
Zayd is **certainly** hardworking.

35.   إن في البيت لزيداً.
At home **Zayd certainly** is.

36.   إن زيداً لكريم.
Zayd is **certainly generous**.

37.   إن زيدا لخلقُه كريم.
Zayd, he is **certainly of** good **character** (or noble **manners**).

38.   إن زيداً ليكرم الضيف.
Zayd is **certainly hospitable** to his guest.

39.   إن زيداً لفي البيت.
Zayd is **certainly at** home.

40.   إن الكتاب لعندك.
The book is **certainly with** you.

41.   إن الاستقامة لهي مفتاح النجاح.
Honesty **is certainly** the key to success.

7.6. Cases with combinations of أنْ and either قد – لم – لا – لن and their English equivalence

These combinations are really problematic and perplexing as they present complex structure in the SL and their syntactic analysis is rather complicated. These can be best explained in the form of examples to show how they function in the language in use and what their TL equivalence is.

42. أَنْ ليس لك إلا عملك.

It is **that** you have **nothing** but your work.

43. أيحسبون أَنْ لن نقدر عليهم.

They reckon **that** we **cannot** restrict them (or challenge them).

44. أيقنتُ أَنْ لا يفشلُ المجدّ.

I am certain **that** the hardworking person will **never** fail.

45. أيحسب أَنْ لم يره أحد.

He reckons **that no** one will see him.

46. أوقن أَنْ لو جد الإنسان لأفلح.

I am certain (convinced) **that if** man works hard, he will succeed.

Here are exercises that have the superseding auxiliaries إِنَّ and its sisters, along with their English equivalence. It is important to remember that these auxiliaries are used for emphasis, emendation and redressing, to draw similarities, or to express a wish or hope.

" فَلَمْ تَقْتُلُوهُمْ وَلَـكِنَّ الـلـه قَتَلَهُمْ." (*The qur'ān*, 8:17)

a. "It was not you who killed them **but God**" (Haleem, p.111).

b. "It is not you who slew them; **it is Allah**" (Yūsuf 'Alī, p.201).

c. "You killed them not, **but Allāh** killed them" (al-Hilālī and Khan, p.233).

d. "You did not kill them, **God did**" (*my translation*).

Syntactically, translation (c) is most appropriate, showing that balance in the use of the verb 'to kill', only the negative form of the first sentence is grammatically unacceptable. On the other hand, translation (a) is rather too elliptical compared to the non-elliptical style in the ST. The verb 'to kill' is repeated in the ST to give some balance, that stylistic element is missed. Translation (d) creates that

199

balance and presents the correct form of negation in the first clause; therefore, it is most appropriate all round.

Here is a further exercise,

"وَآخِرُ دَعْوَاهُمْ أَنِ الْحَمْدُ لِلَّهِ رَبِّ الْعَالَمِينَ." (*The qur'ān*, 10:10)
a. "**and the last part of their prayer, 'Praise be to God,** Lord of the Worlds' " (Haleem, p.129).

b. "**And the close of their cry will be: 'Praise be to Allah,** the Cherisher and Sustainer of the Worlds!' " (Yūsuf 'Alī, p.235)

c. "**and the close of their request will be:** *Al-Hamdu Lillāhi Rabb-il-'Alamīn* [All the praises and thanks are to Allāh, the Lord of *'Alamīn* (mankind, jinn and all that exists)]" (al-Hilālī and Khan, p.271).

As usual translation (c) is exegetic with a number of brackets to explain the extended meaning of the ST. This technique of al-Hilālī and Khan, though informative for readers who are after the deep interpretation of the holy Book, is sometimes rather distracting as the reader struggles to find what the actual TT – what the end product is. This reason may lie in the use of loan words from the ST (transliterating them) and then explaining in between brackets.

Another interesting exercise is this,

"إِنَّمَا اللـه إِلَـهٌ وَاحِدٌ." (*The qur'ān*, 4:171)
a. "**God is only one God**" (Haleem, p.66).
b. "**for Allah is One God**" (Yūsuf 'Alī, p.115).
c. "**For Allāh is (the only) One** *Ilāh* (God)" (al-Hilālī and Khan, p.139).

200

d. "**For God is the one and only**" (*my translation*).

Translation (a) is afflicted by its repetitiveness. Translation (b) is in a way better, as the translator has resorted to referring to God throughout his translation as *Allah* and so did the third translator, though with a different variation of transliteration (*Allāh*). Translation (c), however, uses also the loan word *Ilāh* alongside its meaning.

A further exercise is this,

"وَأَن لَّيْسَ لِلْإِنسَانِ إِلَّا مَا سَعَى." " (*The qur'ān*, 53:39)
a. "**that man will only have what he has worked towards**" (Haleem, p.348).

b. "**That man can have nothing but what he strives for**" (Yūsuf 'Alī, p.663).

c. "**And that man can have nothing but what he does (good or bad)**" (al-Hilālī and Khan, p.721).

Syntactically speaking, in translation (a) the adverb 'only' is incorrectly positioned before 'have' and it should be *after* that verb in order to give the same sense as that in the ST, that sense and effect is achieved in translations (b) and (c) in this connection. A further minor comment here is the verb سعى and its lexical equivalent 'to work towards', 'to strive for' and 'to do'. The last verb ('to do') is the weakest in this context. The strongest equivalent here is 'to strive for' and then 'to work towards' and finally 'to do'. Another strong equivalent that equals the first is 'to endeavour' – i.e. 'that man can have only what he endeavours to have'.

201

Moving on to another exercise that may be useful to students and translators in terms of the application of what this chapter has covered is,

" عَلِمَ أَن سَيَكُونُ مِنكُم مَّرْضَى." (*The qur'ān*, 73:20)

a. "He knows that some of you will be sick" (Haleem, p.396).

b. "He knows that there may be (some) among you in ill-health" (Yūsuf 'Alī, p.742-43).

c. "He knows that there will be some among you sick" (al-Hilālī and Khan, p.795).

Translation (a) is most appropriate in terms of its compactness and clarity, compared to the other two translations.

Here is yet another exercise on the theme of this chapter,

"قَالَتْ يَا لَيْتَنِي مِتُّ قَبْلَ هَذَا وَكُنتُ نَسْيًا مَّنسِيًّا." (*The qur'ān*, 19:23)

a. "She exclaimed, 'I wish I had been dead and forgotten long before all this!' " (Haleem, p.192).

b. "she cried (in her anguish): 'Ah! Would that I had died before this! Would that I had been a thing forgotten and out of sight!' " (Yūsuf 'Alī, p.360).

c. "She said: 'Would that I have died before this, and had been forgotten and out of sight!' " (al-Hilālī and Khan, p.404).

d. "She said, 'How I wish I was dead before this and was completely forgotten' (*my translation*).

Again there are errors at the syntactic level, grammatically speaking the tenses in the TT need to be accurate. In translation (a), as the ST has a direct speech, then its equivalence should be in the simple present tense and the simple past tense after 'she said' and not the present and the past perfect tenses. It is the present tense of the verb 'to wish' and the simple past for the verbs 'to die' and 'to forget' as in translation (d). The other alternative for expressing a wish in English is to use the conditional structure of the TL sentence, as in the case of translations (b) and (c). However, part of the conditional structure is missing. The conditional structure of the TT in translations (b) and (c) should have been: 'It would have been better, Had I died before this and been forgotten forever.' Another issue in translation (b) is to refer to Mary as 'a thing' of the past which is touching on TL colloquialism.

It is important to note that إن in the nominal SL sentence makes the subject take the diacritic *fatha* and its predicate take the diacritic *dhamma* and this fact is not known to students in practical terms, that is why here are few examples that show which is the SL subject and which is the SL predicate. This certainly affects the student's or translator's comprehension of the ST. Here are few exercises to that effect.

"وَإِنَّ رَبَّكَ لَيَحْكُمُ بَيْنَهُمْ يَوْمَ الْقِيَامَةِ فِيمَا كَانُواْ فِيهِ يَخْتَلِفُونَ." (*The qur'ān*, 16:124)
a. "On the Day of Resurrection your Lord will judge between them as to their differences" (Haleem, p.174).

b. "But Allah will judge between them on the Day of Judgement, as to their differences' (Yūsuf 'Alī, p.325).

c. "Your Lord will judge between them on the Day of Resurrection about that wherein they used to differ" (al-Hilālī and Khan, p.366).

203

Syntactically, all three translations are successfully. But on the semantic or lexical level, there are a couple of points to raise. With regards to the TL equivalence of the phrase يوم القيامة the choice of words matters, though it refers to the Day of Judgment but its exact lexical equivalence is in translations (a) and (c), i.e. 'the Day of Resurrection'. There is also the issue of consistency which is significant in translation. Consistency is met in the use of 'Lord' for رب in both translation (a) and (c), but translation (b) shows no respect to that, and uses instead '*Allah*'; admittedly this is correct as co-referent to God and can still be accepted.

A further exercise about the SL word إن,

"كَمَا أَخْرَجَكَ رَبُّكَ مِن بَيْتِكَ بِالْحَقِّ وَإِنَّ فَرِيقاً مِّنَ الْمُؤْمِنِينَ لَكَارِهُونَ". (*The qur'ān*, 8:5)
a. "For it was your Lord who made you [Prophet] venture from your home for a true purpose, **though a group of the believers disliked it**" (Haleem, p.110).
b. "Just as your Lord ordered you out of your house in truth, **even though a party among the Believers disliked it**" (Yūsuf 'Alī, p.199).
c. "As your Lord caused you (O Muhammad) to go out from your home with the truth; **and verily, a party among the believers disliked it**" (al-Hilālī and Khan, p.231).
d. "For your Lord who made you leave your home for a true purpose, **though a group of the believers detested that**" (*my translation*).
Now syntactically all translations (a-c) are successful. However, there are a couple points to talk about here with regards to the choice of lexis or style. The first comment is that, unlike the other translations (a), (c) and (d), the SL word بيتك and its equivalent in translation (b) is

'house' which has no emotional element in English. That is why English people say, 'Home sweet home' and not 'House sweet house' due to its emotional value.

Here is another exercise,

"ذَلِكَ بِأَنَّ الـلـه هُوَ الْحَقُّ." (*The qur'ān*, 22:6)
a. **"This is because God is the Truth"** (Haleem, p.209).

b. **"This is so, because Allah is the Reality"** (Yūsuf 'Alī, p.396).

c. **"That is because Allāh: He is the Truth"** (al-Hilālī and Khan, p.443).

d. **"That is because God is the Truth"** (*my translation*).

An interesting syntactic point here is the use of the demonstrative pronoun 'this' in translations (a) and (b), which is inappropriate. 'That' is more appropriate here. Another point is in translation (c) where unnecessary repetition is used 'Allāh' and 'He'. As for the lexical aspect, though it is incidental in this textbook, there is the choice of equivalent for the SL word الحق. Now unlike all other translations, translation (b) has chosen 'Reality' which is rather a weak equivalent; 'the Truth' would have been better and stronger.

Here is yet another interesting exercise.

"إِنَّ كَيْدَ الشَّيْطَانِ كَانَ ضَعِيفًا." (*The qur'ān*, 4:76)
a. **"Satan's strategies are truly** weak" (Haleem, p.57).

b. "feeble **indeed is the cunning of Satan**" (Yūsuf 'Alī, p.99).

c. **"Ever feeble indeed is the plot of** *Shaitān* **(Satan)"** (al-Hilālī and Khan, p.121).

d. "**Satan's slyness is certainly** frail" (*my translation*).

At the lexical and semantic level, there is the SL adjective ضعيف which means 'weak' but its other English hyponyms might serve as well – 'feeble' and 'frail'.

The exercise below is useful, as the SL word إنّ is sometimes problematic in the ST as in the first clause highlighted below, where the subject and predicate of إن is not as clear as that in the second clause,

"وَاللّـه يَعْلَمُ إِنَّكَ لَرَسُولُهُ وَاللّـه يَشْهَدُ إِنَّ الْمُنَافِقِينَ لَكَاذِبُونَ." (*The qur'ān*, 63:1)
a. "**God knows that you truly are His Messenger**; God bears witness that the hypocrites are liars" (Haleem, p.374).

b. "**Allah knows that you are indeed His Messenger**, and Allah bears witness that the Hypocrites are indeed liars" (Yūsuf 'Alī, p.707).

c. "**Allāh knows that you are indeed His Messenger**, and Allāh bears witness that the hypocrites are liars indeed" (al-Hilālī and Khan, p.761).

Now is the last exercise in this group which has the SL word لكنّ whose function is the same as that of the SL word إنّ seen above.

"وَمَا رَمَيْتَ إِذْ رَمَيْتَ وَلَـكِنَّ اللّـه رَمَى." (*The qur'ān*, 8:17)
a. "and when you threw [sand at them] it was not your throw [that defeated them] **but God's**" (Haleem, p.111).

b. "when you threw (a handful of dust), it was not your act, **but Allah's**" (Yūsuf 'Alī, p.201).

c. "And you (Muhammad) threw not when you did throw, **but Allāh threw**" (al-Hilālī and Khan, p.233).

Having covered some of the aspects regarding some superseding words functioning auxiliaries إنَّ and its sisters in nominal SL sentence and their English equivalence, it is time to move to yet another type of word that affects the syntax in the SL sentence, and therefore its English equivalence needs to be addressed.

Chapter Eight: 'No' which denies the whole genus لا النافية للجنس in the SL and its TL equivalence

8.1. Undefined subject in nominal SL sentence and its TL equivalence

This negating auxiliary word لا (the 'no' which denies the whole genus) acts in the same way as the superseding auxiliary إنَّ does (See the paragraph 5.1. about the function of the superseding auxiliary word إنّ grammatically speaking, and not like the function of the superseding auxiliary word كان). Its function is to distance the subject from the meaning of the predicate in the SL sentence (Al-Rājiḥī, 167). Its TL equivalence must be produced in two ways depending on the status of the SL subject: The first option is that if the SL subject is undefined, then negation is to be added to the TL subject in the same way as that in the nominal SL sentence, as in the following examples and for clarity the subjects are underlined in both in the SL and TL to elaborate the point made here about the subjects in both languages,

1.   لا إنسانَ مخلّد. (Meaning '**no human being nor his race**')
No <u>man</u> is immortal.

2.   لا رجلَ في البيت. (The predicate of لا is not omitted)
No <u>man</u> is in the house.

3.   لا مجدّين فاشلون.
No <u>hard workers</u> fail in their job. [*masculine*]

4.   لا مجداتٍ فاشلاتٌ.
No <u>hard workers</u> fail in their job. [*feminine*]

5.   لا بائعَ صحفٍ موجودٌ.
No <u>news agent</u> is there.

6.   لا بائعَيْ صحفٍ موجودان.

No <u>two news agents</u> are there.

7. لا بائعي صحفٍ موجودون.

No <u>news agents</u> are there. [*masculine*]

8. لا بائعاتِ صحفٍ موجودات.

No <u>news agents</u> are there. [*feminine*]

9. لا ذا إيمانٍ ضعيف.

No <u>believer</u> is weak.

10. لا كريماً خلقُه مكروهٌ.

No <u>generous man</u> has an obnoxious behaviour.

11. لا خمسةً وعشرين حاضرون.

No <u>twenty-five people</u> are present.

12. لا رجلَ موجودٌ ولا امرأةً.

No <u>man</u> is present, **nor** is there any <u>woman</u> present.

13. لا طالبَ علمٍ مجدٌّ فاشلٌّ.

No <u>student</u> (or <u>scholar</u>) is assiduous and a loser.

14. (لا شكَّ في ذلك Meaning) هو ناجح لا شكٍّ.

He succeeds, **no** doubt (or undoubtedly).

15. لا بأسَ. (لا بأس عليك You say to the patient this sentence, implying)

Not to worry.

16. أحب الكتب ولا سيما كتبُ الأدب. (أو كتبَ الأدب أو كتبِ الأدب)

I love books, **especially** <u>literary books</u>.

17. أحب الكتب ولا مثلَ كتبِ الأدب.

I love books, and **nothing** is like literary books.

It is crucial to note that in Examples 16 and 17 the SL word 'books' has a definite particle to mean 'books in general', that is why its TL equivalence is 'books' and not 'the books'. Another example is for abstract nouns in the SL are defined with a definite particle, and this is a grammatical rule in the SL to refer abstract nouns; but their TL equivalence is also undefined with a definite particle. Here are a couple of examples, الجمال = beauty, الإيمان = faith, التعليم = education, القبح = ugliness.

8.2. Defined subject in nominal SL sentence and its TL equivalence

The other option is when the SL subject is a proper noun, the translation strategy here is that, unlike the SL structure, the TL structure has the TL verb itself and *not* the TL subject being negated, as in Examples 18 and 19.

18.   لا زيد قائم ولا عليّ. (here لا must be repeated before a proper noun)
Zayd is **not** standing, **nor** is <u>Ali</u>.

19.   لا في البيت زيد ولا أخوه.
<u>Zayd</u> is **not** in the house, **nor** is <u>his brother</u>.

Here are few exercises that demonstrate how the SL 'No' denies the whole genus and show its TL equivalence.

" لَا قُوَّةَ إِلَّا بِاللـه." (*The qur'ān*, 18:39)
a. "There is **no power** not [given] by God" (Haleem, p.186).

b. "There is **no power** but with Allah" (Yūsuf 'Alī, p.348).

c. "There is **no power** but with Allāh!" (al-Hilālī and Khan, p.390).

" وَلَوْ تَرَى إِذْ فَزِعُوا فَلَا فَوْتَ وَأُخِذُوا مِن مَّكَانٍ قَرِيبٍ." (*The qur'ān*, 34:51)
a. "[Prophet], if you could only see their terror! **There will be no escape** when they are seized from a nearby place" (Haleem, p.276).
b. "If you could but see when they will quake with terror; but then **there will be no escape** (for them), and they will be seized from a position (quite) near" (Yūsuf 'Alī, p.527).

211

c. "And if you could but see, when they will be terrified **with no escape** (for them), and they will be seized from a near place" (al-Hilālī and Khan, p.581).

A further exercise is the following,

" ذَلِكَ الْكِتَابُ لاَ رَيْبَ فِيهِ هُدًى لِّلْمُتَّقِينَ." (The qur'ān, 2:2)
a. "This is the Scripture in which **there is no doubt**, containing guidance for those who are mindful of God" (Haleem, p.4).
b. "This is the Book; in it is guidance **sure, without doubt**, to those who fear Allah" (Yūsuf 'Alī, p.2).
c. "This is the Book (the Qur'ān), whereof there is **no doubt**, a guidance to those who are *Al-Muttaqūn* [the pious and righteous persons who fear Allāh much (abstain from all kinds of sins and evil deeds which He has forbidden) and love Allāh much (perform all kinds of good deeds which He has ordained)]" (al-Hilālī and Khan, p.3).

d. "That is the Book, **free of** scepticism, it provides true guidance to the pious people" (*my translation*).

First, it is essential to note that ﻻ can be translated as we have seen as either 'no' or 'free of' (*cf.* exercises below). Further, the demonstrative SL pronoun is totally ignored syntactically in the first three translations but in the fourth one. In the SL it is ذلك and in their TLs 'this'. Lexically, the use of 'doubt' or 'skepticism' is a matter of word choice, so is the use of 'Scripture' or 'Book'; though 'Scripture' is in a way a form of 'domestication' in translation, that is making the TT closer to the target reader. 'Scripture' is used here figuratively by the (a) translator, although when capitalized it means according to Webster online dictionary as 'the books of the Bible'. A final semantic point is the SL word المتقين which means 'those who fear

212

God' and not just 'mindful of God', either translation (b) or (d) are closed to the meaning.

A further exercise of لا that denies that whole genus and its English equivalence is this,

" قَالَ لاَ عَاصِمَ الْيَوْمَ مِنْ أَمْرِ الـلـه إلاَّ مَن رَّحِمَ." *(The qur'ān*, 11:43)

a. "Noah said, 'Today there is **no refuge** from what God has commanded, except for those on whom He has mercy' " (Haleem, p.139).

b. "Noah said: 'This day **nothing** can save, from the Command of Allah, any but those whom He has mercy!' " (Yūsuf 'Alī, p.256).

c. "Nūh (Noah) said: 'This day there is **no saviour** from the Decree of Allāh except him on whom He has mercy' " (al-Hilālī and Khan, p.292).

Few comments on the above translations to show students that additions are sometimes necessary to help with the clarity of the TT. The lexical addition is the name 'Noah' or 'Nūh' (a transliteration of the proper name). This type of addition is vital here, that is why all translations (a-c) have included the proper name. Translation (b) has inadvertently dropped the preposition 'on' in 'to have mercy on or upon'. Two more words need to be commented upon regarding the word choice. The SL word أمر has been translated by various translators (a), (b), (c) as 'order' and/or 'command'. Consistency as a strategy is required in translation, particularly when translating a large document, in order to facilitate the target reader's comprehension of the TT. In translation (c) this time round there is yet another TL equivalent 'Decree'. A further minor point is the use of punctuation

213

before a direct speech – with either a colon or a comma. Students and translator, as seen in the above translations above, can use either punctuation marks, so long as they are consistent through their translation.

Another exercise about the SL word لا that denies the whole genus is this,

" فَلاَ رَفَثَ وَلاَ فُسُوقَ وَلاَ جِدَالَ فِي الْحَجِّ." (*The qur'ān*, 2:197)

a. "There should be **no indecent speech**, **misbehavior**, **or quarrelling** for anyone undertaking the pilgrimage" (Haleem, p.22).

b. "let there be **no obscenity**, **nor wickedness**, **nor wrangling** in the *Hajj*" (Yūsuf 'Alī, p.33).

c. "then he should **not have sexual relations** (with his wife), **nor commit sin**, **nor dispute** unjustly during the *Hajj*" (al-Hilālī and Khan, p.42).

The main syntactic comment about the SL word لا and its English equivalent is in translation (a) where the recurrent conjunction 'or' should have been 'nor'. In translation (c) only the second clause should have been 'nor should he' otherwise the grammatical structure is lopsided. As for the lexical aspect, and to clarify the different vocabulary used in translations (a), (b) and (c) one should say what the various words in the SL mean. Based on Edward William Lane's Arabic-English Lexicon which is an excellent Arabic-English dictionary, the first SL word رفث means 'no lewdness' which covers all forms of sexual talk or act, also the second SL word فسوق means 'sinfulness' as one of the meanings or a 'sinful act', and finally the SL

جدال means 'argument' or 'dispute'. Also, with regards to using loan words in translation now the word حج has an English equivalent capitalized Pilgrimage. Now unless the translator explains what that foreign word means after transliterating it, this technique can be considered failure on the side of the translator. Often loan words are kept as they are because they are essential or keywords, but explanation in between brackets is vital.

Here is a further exercise about لا that denies the whole genus and its English equivalence.

" قَالُوا لَا ضَيْرَ إِنَّا إِلَى رَبِّنَا مُنقَلِبُونَ." (*The qur'ān*, 26:50)
a. " 'That will do us **no harm**,' they said, 'for we are sure to return to our Lord' " (Haleem, p.233-34).
b. "They said: '**No matter**! For us, we shall but return to our Lord!' " (Yūsuf 'Alī, p.444).
c. "They said: '**No harm**! Surely, to our Lord (Allāh) we are to return' " (al-Hilālī and Khan, p.492).

Another exercise shows that لا becomes non-functional when the predicate is fronted in the SL, and the translator needs to identify this,

" مِّن قَبْلِ أَن يَأْتِيَ يَوْمٌ لاَّ بَيْعٌ فِيهِ وَلاَ خُلَّةٌ وَلاَ شَفَاعَةٌ." (*The qur'ān*, 2:254)
a. "before the Day comes when there is **no bargaining, no friendship, and no intercession**" (Haleem, p.29).

b. "before the Day comes when **no bargaining (will avail), nor friendship nor intercession**" (Yūsuf 'Alī, p.46).

215

c. "before a Day comes when there will be **no bargaining, nor friendship, nor intercession**" (al-Hilālī and Khan, p.57).

This is just a minor note that at the lexical level, the ST says 'a day' and not 'the day'. Another similar case about the separation of ﻻ from its subject, where it becomes non-functional, is the following exercise,

" لَا فِيهَا غَوْلٌ وَلَا هُمْ عَنْهَا يُنزَفُونَ." (*The qur'ān*, 37:47)
a. "causing **no** headiness **or** intoxication" (Haleem, p.286).

b. "**Free from** headiness; **nor** will they suffer intoxication therefrom" (Yūsuf 'Alī, p.547).

c. "**Neither** will they have *Ghoul* (any kind of hurt, abdominal pain, headache, a sin) from that, **nor** will they suffer intoxication therefrom" (al-Hilālī and Khan, p.599).

The main comment about the SL word ﻻ and its English equivalent here is in translation (a) where the conjunction 'or' should have been 'nor'.

Now having given these exercises about the use of ﻻ and its English equivalence it is to move to some elements in the verbal SL sentence and their TL equivalence.

Chapter Nine: Verbal SL sentence and its TL equivalence

One of the main elements of the verbal SL sentence and for that matter the nominal SL sentence is the subject. This is the case also when finding its English equivalence.

9.1. Subject الفاعل

Unlike the TL sentence (English one), the SL verbal sentence (Arabic one) has the verb at the beginning followed by the subject (the SVO structure in the TL as opposed to the VSO one in the SL) as in the following four simple sentences,

1. قام زيد.
Zayd stood.
2. جاء الطالب.
The student came.
3. جاء الطالبان. جاءت الطالبتان.
The two students (or **Both students**) came. [*masculine and feminine*]
4. جاءت الطالبات. جاء الطلاب.
The students came. [*masculine and feminine*]

But the subject in the SL is sometimes unclear particularly when diacritics are not used, and when the SL sentence is in the passive voice as in Example 5 where the actual subject of the first verb is 'it' referring connotatively to 'the visit', whereas the second subject in the second clause is 'you' and the latter clause is in the active voice; but the former clause is in the passive voice, with the pronoun 'I' as the subject of the passive. Also, the passive voice is more common in the

TL than in the SL, so a shift from active to passive is sometimes preferred.

5.   يُسعدني أن تزورني.
a. I <u>am delighted</u> that **you** have visited me. (In the present tense)
b. I will be delighted when **you** visit me. (In the future tense)
6.   تسعدني زيارتك.
I will be delighted with your visit.

And it is noticeable that when the SL subject in the first clause in Example 5 is referring to an inanimate or abstract noun in the SL ('the visit'), it is advisable to use the separate or detached pronoun ('I') as the subject of that clause as in Examples 5 and 6,

7.   أعجبني ما فعلت.
I liked **what you did.**

Here in Example 7 the subject in the SL is 'what you did' and the object is 'me'; but in the TL it is more common to produce the above equivalence with the subject as the detached pronoun 'I' and the object as 'what you did'. So this shift is clearly favoured as it is more 'natural' in the TL, because the TL equivalence above with that subject-object shift is more appropriate. The same analysis applies to Example 8,

8.   أعجبني فعلك.
a. **Your action** fascinates me.
b. I am fascinated by your action.

Here one should refer to Alan Cruse's book *Meaning in Language* (2000) and his discussion about equivalence between the two translations (a) and (b),

Propositional equivalence between two sentences can be straightforwardly defined as mutual entailment. That is, in effect, equivalent to saying that the two sentences always express the same proposition (provided, of course, that corresponding definite referring expressions are co-referential) (p.30).

So no preference between the two translations here can be made; however, fronting the animate subject to the inanimate or abstract noun acting as subject is the main difference here, therefore translation (b) can be favoured. But how about the following example,

9. أسعدني أنك ناجح.
a. I am delighted that **you** have succeeded.
b. **Your success** delights me.

The second TL equivalence (b) is appropriate and can be used, though not so commonly used. Again the subject-object shift is seen here and it is advisable to do this shift and front the animate to the inanimate or abstract noun in translation. The following example clarifies this point further:

10. (يمكنك الذهاب – الفاعل - Meaning) يمكنك أن تذهب الآن. (al-Rājiḥī, pp.179-81)
a. **You** can go now. (closer to gist translation)
b. **Going** is possible for you now. (literal translation with a stilted style)
c. It is possible for you to go now. (exegetic translation with a 'natural' style)

219

In Example 10, the denotative meaning in the SL can be translated as 'going is possible for you now', but this translation is literal, and literal translation with its corresponding TL grammar is still not favoured by many theorists in translation studies. James Dickins (pp.7-18) mentions different types of translation: Inter-semiotic, intralingual and interlingual translations as well as interlinear, literal, free, and communicative translations.. Dickins writes, 'In literal translation proper, the denotative meaning of words is taken as if straight from the dictionary (that is, out of context), but TL grammar is respected" (p.16).

John Dryden in his translation of Ovid's *Epistles* in 1680 gives three different types of translation: Metaphrase (word-for-word translation), paraphrase (where words are not so strictly followed as the author's sense) and imitation (which is when both words and sense are forsaken, and the translation is more or less very free'). Dryden favours paraphrase and criticizes translators like Ben Johnson who adopt metaphrase (word by word and line by line translation) and considers them as 'verbal copiers' and then Dryden uses his famous simile that literal translation is "much like dancing on ropes with fettered legs – a foolish task" (as cited in Munday, p.25). Peter Newmark's (1981/1986) definition of 'literal translation' is slightly different as it talks about meaning, "If a word for word, primary for primary meaning translation has functional equivalence, any other translation is wrong" (p.137).

Therefore, the equivalence with the subject 'you' in Example 10 is more appropriate. Also another potential equivalence is 'It is possible for you to go now', though the latter is not commonly used in the TL. This example also shows how being closer to what James Dickins calls 'gist translation' is better than to 'exegetic translation'. Dickins (2000) writes explaining Jakobson's interlingual translation, "in general, while translation proper may include elements of gist and exegesis, the dominant mode of translation is one which involves rephrasing between the ST and TT" (p.12); and when explaining intralingual gist and exegetic translation he adds, "an exegetic translation ... is usually longer [than the ST], and can easily shade into general observations triggered by the ST, but not really explaining it" (p.10). A more general explanation is that of Roman Jakobson in his paper 'On linguistic aspects of translation' (1959) who points out, "translation involves two equivalent messages in two different codes" (as cited in Jeremy Munday, 2001, p.37). Here Jakobson does not specify the nature of these two different codes, whether the translation involves gist or exegesis; but Dickins has been more specific saying, "translation proper may include elements of gist or exegesis" (p.12).

The denotative meaning of the example below seems to fit the communicative translation more than the connotative meaning seen in between brackets in the SL:

11. ‏يجوز أن يحضر اليوم. (meaning ‏الحضور‏ ‏يجوز)

221

a. **He** may attend [the class or meeting] today. (Communicative translation)

b. **It** is possible for him to attend [the class or meeting] today. (Communicative translation)

c. **Attendance** is possible for him today. (literal and stilted translation)

The subject 'attendance' in the connotative meaning in the SL should be avoided in translation as the translation will become literal and its style unacceptable compared to translations (a) or (b). The TL equivalence usually opts out for the animate or pronoun 'he', which is yet another proof that this technique is common in the SL and not so in the TL. It is clear that the subject in the SL is changing in the TL, due to the fact that sticking to a similar subject may deem the style of the TL sentence unreadable.

12.   يجب أن تذاكر لتنجح. (Meaning يجب المذاكرة)

a. **You** must revise well in order to succeed.

b. **Revision** must be done well [by you] in order to succeed.

It is vital for the student or translator to decide whether to use the denotative infinitive 'to revise' أن تذاكر or the connotative noun 'revision' المذاكرة. But here translation (a) is more 'natural' in the TL. Let us have a look at the following example which may prove that the inanimate noun acting as subject works well only in formal context,

13.   ينبغي ألا تتدخل فيما لا يعنيك. (Meaning ...ينبغي عدم التدخل)

You ought not to interfere in what is none of your business.

Non-interference in other people's business is a must.

Translation (b) is instructive, so when the SL text is instructive then it is advisable to use this translation, since the word 'you' in translation (a) makes the translation more personal, when that personal effect is intended. To be impersonal in style in translation makes the translation more formal and therefore fits formal context. Here is an example where 'you' is not used, and is arguably instructive,

14. هيهات لنجاح المهمل.

a. **The complacent person** is far from achieving success.

b. Complacency never leads to success.

It is clear that the SL subject is 'success' and the interlinear English translation is 'How far is success from the negligent/complacent person.' Dickins writes, 'interlinear translation is normally only employed where the purpose of the translation is to shed light on the structure of the ST' (16); he also adds that it is 'at the extreme of the SL bias... where the TT does not necessarily respect TL grammar, but has grammatical units corresponding as closely as possible to every grammatical unit of the ST' (p.15).

Unless the subject is changed in the TL, the translation is unacceptable. So translation (a) sounds more appropriate; and indeed translation (b) can only be accepted as exegetic translation, edging close to the extremely free translation, though it sounds more 'natural' and more communicative, but is stigmatized because it is "at the opposite extreme, where there is maximum TL bias... [and usually] the grammar and vocabulary are completely different" (pp.16-17). So it is just as unacceptable as literal translation. However, it must be pointed out that some clients or companies demand this kind of

223

translation for their TL audience, only then can this translation be accepted – provided that its purpose is promotional and its text is used in commercials and it is instructive. The subject here is changed, so are the verb and rest of the sentence and can be considered an adaptation or imitation as Dryden calls it. Dryden does not favour imitation as the translator uses the ST "as a pattern to write as he supposed that author would have done, had he lived in our age and in our country;" by using imitation, the translator is more visible but does "the greatest wrong... to the memory and reputation of the dead" (as cited in Munday, p.25).

So identifying the subject of the SL verbal sentence can be problematic, if the subject is clearly defined or sounds awkward to use in the TL. But, unlike the above examples in this chapter, the subject of a verbal sentence in the SL can sometimes be mysterious as its verb is connotative as in Example 15,

15.   (al-Rājiḥī, p.185) (هذا رجل بالغٌ أبناؤه عشرة Meaning) هذا رجل عشرة أبناؤه.
a. This is a man with ten children. (communicative translation)
b. This man has ten children. (gist translation)
c. This is a man whose children are ten. (literal translation with a glib style)

It is clear that the literal translation here is rather inappropriate and awkward, even far from 'natural' in the TL. One can see that when comparing it to the communicative translation above it.

16.   قلما يصدق الكذوب.

a. Rarely does **the liar** speak the truth.

b. Rarely is **the liar** honest.

c. **It** is rare for the liar to be honest (or to have an honest liar).

قلّما's equivalence is 'very rarely', according to Fischer, (p.140). In the SL the subject of the verbal sentence above is simply 'the liar', and it is the same in the TL in translation (b); but in translation (c), the latter is free translation and the paradox in the object 'honest liar' is nonsensical. Incidentally, identifying the verb in Example 16 is most problematic and needs to be taken care of. There are two verbs in the SL (al-Rājiḥī, p.185), 'to be rare' قلّما and 'to speak the truth' يصدق. The main verb in the TL is either a combination of two words, i.e. an expression consisting of a verb and a noun, 'to speak the truth' or the verb 'to be' along with an adjective 'honest'. This shows that the structure in the SL may not correspond well with that in the TL. Here the student finds that the SL verb يصدق has no one-word equivalent but a group of words, which is an obstacle rather hard to overcome for a junior translator or student. The SL verb is one word, whilst its TL equivalence consists of two words. This corrects the assumption one might have that each SL word must have one TL equivalent. So the translator is not 'fettered and walking on a tight rope with his/her legs fettered' but rather works within a track; this technique works well to convey the message faithfully, when no exact one-word equivalence can be found. Another important point here is what linguists call 'propositional equivalence' between two statements where there is, as Alan Cruses says, "... mutual entailment. That is, in effect, equivalent to saying that the two sentences always express the same proposition (provided, of course, that corresponding definite referring expression are co-referential)" (p.30). What this means is to have the following translation to Example 16, '**You** rarely believe the liar'. The only problem with this translation is introducing a new subject the pronoun 'you'. But how equivalent is this sentence to 'rarely does the liar speak the truth' or 'rarely is the liar honest' is an issue one needs to leave it to linguists to argue semantically and pragmatically.

Another issue in the above example is the verb 'to be rare' which is converted into the adverb of frequency 'rarely', a technique which is acceptable, otherwise the whole TL sentence is stilted as in translation (c).

The same comment applies to Example 17,

17.   طالما ساعد أصدقاءه. (Meaning طال and then ما)
a. **He** often <u>helps</u> his friends.
b. **He** has been <u>helping</u> his friends for a long time.
c. **It** has been long, his help to his friends. (literal translation)

Again no problem here in identifying the subject, but it is problematic to decide which verb to consider as the main verb, طال 'to last long' or ساعد 'to help'. According to Fischer, its equivalence is 'very often' (140) In his search for what Peter Newmark calls 'the core of a thought: logical structure'. He points out,

> In any fussy or obscured syntactic (surface) structure, the translator's job is to find the underlying (deep) structure. In my opinion, the most useful procedure is to discover the

logical subject first, then its specific verb, and let the rest fall into place. The basic structure... is: animate (human) subject plus operator (transitive verb) plus inanimate direct object, and this should be looked for first (1981/1986, p.116).

Now although his prescription or solution is useful here, it cannot be applied fully here. It is clear that the first verb in Example 17 is replaced by an adverb of time 'often' in translation (a) and by the adverbial phrase 'for a long time' in translation (b) to cover that aspect of the sentence; whilst the verb 'to help', which is as Newmark calls it, the main "specific verb" for the "logical subject", has been highlighted in both translations to be the main verb of the TL sentence. But, unlike Newmark's prescription, the object of the sentence in this instance is an animate (human) one 'his friends'. Translation (c), however, uses a different subject or pronoun 'it' instead of 'he' and that translation becomes really awkward when the translator attempts to use two verbs, particularly because the particle ما is considered an infinitive particle in this SL sentence (al-Rājiḥī, p.186). The connotative meaning is that 'liar's honesty is rare' in Example 16, and this translation sounds 'natural' and can be acceptable; but 'his help to his friends has been long' in Example 17 is hardly 'natural' and therefore is totally unacceptable.

Now here are few exercises to understand better how the verbal SL sentence is structured and how its TL equivalence is found in practical terms.

" ثُمَّ عَمُواْ وَصَمُّواْ كَثِيرٌ مِّنْهُمْ." (The qur'ān, 5:71)
a. "but many of them again became blind and deaf" (Haleem, p.75).

227

b. "yet again <u>many of them</u> **became blind and deaf**" (Yūsuf 'Alī, p.131).

c. "yet again <u>many of them</u> **became blind and deaf**" (al-Hilālī and Khan, p.158).

It is not so clear that the underline noun phrase is the subject. Here is a similar exercise which has the subject also as the end of the sentence. Another point is that in British National Corpus (BNC) 'deaf and blind' as a phrase occurs 24 times whereas 'blind and deaf' is less, only 18 times. As these two phrases are close, there is no preference as to which one to use.

" وَأَسَرُّواْ النَّجْوَى الَّذِينَ ظَلَمُواْ." (*The qur'ān*, 21:3)

a. "<u>The evildoers</u> **conferred in secret**" (Haleem, p.203).

b. "<u>The wrong-doers</u> **conceal their private counsels**" (Yūsuf 'Alī, p.382).

c. "<u>Those who do wrong</u>, **conceal their private counsels**" (al-Hilālī and Khan, p.429).

In the SL the subject is repeated, but in the TL it is not; the literal translation of the ST is 'And they conferred secretly, those who treat (others) unjustly'. The previous exercise has the same structure in the SL – i.e. 'Then they again became blind and deaf, many of them."

Here is another exercise about the verbal SL sentence and its TL equivalence,

" ثُمَّ بَدَا لَهُم مِّن بَعْدِ مَا رَأَوُاْ الآيَاتِ لَيَسْجُنُنَّهُ حَتَّى حِينٍ." (*The qur'ān*, 12:35)

a. "In the end they thought it best, after seeing all the signs of his innocence, that they should imprison him for a while" (Haleem, p.147).

b. "Then it occurred to the men, after they had seen the Signs, (that it was best) to imprison him for a time" (Yūsuf 'Alī, p.272-73).

c. "Then it occurred to them, after they had seen the proofs (of his innocence), to imprison him for a time" (al-Hilālī and Khan, p.308).

Two clauses are here and the student and translator need to be aware of them. At another level, lexically the SL word آيات is 'evidence', and one must point out that in English this TL word is in plural, and the other point is that the phrase 'of his innocence' is connotative in the ST but not so in the TT. That is why in translation (c) that phrase is put in between brackets.

A further exercise is this.

" إِذَا السَّمَاء انشَقَّتْ ". (The qur'ān, 84:1)

a. "When the sky cracks" (Haleem, p.415).

b. "When the sky is rent asunder" (Yūsuf 'Alī, p.774).

c. "When the heaven is split asunder" (al-Hilālī and Khan, p.824).

The subject in this SL structure, underlined above, is at the beginning of the Arabic sentence, before the verb, when it usually comes after the verb. On the lexical front, though not the point in question in this book, is the equivalent of السماء which is either 'sky' as in translations (a) and (b) or 'the heaven'. Now the most appropriate lexeme here is 'heaven' the reason being that 'earth' is later mentioned in the same holy chapter. This reminds one of the English collocation 'heaven and earth', and not 'sky and earth'. Another interesting point is the verb

انشقت which can be translated as either 'ripped', 'cracked', 'split' or 'rent'.

The penultimate exercise in this group of exercises is this one

" أَسْمِعْ بِهِمْ وَأَبْصِرْ." *(The qur'ān, 19:38)*
a. "How sharp of hearing, how sharp of sight <u>they</u> will be" (Haleem, p.193).

b. "How plainly will <u>they</u> see and hear" (Yūsuf 'Alī, p.361).

c. "How clearly will <u>they</u> (polytheists and disbelievers in the Oneness of Allāh) see and hear" (al-Hilālī and Khan, p.406).

Clearly, the syntactic structure of translations (b) and (c) are more accurate than that of translation (a). Translation (a) should have been 'How sharp… will they be'. Also, here an interesting collocation, 'see and hear' in English which is more common than 'hear and see' as that in the ST. That is why in translations (b) and (c) 'seeing' is mentioned before 'hearing' and not the other way round. In British National Corpus (BNC) on its website the two words 'see' and 'hear' has occurred respectively 61 times; whereas 'hear and see' has occurred only 16 times in the massive data bank. Here the difference is huge compared to the phrase 'blind and deaf' mentioned earlier. This technique proves that collocations in the ST may not be the same in the TT. A similar example here is that in English one says, 'you and I' and not 'I and you'. The latter is commonly used in Arabic but in English.

Finally, here is a complex exercise where there are more than one verbal clause in the ST and the challenge is to identify the subject before engaging in finding the TL equivalence.

" أَلَمْ يَأْنِ لِلَّذِينَ آمَنُوا أَن تَخْشَعَ قُلُوبُهُمْ لِذِكْرِ الـلـه." (*The qur'ān*, 57:16)

a. "Is <u>it</u> not time for <u>believers</u> to humble their hearts to the remembrance of God" (Haleem, p.360).

b. "Has not <u>the time</u> arrived for <u>the Believers</u> that their hearts in all humility should engage in the remembrance of Allah" (Yūsuf 'Alī, p.684).

c. "Has not <u>the time</u> come for the hearts of those <u>who</u> believe (in the Oneness of Allāh – Islāmic Monotheism) to be affected by Allāh's Reminder (this Qur'ān)" (al-Hilālī and Khan, p.741).

d. "Is not <u>the time</u> for the hearts of those <u>who</u> believe to be submissive when engaged in the remembrance of God" (*my translation*).

One can see that the subject is hard to identify at times. The subject 'it' or 'time' is connotative in the SL, but not so in the TL, that is why it is underlined above. So the word 'time' might become a challenge to the student or the translator as it is implied in the verb يأن. At the lexical level, there is the interesting point about all the translations above that there are variations in the TL equivalent of الله: God, Allah, or Allāh; but certainly 'Lord' is inappropriate here as the SL word رب is not mentioned.

Having now covered the subject in the verbal SL sentence and its TL equivalence it is time to see how the SL pro-agent or the subject of the passive is and what its TL equivalence will be.

231

9.2. Pro-agent or subject of the passive voice نائب الفاعل (Cachia, p.77)

Passive voice is rare in the SL (Arabic) but not so rare in the TL (English). Here

are few examples, it is evident that the passive voice in the TL sounds natural,

but not so in the SL, that is why diacritics are essential and need to be added in

the SL,

The following examples have the passive in both in the SL and TL:

1.   فُهِمَ الدرسُ.
The lesson is understood.

2.   عُلِمَ أن زيدا ناجح.
It is known that Zayd has succeeded.

3.   عُلِمَ نجاح زيد.
Zayd's **success** is known.

4.   مُنِحَ زيد مكافأة.
Zayd is given an award.

5.   سُمي الطفل عليًا.
The baby is called Ali.

6.   أعلِمَ الطالبُ الحضورَ مهماً.
The student is informed how important attendance is.

7.   صيم رمضان.
Ramadan is fasted.

8.   قُضي شهرٌ جميل في لبنان.
A lovely month is spent in the Lebanon.

9.   دُهِشَ
He was astonished.

10,   شُده
He was gob smacked.

11.   شُغِفَ
He was in love with.

12.   أولع
He was infatuated.

13.   هُرِع
He was taken hurriedly.

14.   أهرِع

He was rushed (to hospital).

The phrase in between brackets can be added only if it is appropriate in the context.

15.   عُنِيَ زيدٌ بهذا الأمر.

Zayd was assigned to this matter.

But the skill and rich knowledge of the student or professional translator plays a major part in enhancing the quality of his/her translation. Here is an excellent example which highlights this point,

16.   قيل إن زيداً ناجح.

a. **It** is said that Zayd has succeeded.

b. **Simon says** that Zayd has succeeded. (Socio-cultural equivalence)

c. **A little bird says (or tells me)** that Zayd has succeeded. (Socio-cultural equivalence)

Two points are here worth mentioning: One is that it is clear in translations (b) and (c) that the 'dynamic' equivalence is used and it is based on socio-cultural context; secondly, unlike translation (a) which is in the passive with its pro-agent 'it', the latter translations (b) and (c) are in the active with a direct subject being introduced, this technique has made the TL equivalence more 'natural', although the passive is usually favoured in English. Peter Newmark writes,

> His [The translator's] idiolect at once incidentally expresses his own style
> and character and regulates the *naturalness* of his translation, ensuring that
> is modern and full. The effectiveness of the version is finally dependent on
> the elegance and sensitivity of the translator's command of a rich language
> (p.138). [*my emphasis*]

233

Here is another example in which the active is favoured to the passive in the TL, though the passive is used in the SL,

17.   أُغمي عليه

a. **He** fainted.

b. **He** went into a coma. (exegetic translation)

It must be pointed out that the passive voice in the SL is the active voice in the TL; as the equivalence here is more common and more 'natural' in the TL than in the SL. The same can be said about the following example,

18.   أسِفَ عليه.

They (People) are sorry for him.

Now it is superbly explained by Ryding how "a definite adjective or passive participle, often preceded by the partitive preposition" مِن or preceded by و is commonly used in Arabic. Here are two sets of examples with their original equivalences by Ryding (pp.419-20),

Set One:

-     'ومن المتوقع أن...'

'**It is expected** that...'

-     'من الممكن أنّ...'

'**It is possible** that...'

-     'من المهمّ عدم تقديم الكثير من التنازلات.'

'**It is important** not to offer too many concessions.'

-     'من الطبيعي أن نقوم بزيارة...'

'**It is natural** that we undertake a visit...' (*or simply* 'pay a visit') [*emphasis in original*]

Set Two:

-     'ومعلوم أنّ...'

'It is known that...'

- 'والمستغرب أنّ...'

'The strange [thing] is...' [*emphasis in original*]

- 'وعُلم أنّ...'

'(And) it has been learned that...'

- 'يُشار إلى...'

'It is indicated ...'

- 'ويُذكر أن الأمين العام...'

'(And) it is mentioned that the Secretary General...'

- 'ويتوقع أن يشمل التقرير اقتراحاً...'

'(And) it is expected that the report will include a proposal...'

Such beautiful equivalences are extremely useful to both students and professional translators in order to see how the passive is more common in English than in Arabic, and it is noticeable that these two sets above are commonly used in journalistic style.

Here are few exercises to see the Arabic pro-agent or the subject of the passive and its English equivalence.

"فَإِذَا نُفِخَ فِي الصُّورِ نَفْخَةٌ وَاحِدَةٌ." (*The qur'ān*, 69:13)

a. "And when **the Trumpet is sounded** a single time" (Haleem, p.387).

b. "Then, when **one Blast is sounded** on the Trumpet" (Yūsuf ʿAlī, p.727).

235

c. "then when **the Trumpet will be blown** with one blowing (the first one)" (al-Hilālī and Khan, p.780).

Another exercise is this one,

" وَجُمِعَ الشَّمْسُ وَالْقَمَرُ." (*The qur'ān*, 75:9)

a. "when <u>the sun and the moon</u> **are brought together**" (Haleem, p.399).

b. "And <u>the sun and moon</u> **are joined together**" (Yūsuf 'Alī, p.748).

c. "And <u>the sun and moon</u> **will be joined together** (by going one into the other or folded up or deprived of their light)" (al-Hilālī and Khan, p.800).

It is clear where the pro-agent or the subject of the passive underlined above is and what its English equivalence. Here is another exercise.

" إِنْ هُوَ إِلَّا وَحْيٌ يُوحَى." (*The qur'ān*, 53:4)

a. "The Qur'an is nothing less than a revelation <u>that</u> **is sent** to you" (Haleem, p.347)

b. "<u>It</u> **is** no less than inspiration **sent down** to him" (Yūsuf 'Alī, p.660).

c. "<u>It</u> **is** only a Revelation **revealed**" (al-Hilālī and Khan, p.717).

It is clear in both the ST and TT the use of the pro-agent or the subject of the passive. Translation (c) is closest in terms of the use of the verb and the noun from the same infinitive.

Here is a further exercise to illustrate the use of the SL pro-agent and its TL equivalence.

" ثُمَّ لَتُسْأَلُنَّ يَوْمَئِذٍ عَنِ النَّعِيم." (*The qur'ān*, 102:8)

a. "On that Day, <u>you</u> **will be asked** about your pleasures" (Haleem, p.434).

b. "Then, **shall** <u>you</u> **be questioned** that Day about the joy (you indulged in!)" (Yūsuf 'Alī, p.804).

c. "Then on that Day <u>you</u> **shall be asked** about the delights" (al-Hilālī and Khan, p.848).

Here are more exercises that show the SL pro-agent and its TL equivalence.

" وَإِذَا صُرِفَتْ أَبْصَارُهُمْ تِلْقَاء أَصْحَابِ النَّارِ" (*The qur'ān*, 7:47)

a. "and when their glance falls upon the people of the Fire" (Haleem, p.97).

b. "When their eyes shall be turned towards the Companions of the Fire" (Yūsuf 'Alī, p.174).

c. "And when their eyes will be turned towards the dwellers of the Fire" (al-Hilālī and Khan, p.207).

In translation (a) it is not the pro-agent or the subject of the passive but the subject of the active underlined. This by no means indicates that that translation is inappropriate but rather shows that the passive structure in the SL can be translated into the active one in the TL if it conveys the message truthfully.

Here are the last two exercises in this group and they focus on the verb 'to say'.

"وَإِذَا قِيلَ لَهُمْ لاَ تُفْسِدُواْ فِي الأَرْضِ." (*The qur'ān*, 2:11)

a. "When it is said to them, 'Do not cause corruption in the land' " (Haleem, p.5).

b. "When it is said to them: 'Make not mischief on the earth' " (Yūsuf 'Alī, p.3).

c. "And when it is said to them: 'Make not mischief on the earth' " (al-Hilālī and Khan, p.5).

The other final exercise is this.

"وَقِيلَ يَا أَرْضُ ابْلَعِي مَاءكِ وَيَا سَمَاء أَقْلِعِي وَغِيضَ الْمَاء." (*The qur'ān*, 11:44)

a. "Then it was said, 'Earth, swallow up your water, and sky, hold back,' and the water subsided" (Haleem, p.139).

b. "Then the word went forth: 'O earth! Swallow up your water, and O sky! Withhold (your rain)!' And the water abated" (Yūsuf 'Alī, p.256).

c. "And <u>it</u> **was said**: 'O earth! Swallow up your water, and O sky! Withhold (your rain).' And the water was made to subside" (al-Hilālī and Khan, p.292).

Translation (b) again proves that the passive structure in the ST can be translated into the active one in the ST. So 'the word' is the subject in the TL and not the pro-agent. Now having discussed the Arabic subject of the active and the passive or pro-agent alongside their TL equivalence, it is time to see the Arabic object, its types and their English equivalence.

9.3. Object المفعول به and its types alongside their English equivalence

9.3.1. One direct object in the verb SL sentence and its straightforward equivalence.

Unlike the nominal SL sentence, the verbal SL sentence requires at least one object with its known structure Verb + Subject + Object (VSO), when its verb is transitive. The equivalence of that object is clear in the TL sentence structure Subject + Verb + Object (SVO) as in Examples 1 and 2,

1.   فهمتُ الدرسَ.

I understood **the lesson**.

2.   أود أن أزوره.

I would like to visit **him**.

But sometimes the object of the SL sentence, though just one here, can be unclear particularly when the verbal SL sentence is within a nominal SL one, and therefore its object might appear as if it is a nominal sentence but it is not as in Example 3,

3.   إعدادُك الدرسَ مفيد.

Preparing **the lesson** is useful to you.

Now it is preferable to use the gerund here (which in other cases can sometimes be the present participle) and not the noun 'preparation' in the TL; otherwise the TL equivalence appears to be awkward and 'unnatural' in the TL, let us see the literal translation of Example 3, 'Your preparation of the lesson is useful.' Here the connotative meaning is unclear as to whom that preparation is useful. A similar more complex case is in Example 4,

4.   هو الكاتبُ الكتابَ أمسٍ. (al-Rājiḥī, p.196)

a. He was the one who wrote **the letter** (or note) yesterday.

b. He was the one who drew up **the marriage contract** yesterday.

c. He was the one who wrote **the book** yesterday. (literal translation)

d. He was *the writer of the book* yesterday. (too literal, almost interlinear translation)

In Example 4, it is rather illogical or nonsensical to produce translation (c) or even worse still to use translation (d). The TL equivalence in both translations (c) and (d) does not make sense because one cannot write a whole book in a day (yesterday). So it is semantically unsound to translate this sentence word-for-word. One ought to go deeper into the meaning or message the ST carries before attempting to produce its TL equivalence. As the analysis of this research aims to help in understanding the syntactic complexity of the

SL sentence, which will help in finding an appropriate equivalence; there is no space to give analysis on the semantic level of the SL sentence, with its socio, and cogni-/menti-facts as Basil Hatim calls them in his presentation about translation at a conference in Effat University in November 2012.

In his presentation about the theory of translation Basil Hatim has pointed out that there are three facts: Artifacts, Socio-facts and Menti-facts or Cogni-facts. His presentation is to be published in the conference proceedings of the conference 'The Cultural Impact of Language and Translation' (CILT) which was held in Effat University in Jeddah on 14th November 2012.

Example 4 has homography – and a homograph is a word that has the same spelling but two different meanings (John Lyons, 1981/1999, p.72). The SL words 'الكاتب' and 'الكتاب' are both polysemous ('Polysemous' means having more than one meaning.). The former can mean 'the writer' or the act of writing (the active participle, or the present participle and sometimes gerund in the TL); the latter refers to 'letter', 'note', 'book', or 'marriage contract'. So their equivalence in the TL is problematic.

Another similar problem with homonyms in Arabic translation is when the verbal noun is used as its equivalent is either a gerund or an infinitive, see Ryding's discussion on the verbal noun (Ryding, pp.79-82) e.g.

- دفع التعويض.
'the **payment** of compensation'. (Ryding, p.80) [*my emphasis*]

It must be noted that examples from Ryding are used in her book to explain grammatical rules but in my analysis here and everywhere else in my book are used to explain some translation problems or issues. Now as the short vowels (the diacritical marks) are not added to the ST (Arabic text), the word 'دفع' may look as it is a verb 'to pay' and not a verbal noun 'payment', and therefore translators might produce an altogether different translation saying, He **paid** compensation. Here are two examples of a similar calibre: 'رفع العلم' with its TL equivalence 'the **raising** of the flag' - in Ryding, it is translated in a different context in Ryding's book, i.e. as a verbal noun and not as a sentence (p.81) - or 'he **raised** the flag'; and 'لعب دور' with its TL equivalence '**playing** a role' - also, it is translated in a different context by Ryding, i.e. as a verbal noun and not as a sentence (*Ibid.*) - or 'he **played** a role.'

Another homonym is usually in what Ryding calls 'plural of paucity' as opposed to 'plural that indicates many' (Ryding, p.148), e.g. the plural of 'شهر' 'month' is either 'أشهر' (meaning 'few months') or 'شهور' (meaning 'many months') in the SL. Now the first plural of paucity here is to be avoided, particularly in audiovisual translation, as it can be mistaken for comparative and superlative adjective أشهر (meaning, 'more reputed' or 'more famous'). Now for a good discussion on the word choice in audiovisual translation, see Ahmad Khuddro (1997: 115-30) in *Turjuman* (written in Arabic). He discusses some problematic words such as the spelling of the SL word موسيقى or موسيقا 'music' which can be confusing, as it can mean 'musician' (Egyptian school of spelling 'yā', having no dots

241

underneath) as well as 'music' if spelt with the shortened or abbreviated 'alif' الألف المقصورة.

So the verbal noun in the SL (Arabic) can be misleading when translated into the TL (English). Here are few examples, in which the word 'قارئ' does not necessarily mean in the TL 'reader' but 'the acting of reading' (the active participle, the present participle or gerund depending on the context and corresponding to the TL grammar).

5.   ما قارئ زيدٌ كتاباً.
Zayd is not reading **a book**.

6.   هل قارئ زيدٌ كتاباً؟
Is Zayd reading **a book**?

7.   محمد قارئ كتاباً.
Muḥammad is reading **a book**.

8.   رأيت رجلاً قارئاً كتاباً.
I saw **a man** who was **reading a book**.

In Example 8, the active participle 'the act of reading' (or the present participle) in the SL sentence is the second object of the verbal sentence, followed by yet another object 'a book'. This subtle difference between the active participle (the act of reading) and the noun (the reader) needs to be identified during the syntactic analysis of the SL, otherwise the translator or student might fail in the process and produce a semantically incorrect translation.

9.   هو حمّالٌ أعباءَهم.
a. He carries **all their burdens**.
b. He takes on his shoulders **all their burdens** (or **responsibilities**).

Here one is tempted to compare this with إمرأته حمّالةَ الحطبِ 'his wife, the firewood-carrier' (*The qur'ān*, 111:4) [*Haleem's translation*]. This Arabic syntactic structure is completely different ; in his analysis of this structure Fischer (2002) writes, 'In pre-classical Arabic, substantives occur on occasion in the definite appositional accusative' (199).

It is worth noting that the SL word 'حمّال' has two meanings: 'carrying' and 'porter'. The translator might mistakenly choose the word 'porter'. Indeed, all present participles or gerunds in the SL sentence can be easily misunderstood structurally or syntactically, as seen in the above examples. So one should look carefully and distinguish between the present participle and the verbal noun in the SL, and then decide how to re-encode or rephrase using the TL equivalence.

Two direct objects in the verb SL sentence and their equivalence

At times two objects are found in the verbal SL sentence, whose verb requires multiple valents – that is it requires not only one subject but also two or even three objects. The verb 'give', for example, is transitive in both the SL and TL; and therefore it is easy to transfer the message across. There are other verbs of similar nature as in the following examples,

10.   أعطيت زيداً كتاباً.
I gave **Zayd a book**.
11.   منحه وساماً.
He gave **him a badge**.

243

12. وهبه كتاباً.

He gave **him a book**.

As demonstrably seen in Examples 10-12, the two objects in each SL sentence are clear and their TL equivalence are also two straightforward objects, but they become more difficult to identify in Examples 13 and 14 below, though the two objects in each SL sentence are obvious to the trained eye of the source reader,

13. ألبسه قميصاً.

He got **him** dressed **in a shirt**.

14. كساه ثياباً فاخرة.

He dressed **him in fine clothes**.

The first object in both examples is a connected pronoun (suffixed) ضمير متصل, and needs to be identified first before thinking about the second object when translating such sentences.

Two direct objects for verbs of heart or mental verbs أفعال القلوب

Now this is what Cachia called them (p.76); whilst Ryding calls them 'verbs of perception or cognition' (p.682).

It is clear that objects are directly linked to the type of verb used. Some verbs require not only bivalent (a subject and one object) but further valents (a subject and two or more objects). Verbs of heart require two direct objects in the verbal SL sentence – further valency. See a whole discussion in the chapter on Lexis and Syntax in David Singleton's (2000) *Language and the lexicon: An introduction*, in which there are monovalents (some verbs require only a subject as the verb is 'the fundamental or central element of the sentence'), bivalents (verbs requiring both a subject and one direct object) and further valents (verbs requiring more than one object). Also these verbs are of two types, one indicating certainty and the other indicating probability (al-Rājiḥī, pp.200-03). Both types are transitive verbs, which require two objects as well.

Verbs of heart used to indicate certainty

Even though the discussion or syntactic analysis here is about identifying the two objects of a verbal SL sentence, it is vital for the student or translator to recognise the verbs of heart or mental verbs when they indicate a sense of certainty. Here are few examples with these verbs underlined whereas the objects are done in bold in order to understand their positions or status, and the same is done for their TL equivalence,

1.   علمتُ الجدَّ سبيلَ النجاح.
I <u>learnt</u> that **working hard** was really **the way** to success.

2.   رأيت الجدَّ سبيلَ النجاح.
I <u>saw</u> that **working hard** was really **the way** to success.

3.   وجدت الإهمالَ طريقاً إلى الفشل.
I <u>found</u> **negligence** (or **complacency**) to be **the** (inevitable) **way** to failure.

Before discussing these three examples in detail, it is vital to point out that verbs of heart with their two direct objects in the SL are more problematic in translation than those in the earlier set of verbs (see *para.*9.3.1 'Two direct objects'); and therefore, their equivalence can be either a clause acting as object in the main clause ('I knew that...' or 'I saw that...'), whereas the two direct objects are transferred in the TL by shifting the position of one of the two to be a subject ('working hard') whilst the other object ('the way...') keeps its position as object in the secondary clause, as seen in Examples 1 and 2.

Furthermore, looking closely at Example 3 shows that the adjective 'inevitable' with its negative connotative meaning is added to emphasize the sense of certainty, and interestingly, unlike that in the SL, this adjective is commonly used in the TL, presumably since the SL word حتما 'inevitable' has religious connotative meaning – as it is believed that everything in life is pre-destined and therefore may not *inevitably* happen. This can be easily proven in the SL by checking up the concordance of that word in *The qur'ān*. The word حتما 'inevitable' is only mentioned once in the SL corpus. See Chapter 19, verse 71: 'A decree from your Lord which must be fulfilled.' The translation does not mention the word 'inevitable' in the translation, though it is used in the SL verse. However, that word ('inevitable') is used with a capital letter in Haleem's translation of the title of Chapter 69 as well as in the first 3 verses of that chapter: 'The Inevitable Hour! What is the Inevitable Hour? What will explain to you what the Inevitable Hour is?'

But in British National Corpus on its website regarding the TL the frequency of 'inevitable' is 2682 times (http://corpus.byu.edu/bnc/).

4.　　دَرَيتُ الإيمانَ أساسَ النصر.

a. I <u>realised</u> **faith** was **the basis** of victory.

b. I realised **victory** was **based on faith**.

In Example 4, the same comment can be said about the use of two clause, a main one and secondary one, as seen in Examples 1 and 2. Furthermore, translation (b) has the same propositional equivalence as translation (a), so long as they both have 'mutual entailment', as Alan Cruse (2000, p.30) says, as it is 'the same proposition (provided… that corresponding definite referring expressions are co-referential)'. Translation (b) might be more appropriate as it is in the passive voice, which is common and more 'natural' in the TL. Here are more examples which show how the two direct objects are translated,

5.　　جعلتُ زيداً كريماً. (Meaning 'I believed'; see al-Rājiḥī's explanation of the SL verb 'to believe', p.201).

I <u>believed</u> **Zayd** was actually **generous**.

6.　　ألفيتُ الإخلاص خلقاً كريماً.

I <u>realised</u> **one's loyalty** was really a **fine characteristic**.

7.　　تعلَّمْ الجِدَ سبيلَ النجاح. (Meaning 'know that'; see al-Rājiḥī's explanation of the SL verb of heart 'to know' used here, p.201).

<u>Know</u> **that working hard** is, in fact, **the way** to success.

It is essential to show that certainty in the TL by using adverbs such as 'really', 'actually', and 'in fact'. It is worth noting that the verb in Example 5 means 'to believe' and not 'to make' or 'to begin'; also the verb in Example 7 means 'to know' and not 'to learn'.

247

Verbs of heart used to indicate probability or preponderance (For explanation see al-Rājiḥī, p.201 and see the term in Cachia, p.75)

Again, the job of identifying the two direct objects of the verbal SL sentence is vital, as some verbs of heart or mental verbs require further valents, i.e. the use of two objects, and they also can refer to probability which needs to be highlighted in the TL, e.g.

8. ظننتُ زيداً كريماً.

I <u>guessed</u> Zayd was **generous**.

9. يظن البخيل السعادة في جمع المال.

The miser <u>thinks</u> **happiness** is in hoarding (or stashing away) money.

10. خِلت زيداً كريماً.

I <u>thought</u> of **Zayd being generous.**

11. حسبتُ زيداً كريماً.

I <u>considered</u> Zayd to be **generous.**

(Also, I thought of **Zayd being generous**.)

12. زعمت زيداً كريماً.

I <u>assumed</u> Zayd to be **generous.**

13. عددت زيداً صديقاً.

I <u>considered</u> **Zayd a friend.**

14. أُظنني قد صدَقتُ

a. 'I <u>consider</u> **myself to have spoken the truth**' (Fischer, p.221). [*my emphasis*]

b. I <u>believe</u> **I have spoken the truth.**

So the solution in the TL is either to replace the two direct objects in the SL with a secondary clause acting as object to the main clause or as two direct objects; this depends on which option is more 'natural' in the TL.

Moreover, it is vital to note that Example 14 has clearly two translations: translation (b) is acceptable, though the TL equivalence has only one object which is the clause, whilst the other object 'myself' is connotative. A further use of the verb ظن and its TL equivalence is elaborated in Fischer's example (Example 14). Also, it is interesting to point out that the SL verb 'اعتبر' and its TL equivalence have the same function in both languages, and here is another example of the verb 'to consider' and it is given by Ryding,

- 'يعتبرونهم نجومهم المفضلين'

'They consider **them their favourite stars**' (Ryding, p.71). [*emphasis in original*]

- 'يعتبرونكم الرواد'

'They consider **you** (m.pl.) **the pioneers.**' (Ryding, p.32) [*my emphasis*]

One must point out that though the example in her book is used in a different context the focus here is on translation and not on its phonetically significant as Ryding is doing in this particular example. One of the translation loss is highlighted here in Ryding's example, where she inserts the acronym 'm.pl.' (meaning, 'masculine plural') in between brackets for the purpose of explaining a grammatical rule as her book deals with Arabic grammar and not with translation. For further examples along with their equivalence to enrich students' and professional translators' knowledge, on can refer to Karin C. Ryding (2005, pp.68-72).

So it is vital that verbs of heart must be first identified by students and professional translators, in order to know how many direct objects are used and then 're-encoded' in the TL. That process of decoding and

249

're-encoding' is discussed by Frank Pöchhacker (2004) in *Introducing interpreting studies* points out, "based on the analogy of electrical signal transmission [in the late 1940s by Claude Shannon and Warren Weaver], Translation was viewed as a combined decoding and encoding operation involving the switching of linguistic code signals" (p.54), by using verbs which have further valents following valency grammar, as discussed by David Singleton (2000) in his book *Language and the Lexicon*.

Two objects for verbs of transmutation or factitive verbs أفعال التصيير أو التحويل

Cachia calls فعل تحويل as verb of transmutation which is an appropriate equivalence (pp.75,76), whereas Ryding (p.682) calls such verbs as 'verbs of transformation' which is just appropriate. In the SL, factitive verbs which require two objects need to be recognised by students and professional translators during the process of their syntactic analysis, but their equivalence might not be a verb in the TL that requires two objects but just one direct object followed by the rest of the sentence. Here are few examples alongside their equivalence,

15. صيّر الحائك القماش ثوباً.
The tailor has <u>made</u> **a dress** <u>out of</u> the material.

16. هذا المصنع يجعل القشّ ورقاً.
This factory <u>turns</u> **hay** <u>into</u> paper.

17. اتخذ الرجلُ الجبلَ ملجأً.
The man <u>took</u> **the mountain** <u>as</u> refuge.

18. ترك المعتدون القرية أطلالاً.
The aggressors <u>left</u> **the village** <u>in</u> ruins.

So identifying factitive verbs underlined above, alongside certain prepositions, does help to find an appropriate TL equivalence but that equivalence by default needs to correspond to the TL syntax still and not just stick too closely to the SL syntax. One must analyse the SL syntax correctly for the purpose of understanding the message first, before forming the TL text with its lexical equivalence and corresponding syntax, as evident in Examples 15-18 (with their TL equivalence). However, the phrasal verbs 'make out of', 'turn into', and 'take as' must by default have two objects in the TL, but the last verb 'leave (something) in ruins (or in tatters)' is not phrasal but the whole expression is collocational or idiomatic. Therefore, the translator or student needs to take special care of that as well.

Verbs of heart in the interrogative form and negation in the SL sentence alongside their TL equivalence

Now let us discuss how SL verbs of heart or mental verbs are translated when they are in the interrogative or in negation.

SL verbs of heart in the interrogative form

In the interrogative form the verb 'دري' or 'علم' (to 'know' or 'come to one's knowledge') requires further valents (i.e. two objects) in the verbal SL sentence, and therefore it is harder to identify by the student or translator as these valents are mentioned within a nominal secondary SL clause in the sentence, as in the following example,

19.   لا أدري أزيد حاضر أم غائب.

a. I do not know **whether Zayd** is **present or not.** (communicative translation with a formal style)

b. I don't know **whether Zayd** is **present or absent.** (literal translation with a colloquial style)

Here the nominal clause in its interrogative form with its subject and two predicates, acts implicitly as the two objects to the verb 'know' in the verbal sentence (al-Rājiḥī, p.208). Also, it is clear that translation (b) has colloquial language (the truncated or short form of 'do not') and is literal (with its rather childlike wording 'present or absent' and not being elliptical).

SL verbs of heart in negation

Like Example 19, the SL verb 'درى' or 'علم' (to 'know' or 'come to one's knowledge') requires further valents, i.e. one subject and two objects in negation. But these two objects are implicitly mentioned in the nominal secondary clause (al-Rājiḥī, p.208) and need to be identified in the SL syntax by students or professional translators first before finding the most appropriate equivalence in the TL sentence. Here is an example,

20.   علمتُ ما زيدٌ بخيل.

I knew Zayd is **not** mean.

Another example with the use of 'might' (meaning, perhaps) can be analysed in the same way as Example 20 with the nominal clause acting as further valents to the verb 'know' (al-Rājiḥī, p.209).

21.   لا أدري لعل الأمر خير.

I do not know, this thing **might** be good.

Here are other examples where the nominal clause in the SL has the two objects

to the transitive verbs 'know', 'notice' or 'see', and 'reckon',

22.   أعلم كم كتابٍ قرأ زيد.

I know **how many books** Zayd has read.

23.   رأيتُني راغباً في السفر.

You see **me keen to travel**.

24.   (أتظن, meaning) أتقول زيداً قادماً اليوم؟

Do you reckon **Zayd is coming** today?

In Example 25 the verb تقول means 'to reckon' but when that verb is used in a

conditional sentence it means 'to say', and in this case it becomes bivalent,

requiring only one object (al-Rājiḥī, p.212),

25.   تسألني عن طريق النصر فأقول الإيمانَ.   [emphasis in original]

You ask me about the way to victory, **I say** Faith.

Clearly, the verb 'say' in the SL is polysemous, and therefore students and

professional translators need to identify which meaning is intended in the

sentence before they attempt to translate such a tricky verb, as it can be a verb of

heart and a proper transitive 'normal' verb that requires one object only.

Here are other verbs of hearts which are similar to the two verbs 'to know' and

'to see', but demand <u>three</u> objects in the SL (al-Rājiḥī, p.215), such as أنبأ، أخبر 'to

inform', 'to tell', clearly defined in the SL. It is vital that students or translators

are aware of this syntactical rule before translating such verbs into English. Here

is an example with its equivalence,

26. أعلمتك زيدا كريماً.

I have informed **you, Zayd is generous.**

It is clear that the three objects in this SL sentence are not so in the TL

equivalence, the first object in the TL grammar here is 'you' and the clause 'Zayd

is generous' stands for the other two objects. The same can be said about the

following two examples,

27. أنبأت زيداً أخاه ناجحاً.

I have told **Zayd, his brother has succeeded.**

28. نُبِّئتُ زيداً ناجحاً.

I was told Zayd had succeeded.

It must be noted that in Example 28 the SL sentence is in the passive voice, and

the subject of the passive is 'I', but had the SL sentence been written in the active

voice, then the 'I' is the first object ('someone told **me**') and the other two objects

are 'Zayd' and 'success'. One can see that a shift in translation is sometimes

required to make the sentence acceptable by its readers. De Beaugrande talks

about 'acceptability' as one of the seven standards of textuality *Introduction to*

text linguistics (1981). He writes, "The notion of ACCEPTABILITY as the text

receivers' attitude in communication" (p.129).

Here are few exercises that show the Arabic object(s) and their English

equivalence. Here is one with two objects,

"وَإِنِّي لَأَظُنُّكَ يَا فِرْعَونُ مَثْبُورًا." (*The qur'ān*, 17:102)

a. "I think **that you, Pharaoh, are doomed**" (Haleem, p.181).

b. "I consider **you** indeed, O Pharaoh, **to be one doomed** to destruction". (Yūsuf 'Alī, p.340).

c. "And I think **you are**, indeed, O Fir'aun (Pharaoh) **doomed** to destruction (away from all good)!" (al-Hilālī and Khan, p.383).

Translation (b) shows the two TL equivalents to the two SL objects, but the other two translations (a) and (c) are not so clear.

Here is another exercise with a couple of SL objects and their TL equivalence.

"لَا تَحْسَبُوهُ شَرًّا لَّكُم."(The qur'ān, 24:11)

a. "do not consider **it a bad thing** for you [people]" (Haleem, p.221).

b. "think **it** not **to be an evil** to you" (Yūsuf 'Alī, p.420).

c. "Consider **it** not **a bad thing** for you" (al-Hilālī and Khan, p.468).

It is clear where the two TL objects are, and even clearer when the verb 'to consider' is used in English.

A further exercise of SL objects and their TL equivalence is this,

"وَجَعَلُوا الْمَلَائِكَةَ الَّذِينَ هُمْ عِبَادُ الرَّحْمَنِ إِنَاثًا." (The qur'ān, 43:19)

a. "They consider **the angels** – God's servants – **to be female**" (Haleem, p.317).

b. "And they make into females angels who themselves serve Allah" (Yūsuf 'Alī, p.605).

c. "And they make **the angels** who themselves are slaves of the Most Gracious (Allāh) **females**" (al-Hilālī and Khan, p.662).

Here is a similar exercise which has two objects in the SL as well as their equivalence in the TL.

"وَاتَّخَذَ اللـه إِبْرَاهِيمَ خَلِيلاً." (The qur'ān, 4:125)

a. "God took **Abraham as a friend**" (Haleem, p.62).

b. "For Allah did take **Abraham for a friend**" (Yūsuf 'Alī, p.108).

c. "And Allāh did take **Ibrāhīm** (Abraham) **as a Khalīl** (an intimate friend)!"
(al-Hilālī and Khan, p.130).

A further exercise is this,

"لَوْ يَرُدُّونَكُم مِّن بَعْدِ إِيمَانِكُمْ كُفَّاراً حَسَدًا." (The qur'ān, 2:109)

a. "[many of the People of the Book wish] they could turn **you** back to **disbelief**
after you have believed, **out of their selfish envy**" (Haleem, p.13).

b. "[Quite a number of the People of the Book wish] they could turn **you**
(people) back to **infidelity** after you have believed, **from selfish envy**" (Yūsuf
'Alī, p.18).

c. "[many of the People of the Book wish] they could turn **you** back **to disbelief**
after you have believed, **out of their selfish envy**" (al-Hilālī and Khan, p.13).

Another exercise of the SL objects and their TL equivalence.

"وَتَرَكْنَا بَعْضَهُمْ يَوْمَئِذٍ يَمُوجُ فِي بَعْضٍ." (The qur'ān, 18:99)

a. "On that Day, We shall let **them surge** against each other like waves" (Haleem,
p.189).

b. "On that day We shall leave **them to surge** like waves on one another" (Yūsuf
'Alī, p.355).

c. "And on that Day [i.e. the Day Y'jūj and Ma'jūj (Gog and Magog) will come
out], We shall leave **them to surge** like waves on one another" (al-Hilālī and
Khan, p.399).

Here is yet another exercise which shows one Arabic object and its English
equivalence.

"لَقَدْ عَلِمْتَ مَا هَؤُلَاء يَنطِقُونَ." (The qur'ān, 21:65)

a. "You know very well **these gods cannot speak**" (Haleem, p.206).

b. "You know full well **that these (idols) do not speak!**" (Yūsuf ʿAlī, p.389).

c. "Indeed you [Ibrāhīm (Abraham)] know well **that these (idols) speak not!**" (al-Hilālī and Khan, p.436).

A further more interesting and complex exercise which has more than one Arabic object alongside their English equivalence.

" كَذَلِكَ يُرِيهِمُ الـلـه أَعْمَالَهُمْ حَسَرَاتٍ عَلَيْهِمْ." (*The qurʾān*, 2:167)

a. "In this way, God will make **them** see **their deeds as a source of bitter regret**" (Haleem, p.19).

b. "Thus will Allah show **them (the fruits of) their deeds as (nothing but) regrets**" (Yūsuf ʿAlī, p.27).

c. "Thus Allāh will show **them their deeds as regrets** for them" (al-Hilālī and Khan, p.33).

It is clear that there are three objects in the SL, and they are a challenge for translators and students, who should be extremely careful when analysing the ST, in order to find the most appropriate equivalent objects in the TL.

The final exercise here is this exciting one as it has more than one Arabic object.

"إِنِّي أَرَانِي أَعْصِرُ خَمْرًا." (*The qurʾān*, 12:36)

a. "I dreamed that I was pressing grapes" (Haleem, p.147)

b. "I see **myself** (in a dream) **pressing wine**" (Yūsuf ʿAlī, p.273).

c. "Verily, I saw **myself** (in a dream) **pressing wine**" (al-Hilālī and Khan, p.308).

257

Now translation (a) shows one object in the TL, whereas translations (b) and (c) are more appropriate for they have used two objects in English. At the lexical level, the word خمر being squeezed or pressed might sound inappropriate as 'wine' cannot be pressed but 'grapes' can. So translation in this sense is most appropriate lexically.

Now having discussed the multiple SL objects and their TL equivalence, it is time to see how the accusative of specification or particularisation.

9.3.2. Accusative of specification or particularisation المفعول به على الاختصاص

This object is called by Cachia (p.35). The object in the verbal SL sentence is the one whose verb 'to specify' must be dutifully deleted, as it is implicitly or connotatively understood in the SL (al-Rājihī, p.218). This object to the deleted verb (meaning, 'I specify') usually occurs after a pronoun, and refers to a certain person, group or characteristic. Now this object in the TL is sometimes inserted in parenthesis or in between two commas as in the following examples,

1. نحن المسلمين موحّدون.
We, **Muslims**, believe in the oneness of God.

2. نحن جنودَ الجيش ندافع عن الوطن.
We, **the soldiers**, defend our homeland.

3. أنا زيداً أدافع عن الحق.
I, **Zayd**, fight for the truth.

4. أنا – أيُّها العربيُّ – كريم. (Meaning, 'being myself an Arab')
I, **the only Arab** (here), am generous.

5. أنا – أيتها الطالبة – أسعى إلى العلم.

I, **the only female student** (here), endeavour to get knowledge.

So the word or phrase in parenthesis in the TL is the appropriate equivalence of this object of specification, though that TL word or phrase acts as 'substitute' to the subject. And the substitute itself in the SL is a secondary clause (al-Rājiḥī, pp.220-21). Now it is also vital to point out that Examples 4 and 5 show how the accusative of specification (the substitute of the subject) refers to *the one and only* of his/her group here.

9.3.3. Object for cautioning or instigation in the verbal SL sentence and its equivalence

Another kind of object in the verbal SL sentence is the one used for cautioning or instigation (al-Rājiḥī, p.222) and, like the verb of the accusative earlier, its verb is also omitted on purpose. Here are few examples,

6. الإهمالَ الإهمالَ فإنه طريق الفشل.
a. <u>Beware of</u> **negligence**, as it is the way to failure. (communicative translation)
b. **Negligence, negligence** as it is the way to failure. (literal translation)
c. **Negligence** is the way to failure. (communicative translation)

The initial syntactic analysis of the SL shows that there are two clauses, the first of which has the verb missing because it is connotative whilst the second clause is a nominal one and can stand alone. Now the student or translator might analyze the whole sentence as the subject 'negligence' being repeated three times ('negligence, 'negligence,' and 'it'), the third repetition is anaphoric (Baker, p.178), using 'it'. As for the literal translation of the above example, it is clear that it is not grammatically acceptable in the TL, because it makes no sense. But when rephrased the TL equivalence becomes acceptable stylistically, because tautology is a stylistic feature in the SL and it is advisable not to transfer it, except when that feature is intended for its surface value.

In translation (a), though the repetition of the object twice ('negligence') in the SL - as al-Rājihī writes that repetition is stylistic and merely emphatic (p. 222) - can be ignored in the TL equivalence, when the stylistic feature (tautology) is essential or there is space limitation on the screen as in the case of audiovisual translation, such as subtitling. However, the verb 'beware of' in the SL is connotative, but needs to be denotative in the TL. Translations (a) and (c) have two different characteristics, the TT is either done by addition or omission respectively, with the former using exegetic translation and the latter using gist translation. See Dickins' discussion (2002) on translation by omission or by addition (pp.23-4). Translation (a) has the *addition* of 'beware of', whereas the other communicative translation (c) has the *omission* of 'as it'. Also, both ignore the element of repetition, with the former using exegetic translation and the latter using gist translation.

In Example 7, no unlike Example 6, there are two objects to the connotative verb 'to be',

7.   الجدَّ والاستقامةَ فإنهما طريق النجاح.
a. Be **hard-working and honest**, as they are the way to success. (exegetic translation)
b. **Working hard and honesty** are the way to success. (gist translation)
c. **Working hard and honesty**, as they are the way to success. (literal translation)

The initial syntactic analysis reveals that the connotative verb in the SL has its two objects which are nouns. Also, the two objects are used for instigation. But what about their TL equivalence? There is a translation shift in word class from noun to adjective in translation (a); but in translation (b) that shift is not required but the phrase 'as they' must be omitted. It is worth noting that the use of a comma in translation (c) might make the TT acceptable. Both translations (a) and (b) are communicative, but translation (c) might sound right but taken out context it is rather literal and therefore unacceptable in its current form.

The following example is not dissimilar to the previous examples above, it also has two objects. But what about their equivalence?

8.   نفسَك نفسَك فإنها أمّارة بالسوء.
a. **Self, self**, as it incites you to evil. (literal translation)
b. **Your soul, your soul**, might incite you to evil. (communicative translation)
c. Guide **your soul**, as it might incite you to evil. (communicative translation)

261

In (a) above there is an allusive meaning to *The qur'ān*, Chapter 12, verse 53: 'for man's very soul incites him to evil.' This SL sentence number 8 is completely different to the known saying in TL, "look after number one"; but rather it is quite the opposite. One is warned of being rather 'evil' because of his/her 'soul' or 'self'. The implication is that one must guide one's own 'soul'. Now the two objects in the SL are totally ignored in translations (a) and (b). But they are appropriately combined into one in translation (c). The repetition or tautology is a stylistic feature which must be adhered to, when at all possible. Another misleading feature is word choice. The word 'نفسك' might be mistakenly translated as the reflexive pronoun 'yourself'; but obviously, the SL sentence does not refer to that pronoun, that is why 'self' or 'soul' is used. The connotative meaning in the SL is your 'soul' might misguide you or might lead you to evil as it is mentioned in the *Qur'ān* (al-Rājiḥī, p.222).

Tautology is usually used for emphasis in the TL but this repetition in the SL also shows that these are two objects to a connotative verb. But this connotative verb is elusive at times, as it can mean 'beware of' or 'take care of', as in the following example,

9.   أخاك أخاك.
a. **Your brother, your brother.** (literal translation)
b. <u>Take care of</u> **your brother.** (communicative translation, but risky)
c. <u>Beware of</u> **your brother.** (communicative translation, but risky)

Again the two objects are appropriately combined in translation (b). It must be noted that literal translations in Examples 6-9 might make sense if put in a certain context. In Example 9, translation (a) though literal seems acceptable as an utterance and not as a verbal sentence. The syntactic analysis of the SL shows that it is a verbal sentence with two objects, that is why translation (a) might be unacceptable. Also, tautology or repetition is a stylistic feature which should be adhered to in translation (a) as it is an utterance; but repetition is certainly not required in translation (b).

Another crucial point is that the intentionally omitted verb of the two objects can be either 'beware of' or 'take care of' in a *positive* or *negative* sense: 'Beware of your brother' or 'Take care of your brother'. Neither TL versions can be used here as the context is unclear, and therefore translation (a) is most appropriate to avoid any confusion in meaning. So translations (b) and (c) though communicative are risky, unless the SL context is absolutely clear, then one of them will do. Now the positive and negative messages are clearer in Example 10 below, in which the conjunction 'and' has joined the two objects together (in earlier examples they are joined with a comma),

10.   نفسك والشهوة فإنها تقودها إلى الهلاك.
a. Look after **your soul** and beware of **your voluptuous desire** (al-Rājihī, p.224), as the latter leads to one's self destruction. (communicative, exegetic translation)
b. Care for **your soul and voluptuous desire,** as the latter leads to disaster. (communicative and less exegetic translation)

263

There are two points here: One is that the anaphoric reference in the second clause goes back to 'desire'; the second point is that this translation is exegetic, adding the connotative verbs 'look after' and 'beware of' in the TL, along with their objects. Another option is translation (b) with the use of one denotative verb 'care for' and its two objects.

11.   إيّاك وإيّاك الإهمال.

a. I warn you not to be negligent (al-Rājiḥī, pp.224-25). (communicative, exegetic translation)

b. No negligence will be tolerated. (free translation)

Tautology or repetition is a stylistic feature which should be adhered to, when possible unless it is used for emphasis. The initial syntactic analysis of Example 11 shows that the connotative SL verb 'beware of' has two objects, since the second object 'إياك' is repeated just for emphasis. That repetition is necessary as we see in translation (a); translation (b) can be considered as free translation, or even an adaptation, which is rather risky and may not be accepted, unless the text type is instructive and accepts such a style. Another similar example with the same meaning to the one above is this,

12.   إيّاك من الإهمال.

<u>I warn</u> **you** not to be negligent.

Here is the initial syntactic analysis of the SL: The connotative subject 'I' and verb 'to warn' in the SL must be denotative in the TL; but the object 'إياك' 'you' is certainly clear. Also there is a translation shift in word class or parts of speech from noun in the SL to adjective in the TL, but the meaning is appropriately conveyed.

So this is the strategy to be adopted when translating objects for cautioning or instigation in the verbal SL sentence.

9.3.4. Unrestricted object, or absolute object المفعول المطلق

So do Cachia calls it (p.78); whereas Fischer calls it 'Absolute Object' (p.195). This absolute object is yet another object to understand in the SL before attempting to find its TL equivalence, which is usually an adverb in the TL. Here are few SL examples with TL equivalence,

1.   عمّر المسلمون الأرض تعميراً.

Muslims **built** the land **extensively**.

2.   رحل المستعمر رحيل الذليل.

The colonizer **left in a really** humiliated **manner**.

3.   هذا الرجل محبوب حباً شديداً بين قومه.

This man is **greatly loved** by his people.

4.   كلّمني زيد كلاماً مفيداً.

Zayd's **talk** to me has been **really** useful.

5.   إغتسل غسلاً.

He **bathed properly**

Or: He **washed thoroughly**.

6.   استمع سماعاً حسناً.

He **listened well**.

OR: He was **really** a good listener.

7.   توضأ وضوءاً.

His **abolition** is **done really well**.

Fischer also uses a similar example, ضُرب ضرباً with its appropriate equivalence which is an adverb, 'He…was **really** hit' (Fischer, p.195). Another possibly more appropriate one is 'He was **badly** beaten/hit.' So it is clear that the strategy to be used in translation is to find its adverbial equivalence, with adverbs such as 'badly', 'really',

265

'definitely', 'truly', 'completely' and 'overwhelmingly' in most cases. Here are more examples to clarify this point further,

8.   افترق فرقة.

He was **completely detached**.

9.   انتصر نصراً مؤزراً.

He **achieved** an **overwhelmingly** great **victory**.

OR: His victory was overwhelming.

10.   اعمل بجد ثم روّح عن نفسك بعض الترويح.

Work hard, then **enjoy** yourself **a little**.

11.   جلس زيدٌ القرفصاء.

Zayd sat **in a crouching position**.

12.   رجع القهقرى.

He retreated **in a miserable manner**.

OR: He retreated **badly**.

13.   إني أعرفه يقيناً.

I **truly** know.

14.   هذا كتابي قطعاً.

This is **definitely** my book.

15.   كنت سعيداً به حقاً.

I was **really** happy with him.

16.   لم أره البتة.

I have never seen him **at all**.

17.   أإهمالاً وأنت مسؤول؟ (أتهمل إهمالاً؟)

You are **extremely** negligent (complacent) though you are in charge?

Also it might be confusing to students and professional translators when the unrestricted or absolute object implies repetition of an action many times in the SL. The TL equivalence can be either using the same type of repetition or formulating an equivalence more common in the TL, using the verb 'to do' and not necessarily the obvious equivalence of the verb 'to read'. So the TL verb 'to do' is to be followed by the number of actions, e.g.

18.   يقرأ عليّ تلك القراءة التي يسمعها من الأستاذ.

Ali **reads in the same way** as he heard it from his teacher.

19. قرأت الكتاب قراءتين.
a. I **read** the book **twice**.
b. I did **two readings** of the book.

A similar example is given by Fischer, رمى رميتين. 'He shot **two shots**' (Fischer, p.195). Notice that the verb and the object here are the same in both the SL and TL. But it is not always the case that students and professional translators find such exact equivalence, as in the following:

20. قرأت ثلاث قراءات.
a. I **read** it **three times**.
b. I **did** three **readings**.

21. قابلته خمسين مقابلة.
a. I **met** him **fifty times**.
b. I **did** fifty **interviews**.

It is clear that in English the verb 'to read' and the object 'reading' are not often used, so one needs to either use the verb 'to do' and then use the object 'readings' or 'interviews' as in translations (b) in both Examples 20 and 21.

It gets harder to identify the unrestricted object when the verb is connotative and, therefore, omitted in the SL, but needs to be there in the TL. Here it is vital that students and professional translators analyse the SL sentence syntactically correctly, in order to find its appropriate equivalence. Here are few examples.

22. صبراً، لا جزعاً.
<u>Be</u> extremely patient, and <u>feel</u> no fear at all.

23. حمداً وشكراً لا كفراً.

Be **extremely grateful**, <u>be</u> **extremely thankful** but **never** be blasphemous.

24.　ويحَه... وويلَه. (الفعل أهمَل) (al-Rājihī, p.234)

He <u>is</u> **extremely complacent**, <u>woe</u> **unto** him.

25.　لبيك (ألبي لبيك، أي تلبية بعد تلبية) (Ibid.)

Here I am! **Often** at your service.

26.　سَعْدَيْك (أي أساعد مساعدة بعد مساعدة) (Ibid.)

Help <u>is</u> **often** at hand.

27.　حنانيك (أي تحنن) (Ibid.)

Be **extremely kind** to me.

28.　دواليك (أداول دواليك) (Ibid.)

<u>Be</u> at your command **any time**.

It is clear in the above examples that the TL verb is problematic, and needs to be found, the most obvious equivalence is to use the verb 'to be'.

Another issue with the absolute object is when it comes to the use of the word 'God' in the SL no adverb is required as it is connotative in the TL.

29.　اللـهم نصراً. (انصرنا نصراً) (al-Rājihī, p.233)

a. God help us achieve **victory**.

b. God help us **win victoriously**.

30.　سبحانَ اللـه (تنزيها لله وبراءة له من السوء) (al-Rājihī, p.234)

a. **Praise be** to God!

b. God **be praised**! (See Hans Wehr, 393)

31.　معاة اللـه (استعانة به ولعبوءا إليه) (al Rājihī, p.234)

God **help** (protect) me.

Hans Wehr translates Example 31 differently: 'God forbid!' and 'God save (protect) me (us) from that' (p.656).

32.　حاشَ اللـه (تنزيهاً له). أو حاشا لله.

God **forbid**!

This is how Hans Wehr in his *A dictionary of modern written Arabic* (1974) translates this expression (p.180). See al-Rājihī (p.234) and Fischer (p.170) for exception and restriction.

To sum up, the adverb in the TL seems to be most appropriate equivalence to the absolute object in the SL. Also, it is a hard task for students and translators to identify the absolute object first when its verb in the SL is connotative, and it needs a verb in the TL, which can be at time the verb 'to be'.

Here are few exercises to show how the accusative of specifications or particularisation is in the SL and what is its TL equivalence.

"فَإِنِّي أُعَذِّبُهُ عَذَابًا لاَّ أُعَذِّبُهُ أَحَدًا مِّنَ الْعَالَمِينَ." (*The qur'ān*, 5:115)
a. "[but anyone who disbelieves after this] will be **punished** with **a punishment** that I will not inflict on anyone else in the world" (Haleem, p.79).

b. "I will **punish** him with **a penalty** such as I have not inflicted on any one among all the peoples" (Yūsuf 'Alī, p.139).

c. "then I will **punish** him **a torment** such as I have not inflicted on anyone among (all) the *Ālamīn* (mankind and jinn)" (al-Hilālī and Khan, p.168).

Another interesting exercise that has the accusative of specification or particularisation is this,

"وَكَلَّمَ اللَّهُ مُوسَى تَكْلِيمًا." (*The qur'ān*, 4:164)
a. "To Moses God **spoke directly**" (Haleem, p.65).
b. "To Moses Allah **spoke direct**" (Yūsuf 'Alī, p.114).

269

c. "and to Mūsā (Moses) Allāh **spoke directly**" (al-Hilālī and Khan, p.138).

d. "and God **spoke** to Moses in an **outspoken** manner" (*my translation*).

Translation (d) tentatively gives a closer accusative to that in the ST, this is not seen in translations (a-c)..

"صَلُّوا عَلَيْهِ وَسَلِّمُوا تَسْلِيمًا." (*The qur'ān*, 33:56)

a. "so, you who believe, bless him too and **give him greetings of peace**" (Haleem, p.271).

b. "Send your blessings on him, and **salute him with all respect**" (Yūsuf 'Alī, p.517).

c. "Send your *Salāt* on (ask Allāh to bless him) him (Muhammad), and (you should) greet (salute) him with the Islāmic way of greeting (salutation i.e. *As-Salāmu 'Alaikum*)".

d. "Send him [Prophet] your blessings and **salute** him the **best salutation** ever" (*my translation*).

As usual translation (c) is overloaded with phrases and loan words that are extremely useful for the interpretation of the ST, as it is an exegetic translation. Translation (d) is most compact and appropriate as the accusative is absolutely clear.

A further exercise of the accusative of specification or particularisation is this one below.

"فَأَخَذْنَاهُمْ أَخْذَ عَزِيزٍ مُّقْتَدِرٍ." (*The qur'ān*, 54:42)

a. "so We seized them with all Our might and power" (Haleem, p.351).

270

b. "but We seized them with such Penalty (as comes) from One Exalted in Power, able to carry out His Will" (Yūsuf 'Alī, p.668).

c. "so We **seized** them with a **Seizure** of the All-Mighty, All-Capable (Omnipotent)" (al-Hilālī and Khan, p.726).

Another exercise is this,

"فَلَا تَمِيلُوا كُلَّ الْمَيْلِ." (The qur'ān, 4:129)

a. "but do not ignore one wife altogether" (Haleem, p.63).

b. "but turn not away (from a woman) altogether" (Yūsuf 'Alī, p.109).

c. "so do not incline too much to one of them" (al-Hilālī and Khan, p.131).

d. 'so do not **incline** showing **too much inclination** towards one of them' (*my*

translation).

The accusative in the SL is slightly ignored in the first three translations, and need to be redressed to show it in the TL.

More exercises certainly help to understand the implementation of the theoretical part of the chapter, here are more of them.

"فَاجْلِدُوهُمْ ثَمَانِينَ جَلْدَةً." (The qur'ān, 24:4)

a. "**strike** them **eighty times**" (Haleem, p.220).

b. "**flog** them with **eighty stripes**" (Yūsuf 'Alī, p.419).

c. "**flog** them with **eighty stripes**" (al-Hilālī and Khan, p.467).

Another interesting exercise with the accusative of specification or particularisation is this one below.

"وَقُل رَّبِّ أَنزِلْنِي مُنزَلًا مُّبَارَكًا وَأَنتَ خَيْرُ الْمُنزِلِينَ." (The qur'ān, 23:29)

271

a. "say, 'My Lord, let me land with Your blessing: You are the best one to bring [us] to land' " (Haleem, p.216).

b. "And say: 'O my Lord! Enable me to **disembark** with your blessing: for You are the Best to enable (us) to disembark' " (Yūsuf 'Alī, p.409).

c. "And say: 'My Lord! Cause me to **land** at a blessed **landing-place**, for You are the Best of those who bring to land" (al-Hilālī and Khan, p.457).

Here is a further exercise about the accusative of specification in Arabic and its English equivalence.

"إِذَا زُلْزِلَتِ الْأَرْضُ زِلْزَالَهَا." (*The qur'ān*, 99:1)

a. "When the earth is **shaken** violently in its **[last] quaking**" (Haleem, p.431).

b. "When the earth is **shaken** to her **(utmost) convulsion**" (Yūsuf 'Alī, p.801).

c. "When the earth is **shaken** with its **(final) earthquake**" (al-Hilālī and Khan, p.845).

The final and most interesting exercise in this group is this,

"وَتَأْكُلُونَ التُّرَاثَ أَكْلًا لَّمًّا (19) وَتُحِبُّونَ الْمَالَ حُبًّا جَمًّا (20)". (*The qur'ān*, 89:19-20)

a. "you consume inheritance greedily, and you love wealth with a passion" (Haleem, p.421).

b. "And you **devour** inheritance – **all with greed**, (19) And you **love** wealth with **inordinate love!** (20)

c. "And you **devour** the inheritance **all with greed**. (19) And you **love** wealth with **much love** (20)" (al-Hilālī and Khan, p.835).

Having now finished with the accusative of specification or particularisation, it is time to see how the cognate accusative is used in the SL and what its equivalence is in the TL.

9.3.5. Causative Object, also known as Cognate accusative المفعول لأجله (Cachia, p.78)

The causative object is an infinitive noun which is used to show the *cause* of the action (al-Rājiḥī, p.236). As soon as students and professional translators identify the cause of the action in the SL sentence, they will find its appropriate equivalence straightforward as evident in the following examples,

1.   قمت إجلالاً لأستاذي.

I stood up as **a sign of respect for** my teacher (or professor).

2.   يجتهد زيد طلب التفوق (أو زيد مجتهد طلباً للتفوق).

Zayd studies hard **in a quest for** supremacy (or superiority).

(Or, Zayd is studious in a quest for supremacy).

3.   لزوم البيت طلبَ الراحةِ ضرورة بعد العمل الشاق.

Staying at home is necessary **to get some rest** after doing some hard work.

4.   هو محبوب إكراماً لأخيه.

He is popular, **courtesy of** (or **thanks to, in honour of**) his brother.

5.   هو مقدام في الحرب طلباً للشهادة أو النصر.

He is courageous in the battlefield **in a quest for** either martyrdom or victory.

6.   صهْ إجلالاً للقرآن.

Be quiet as **a sign of respect for** the *Qurʾān*.

273

So, as soon as the cause or reason is identified in the SL sentence, its equivalence becomes easy, using 'as a sign of', 'in a quest for' or 'thanks to' to name a few.

Here are three exercises to show how the causative object or cognate accusative is used in Arabic and what its English equivalence is.

"يَجْعَلُونَ أَصَابِعَهُمْ فِي آذَانِهِم مِّنَ الصَّوَاعِقِ حَذَرَ الْمَوْتِ." (The qur'ān, 2:19)

a. "[like people who...] put their fingers into their ears to keep out the thunderclaps **for fear of** death" (Haleem, p.5).

b. "they press their fingers in their ears to keep out the stunning thunder-clap, the while they are **in terror of** death" (Yūsuf 'Alī, p.4).

c. "They thrust their fingers in their ears to keep out the stunning, thunder-clap **for fear of** death" (al-Hilālī and Khan, p.5).

Now syntactically it is clear and highlighted in bold the two types of Arabic objects used. The only lexical concern is the use of the term 'thunder-cap', what about 'thunderbolt'? Also the choice of the verb in the TL ('to put', 'to press', and 'to thrust') is also vital. The first two verbs are more appropriate than the last one, because 'to thrust' has the element of force which is not seen in the SL: the interlinear translation is 'They made their fingers go in their ears to keep out the (sound of) thunderbolts for fear of death'. This helps in assessing the word choice in the above translations. The second exercise is this one about the causative object or cognate accusative in the SL and its TL equivalence.

" وَدَّ كَثِيرٌ مِّنْ أَهْلِ الْكِتَابِ لَوْ يَرُدُّونَكُم مِّن بَعْدِ إِيمَانِكُمْ كُفَّاراً حَسَدًا مِّنْ عِندِ أَنفُسِهِم مِّن بَعْدِ مَا تَبَيَّنَ لَهُمُ الْحَقُّ." (The qur'ān, 2:109)

a. "Even after the truth has become clear to them, many of the People of the Book wish they could turn you back to disbelief after you have believed, **out of their selfish envy**" (Haleem, p.13).

b. "Quite a number of the People of the Book wish they could turn you (people) back to infidelity after you have believed, **from selfish envy**, after the Truth has become manifest unto them" (Yūsuf ʿAlī, p.18).

c. "Many of the people of the Scripture (Jews and Christians) wish that if they could turn you away as disbelievers after you have believed, **out of envy from themselves**, even after the truth (that Muhammad is Allāh's Messenger) has become manifest unto them" (al-Hilālī and Khan, p.21).

The last exercise here is this.

" ثُمَّ قَفَّيْنَا عَلَى آثَارِهِم بِرُسُلِنَا وَقَفَّيْنَا بِعِيسَى ابْنِ مَرْيَمَ وَآتَيْنَاهُ الْإِنجِيلَ وَجَعَلْنَا فِي قُلُوبِ الَّذِينَ اتَّبَعُوهُ رَأْفَةً وَرَحْمَةً وَرَهْبَانِيَّةً ابْتَدَعُوهَا." (*The qurʾān*, 57:27)

a. "We sent other messengers to follow in their footsteps. After those We sent Jesus, son of Mary: We gave him the Gospel and put **compassion and mercy** into the hearts of his followers. But **monasticism** was something they invented" (Haleem, p.361).

b. "Then, in their wake, We followed them up with (others of) Our Messengers: We sent after them Jesus[,] the son of Mary, and bestowed on him the Gospel; and We ordained in the hearts of those who followed him **Compassion and Mercy**. But the **Monasticism** which they invented for themselves" (Yūsuf ʿAlī, pp.686-87).

c. "Then, We sent after them Our Messengers, and We sent ʿĪsā (Jesus) – son of Maryam (Mary), and gave him the Injeel (Gospel). And We ordained in the hearts of those who followed him **compassion and mercy**. But the **monasticism** which they invented for themselves" (al-Hilālī and Khan, p.744).

275

It is vital that translators and students are not only aware of the cognate accusative in the SL but also can easily convey that in the TL. Now having seen how this type of object works in Arabic and what its English equivalence is, it is time to know something about adverbial objects whether that of time or place and their TL equivalence.

9.3.6. Adverbial object المفعول فيه, or adverb of time and place ظرف مكان وزمان with its TL equivalence (Cachia, p.61)

The syntactic SL analysis is always a necessity before students and professional translators can find an appropriate TT.

Occurrence in time

This is the term Cachia uses (p.61). When students and translators identify that occurrence in time in the SL sentence through their syntactic analysis, an appropriate TL equivalence can be straightforward. Here are examples with an object referring to *an occurrence in time*,

1.   المؤمن يخشى **يومَ القيامة**.
The believer fears **the Day** of Judgement.
2.   يحضُر أحمد **غداً**.
Ahmad will come **tomorrow**.
3.   السفرُ **غداً**.
Travel is going to be **tomorrow**.

It is worth noting that the present tense in the SL in Examples 2 and 3 has been shifted to the future in the TL, which is acceptable due to the use of the adverb 'tomorrow'.

4.   السهرُ ليلاً مرهق.

Staying late **at night** is exhausting/trying.

5.   المحل مفتوحٌ صباحاً ومغلقٌ مساءً.

The shop is open **in the morning** and closes **in the evening**.

Here it is important to note that there is no need to use parallelism, the way it is in the SL: The words 'مفتوح' and 'مغلق' may not have the same parallelism in the TL 'open' and 'closed' but rather have one as an adjective 'open' and the other is a verb 'to close'.

6.   الكريم كريم **طولَ** حياته.

A generous person is always so **all** his life.

It is vital to note here that the possessive pronoun 'his' is used, because in Arabic it refers to both male and female.

Here are further examples of adverbial object

7.   الكتاب **ساعةَ الوحدة** خير جليس.

a. **When you feel lonely** the book is your best friend. (communicative translation)

b. **At the lonely hour**, the book is your best friend. (literal translation)

8.   انتظرتك **انصرافَ** الطلاب. (Meaning, '**at the time of** students' leaving school; al-Rājihī, p.245.)

I waited for you **at the time of** students leave school.

9.   قرأت **بعض** الوقت.

I read for **some** time.

10.   قرأت **ثلاث** ساعات.

I read for **three** hours.

11.   كم سعدنا **إذ** نحن أطفال. (Meaning, '**when** we were kids'; al-Rājihī, pp.246-47)

How happy we were **when** we were kids.

12.   نجح **إذ** ذاكر.

He succeeded **since** he had studied.

13.   إذا جئت أكرمتك.

a. **When** you come I will show you my hospitality.

277

b. **When** you come I will show you how hospital I am.

c. When you come I will be generous to you.

The difference between translations (a) and (b) is just a matter of style. But perhaps translation (c) is the closest in meaning and form to the SL, that is why is most appropriate.

14.   " وَاللَّيْلِ إِذَا يَغْشَى." (*The qur'ān*, 92:1)

a. "By the covering night" (Haleem's translation).

b. "By the night **as** it envelops." (al-Hilālī and Khan's translation).

It is clear in Example 14 that translation (b) is more appropriate as it makes the adverb of time clearer.

15.   بينما أقرأ حضر صديقي.

While I was reading my friend came.

16.   بينا زيدٌ نائم حضر أخوه.

Whilst Zayd was asleep, his brother came.

Fischer in his book on classical Arabic grammar shows no difference between بينا and بينما; here are two examples from his book with their TL equivalence:

'بينا أنا ذات يوم جالس إذ أقبَلَتْ عليَّ.' with its TL equivalence, '**While** I sat there one day, she approached me' [*my emphasis*]; 'بينما نحن نمشى إذ عرضَ رجلٌ' with its TL equivalence, '**While** we were walking along, a man suddenly appeared' [*my emphasis*]; and 'بينا الناسُ قد أجمعوا للحرب تداعَوا إلى الصلح.' with its TL equivalence, '**While** they resolved to go to war, they suddenly called upon one another for peace' (Fischer, p.226). [*my emphasis*]

17.   يذهب زيد إلى المكتبة بين وقت وآخر.

Zayd goes to the library **every now and then**.

18.   انتظرْ ريثما يحضر عليّ.

You wait **till** Ali arrives.

19.   عند الامتحان يكرم المرء أو يهان.

At the exam the student will either be rewarded or humiliated.

20.   لما حضر زيد خرج أهله لاستقباله.

When Zayd came, his family (or parents) went out to meet him.

21.   حضرت منذ سافر زيد.

I came **when** Zayd travelled.

22.   حضرت مذ يومان. (Meaning, 'Two days' is the predicate, 'the period of my

attendance is **two days**'; al-Rājiḥī, p.254.)

a. I came two days **ago**.

b. Two days **ago** I came. (fronting the adverbial object)

There is no real difference between the two translations (a) and (b); it is just a

matter of style.

23.   لم يكذب حسام قط.

Ḥusām **never** lied.

Here the SL sentence can be read in two different ways due to the lack of

diacritics: One of which is that has been translated above and the second one is

to translate it as "Ḥusām did not write [the word] 'a cat' ". See the discussion

about the word 'قط' as homonym in appendix I.

Another example is this.

24.   زيد مجدٌّ لدن دخل المدرسة.

Zayd was assiduous **when** he entered school.

See also Fischer's example: 'من لدن ابتدائه إلى تمامه' with its TL equivalence, 'From

its beginning to its end' (p.165).

Occurrence in place.

Like the occurrence in time, *an occurrence in place* in the SL sentence must be identified before attempting to translate or find its TL equivalence, e.g.

25.   اشتريت الكتاب من مكتبة أمام الجامعة.
I bought the book from a bookshop **opposite** the university.

26.   طرحه أرضاً.
He threw him **to the ground**.

It is clear that the TL equivalence needs to correspond to the TL grammar and not the SL grammar. That is why the preposition 'to' is added. So the SL word 'أرضا' is an adverbial object of place; its TL equivalence is a propositional phrase 'to the ground'. Even though the syntactic analysis of the SL sentence reveals the adverbial object; its equivalence respects the TL grammar or syntax in order to make that equivalence acceptable.

27.   سرت ميلاً.
I walked **a mile**.

With regards to distance it is advisable to convert 'mile' to 'kilometre', when translating from English into Arabic, although it is considered a kind of 'domestication' (to use Venuti's term, 1995), but there is no hidden agenda for that conversion, it is just to bring the image close to the target reader's mind. Venuti (1995) wrote, "The aim of translation is to bring back a cultural other as the same, the recognizable, even the familiar; and this aim always risks a wholesale domestication of the foreign text, often in highly self-conscious projects, where translation serves an appropriation of foreign cultures for domestic agendas, cultural, economic, political" (pp.18-19). Nida (as cited in Venuti, 1995) believed in the fluent strategy in the translation theory that 'involves domestication', and added, "the translator must be a person who can draw aside the curtains of linguistic and cultural differences so that people may see clearly the relevance of the original message" (p.21).

28. جلست مجلس زيد.
I sat **in Zayd's place.**

29. جلس زيد بين أصدقائه.
Zayd sat **amongst** his friends.

30. دع هذا الأمر بينَك وبين أخيك.
Keep this matter **between** you and your brother.

31. جلست حيث جلس زيد.
I sat **where** Zayd used to sit.

32. الكتاب عندك.
a. **You have** the book. (communicative translation)
b. The book **you have.** (communicative translation)
b. The book is **at yours** [at your place]. (literal translation)

Here in translation (a) there is a shift from the nominal sentence in the SL to the verbal one in the TL. Also there is another shift from the use of 'the book' as subject in the SL to its new position as an object in the TL. In Translation (b) there is fronting of the object ('the book'), which is in fact the subject of the nominal SL sentence. The difference between translation (a) and translation (b) is that it is a matter of style. The literal translation (c), however, is unacceptable as it has a stilted and awkward style.

33. الكتاب لدى زيد.
a. The book is **with** Zayd. (literal translation)
b. The book is at Zayd's. (literal translation)

a. The book is **with** Zayd. (literal translation)

b. The book is at Zayd's. (literal translation)

c. Zayd has the book. (communicative translation)

Translation (a) is the least acceptable as it is literal, and hardly used in English. The second translation (b) is acceptable if the meaning intended is or the context suggests that 'the book' is certainly 'at Zayd's house/place'. Translation (c) is the most acceptable of them all. However, there is a positional shift of the word 'the book' from the subject in the SL sentence, to the object in the TL. Another permissible shift here is the nominal SL sentence which is converted to a verbal one in the TL. Syntactically speaking, 'Zayd' who assumes the genitive form in the SL has taken the position of the subject instead in the TL. Here is an example which combines two *occurrences in time and place*,

34.   انتظرتك يوم الخميس أمام البيت.

I waited for you **outside** (or **in front of**) the house on **Thursday**.

Clearly, its TL equivalence is straightforward, i.e. no translation shifts are used to convey the SL message across.

In short, occurrences in time and place are adverbial objects which can be kept as they are the TL or have them shifted with the nominal SL becoming a verbal TL one; and the SL subject becoming an object as in translation (c) of Example 33.

Here are exercises showing how adverbial objects in Arabic are handled and how their English equivalence is produced.

"يِبِيرُوا فِيهَا لَيَالِيَ وَأَيَّامًا آمِنِينَ." (*The qur'ān*, 34:18)

a. "Travel safely in this land **by night and by day**" (Haleem, p.273).

b. "Travel therein, secure, **by night and by day**" (Yūsuf ʿAlī, p.523).

c. "Travel in them safely both **by night and day**" (al-Hilālī and Khan, p.575).

'Day' collocates more frequently with 'night' in English about 3 times more than 'night with 'day'. In British National Corpus over 300 times is the collocation 'day and night' compared to 'night and day' which is just over 100 times.

Another exercise which demonstrates how the adverbial object (that of time or place) is used in Arabic and what its English equivalence is.

"وَسَبِّحُوهُ بُكْرَةً وَأَصِيلًا." (*The qur'ān*, 33:42)

a. "and glorify Him **morning and evening**" (Haleem, p.269).

b. "And glorify Him **morning and evening**" (Yūsuf ʿAlī, p.515).

c. "And glorify His Praises **morning and afternoon**" [the early morning (*Fajr*) and 'Asr prayers]" (al-Hilālī and Khan, p.567).

d. "And glorify Him **early morning and late afternoon**" (*my translation*).

The adverbial object is a hyponym for 'morning and evening'. Translations (a) and (b) use the general or superordinate, whilst translation (c) attempts to be more appropriate. Whereas translation (d) is more accurate and exact – therefore it is the most appropriate.

"وَالضُّحَى (1) وَاللَّيْلِ إِذَا سَجَى." (*The qur'ān*, 93:1-2)

a. "By **the morning brightness**, and by **the night** when it grows still" (Haleem, p.425).

283

b. "By **the Glorious Morning Light**, And **by the Night** when it is still" (Yūsuf 'Alī, p.793).

c. "By **the forenoon (after sunrise)**. (1) By **the night** when it darkens (and stand still)" (al-Hilālī and Khan, p.840).

d. "By **the late morning**, and by **the night** when it is tranquil" (*my translation*).

Incidentally from the lexical perspective, it is important to know in the above exercise the hyponyms of the word 'morning', such as 'dawn' 'early morning', and 'late morning' here.

Adverbial objects, those of place are in the following exercise.

" وَفَوْقَ كُلِّ ذِي عِلْمٍ عَلِيمٌ." (*The qur'ān*, 12:76)
a. "**Above** everyone who has knowledge there is the One who is all knowing" (Haleem, p.150).

b. "but **over** all endued with knowledge is One, the All-Knowing" (Yūsuf 'Alī, p.279).

c. "but over all those endowed with knowledge is the All-Knowing (Allāh)" (al-Hilālī and Khan, p.314).

d. "**Above** every knowledgeable person is the Knowable" (*my translation*).

Another adverb of place or position is the following exercise.

" وَهُوَ الْقَاهِرُ فَوْقَ عِبَادِهِ وَهُوَ الْحَكِيمُ الْخَبِيرُ." (*The qur'ān*, 6:18)
a. "He is the Supreme Master **over** His creatures, the All-Wise, the All-Aware" (Haleem, p.81).

b. "He is Irresistible, (watching) **from above** on His worshippers; and He is the Wise, acquainted with all things" (Yūsuf 'Alī, p.143).

c. "And He is the Irresistible, (Supreme) **above** His slaves, and He is the All-Wise, Well-Acquainted with all things" (al-Hilālī and Khan, p.171).

A further exercise on the adverb of place is this one.

" وَأَنَّا كُنَّا نَقْعُدُ مِنْهَا مَقَاعِدَ لِلسَّمْعِ." (*The qur'ān*, 72:9)

a. "we used to sit **in places there**, listening" (Haleem, p.393).

b. "We used, indeed, to sit **there in (hidden) stations**, to (steal) a hearing" (Yūsuf 'Alī, p.738).

c. "And verily, we used to sit **there in stations**, to (steal) a hearing" (al-Hilālī and Khan, p.791).

d. "And verily, we used to sit **in places there**, to overhear" (*my translation*).

Another adverbial object, that of place, is found in the following exercise.

" وَلَا تَجْهَرْ بِصَلَاتِكَ وَلَا تُخَافِتْ بِهَا وَابْتَغِ بَيْنَ ذَلِكَ سَبِيلاً." (*The qur'ān*, 17:110)

a. "[Prophet], do not be too loud in your prayer, or too quiet, but seek **a middle way**" (Haleem, p.182).

b. "Neither speak your Prayer aloud, nor speak it in a low tone, but seek **a middle course between**" (Yūsuf 'Alī, p.341).

c. "And offer your *Salāt* (prayer) neither aloud nor in a low voice, but follow **a way between**" (al-Hilālī and Khan, p.384).

A similar adverb of place is in this exercise below.

" قُلْ أَيُّ شَيْءٍ أَكْبَرُ شَهَادَةً قُلِ اللَّـهُ شَهِيدٌ بَيْنِي وَبَيْنَكُمْ." (*The qur'ān*, 6:19)

a. "Say, 'What counts most as a witness?' Say, 'God is witness **between** you and me" (Haleem, p.81).

b. "Say: 'What thing is most weighty in evidence?' Say: 'Allah is witness **between me and you**' " (Yūsuf 'Alī, p.143).

285

c. "Say (O Muhammad): 'What thing is the most great in witness?' Say: 'Allāh (the Most Great!' is Witness **between me and you**" (al-Hilālī and Khan, p.171).

In translation (c) the superlative adjective 'the most great' breaks a grammatical rule in the TL but 'the greatest' is grammatically correct. Also, grammatically there is an error, in the word order it is 'between you and I' and not 'between I and you'; the latter is rather rude in English. Also, another common English error is to say 'me and you' or 'you and me' as in translations (a), (b) and (c). One should say in English 'I and you'. also note that many students and translators show no respect to that collocational element here. In English it is 'you and I' and not 'I and you' as the latter is rather rude.

" وَبَشِّرِ الَّذِينَ آمَنُواْ أَنَّ لَهُمْ قَدَمَ صِدْقٍ عِندَ رَبِّهِمْ." (*The qur'ān*, 10:2)
a. "[he should] give glad news to those who believe, that they are on a sure footing **with their Lord**?" (Haleem, p.128).

b. "[he should] give the good news to the Believers that they have **before their Lord** the lofty rank of Truth" (Yūsuf 'Alī, p.234).

c. "and [You should] give good news to those who believe (in the Oneness of Allāh and in His Prophet Muhammad) that they shall have **with their Lord** the rewards of their good deeds?" (al-Hilālī and Khan, p.269).

Lexically, translation (a) uses an unusual adjective 'glad' for the noun 'news'; it would have been more appropriate to say 'good news'. In translation (b) it is the issue of choosing a different structure to that in the SL – i.e. the ST says, 'those who believe' and the TT says, 'the Believers'. Translation (a) does just that, with the TT structure corresponding to the ST one. So translation (c) is the most appropriate, though it uses the exegetic approach.

The penultimate exercise is this one below with its Arabic adverbial object and English equivalence.

" وَلاَ أَقُولُ لَكُمْ عِندِي خَزَآئِنُ الـلـه." (The qur'ān, 11:31)

a. "I am not telling you that **I hold** God's treasures" (Haleem, p.138).

b. "I tell you not that **with me** are the Treasures of Allah" (Yūsuf 'Alī, p.254).

c. "And I do not say to you that **with me** are the Treasures of Allāh" (al-Hilālī and Khan, p.291).

It is clear in translations (b) and (c) that the adverbial object can have an equivalent which is in the form of a prepositional phrase, and it can also be converted into a verbal clause as in translation (a) – 'I hold....' The final exercise in this group is this one which has the adverb of place.

" وَنُقَلِّبُهُمْ ذَاتَ الْيَمِينِ وَذَاتَ الشِّمَالِ." (The qur'ān, 18:18)

a. "We turned them over, **to the right and the left**" (Haleem, p.184).

b. "and We turned them **on their right and on their left sides**" (Yūsuf 'Alī, p.344).

c. "And We turned them on **their right and their left sides**" (al-Hilālī and Khan, p.387).

Now having seen how the adverbial objects functions in the SL and what its equivalence is in the TL, it is time to move to another type of object, i.e. concomitant object.

9.3.7. Concomitant object المفعول معه

This Arabic object has its equivalence as 'concomitant' in Cachia, (p.78). The concomitant object in the SL occurs after a conjunction; and its TL equivalence is also considered as the rest of the sentence, which can be an object preceded by conjunctions such as 'and', 'with' or 'along with'. It is worth noting that the word 'concomitant' is defined by Merriam-Webster as "accompanying especially in a subordinate or incidental way". Here are few examples of the concomitant object and their equivalence,

1.   سرت والشاطئ.

I walked <u>along</u> **the beach**.

2.   أنا سائر والشاطئ.

I am walking <u>along</u> **the beach**.

3.   زيدٌ مُكرَمٌ وأخاه.

Zayd, <u>with</u> **his brother**, is generous.

4.   سيرُك والشاطئَ في الصباح مفيد.

Walking <u>alongside</u> **the beach** in the morning is useful.

5.   (أمهل نفسك مع المريض ,Meaning) رويدَك والمريض.

Take it easy on yourself <u>and</u> **the patient**.

It is interesting that Fischer (2002) also translates the phrase رويدك as 'take it easy' (171). But the following example is trickier to identify its concomitant object in the SL and therefore its equivalence will be difficult to find.

6.   كيف أنت والامتحانَ؟

How are you <u>and</u> **your exam?**

This means 'how are you doing **in your Exam**', this is being explained by al-Rājiḥī (1988, p.259). Here is another example which creates a similar difficulty when finding its TL equivalence.

7.   ما لك وعلياً؟

What is up with you <u>and</u> Ali?

The difficulty has risen because there is no such object in the TL. Therefore, it is vital to identify the object along with its conjunction in order to find its most appropriate equivalence.

9.3.8. Denotative of state or circumstantial accusative الحال

The former English equivalence is given by Cachia (p.34), and the latter by Fischer (p.196). This accusative shows the state of the agent one is referring to whether it is a subject or an object, as al-Rājiḥī points out (1988, p.260). The translator has the task of identifying *the state or manner of the agent*, as this will help find the most appropriate equivalence in the TL. Here are few examples to elaborate this point,

1.   أقبل زيد **ضاحكاً**.
Zayd came **laughing**.

2.   الخضروات – **طازجةً** – مفيدةٌ.
Vegetables, **when fresh**, are full of benefits.

3.   (Describing the house).أعجبتني شرفةُ البيت **فسيحاً**.
I liked the patio of the house, **being spacious**.

4.   أعجبتني مقالةُ زيدٍ **موضحاً**.
I have enjoyed reading Zayd's article, **in its explanatory style**.

5.   أعجبني كتابة الكتاب **واضحاً**.
I liked the writing of the book, **in its elaborating style**.

The above examples show the state of vegetables, the patio, and the article or the writing, which has helped in finding its most appropriate equivalence. Here are more examples about the *manner or state of the agent*,

6.   تعجبني قراءته مجوّداً.

I liked his reading, **being a recitation**.

7.   هذا طالبٌ كاتبٌ مقالتّه واضحةً.

This student writes his article **in a clear style**.

8.   هذه مقالةٌ مكتوبٌ موضوعُها واضحاً.

This article is written with a **clear** theme in mind.

9.   حاولت جُهدي.

I tried **my very best**.

10.   سعيت في الأمر طاقتي.

I endeavoured in this matter **as much as I can**.

11.   هذا عملك ممتازاً.

This is your work, being **excellent**.

12.   ليت المواطن – مثقفاً – يساعد غير المثقفين.

I wish the citizen, **who is educated**, helps the uneducated.

13.   جرى زيدٌ خوفاً.

Zayd ran **out of fear (being frightened)**.

14.   كأن زيداً – خطيباً – ساحرٌ يأخذ بالألباب؟

As if Zayd, being **an orator**, is a magician who is capable of convincing the highly intelligent people.

15.   الموضوع أمامك واضحاً.

a. The topic is before you, being **clear**. (literal translation)

b. The topic before you is clear. (communicative translation)

It is obvious that the communicative translation (b) is more appropriate. The same can be said about the communicative translation of the example below,

16.   الموضوع في ذهنه واضحاً.

The topic in his mind is **clear**.

Another set of examples shows how the circumstantial accusative is identified. It is 'when one is moving **in a group**', for instance; but this is clearer below

17. سلمته الكتاب يداً بيد.

I gave him the book **by hand**.

18. دخلوا القاعة ثلاثةً ثلاثة.

They entered the hall **in threes**.

19. تم عدد الطلاب ثلاثين طالباً.

The number of students has reached **thirty**.

20. ذهبت وحدي.

I went **alone**.

21. ادخلوا الأولَ فالأولَ.

Enter **one by one**.

22. جاءوا قضّهم بقضيضهم. (يعني كاسرهم مع مكسورهم)

They all came, **the weakest and the most powerful**.

Another example of the circumstantial accusative is this,

23. رجع زيدٌ عودَه على بدئه.

a. Zayd returned **to the starting point**.

b. Zayd is back **to square one**.

Translation (b) of Example 24 is more idiomatic than translation (a); yet it can be a more appropriate equivalence to another SL sentence, i.e. "رجع زيد إلى نقطة الصفر". There is an example by Ryding (2005) which is also interesting to discuss, 'علينا أن نبدأ من الصفر' with its original equivalence 'We have to begin from zero' (p.383) which can be back translated 'begin from **square one**'. To emphasize the idiomatic equivalence more, here is another example of an idiomatic expression 'من الألف إلى الياء' with its original equivalence 'beginning to end' (p.383) and its more appropriate one is certainly 'from A to Z'.

291

Here are a couple more examples of the circumstantial accusative along with their TL equivalence,

24.   خلق الـلـه رقبة الزرافة **طويلةً**.

God has created the neck of the giraffe **to be long**.

25.   "وَهُوَ الَّذِي أَنْزَلَ إِلَيْكُمُ الْكِتَابَ **مُفَصَّلاً**." (*The qur'ān*, 6:114)

"He who has sent down for you [people] the Scripture, **clearly explained?**"

Prepositional phrase is acting as 'denotative of state or circumstance' الحال

This is how Cachia terms it (p.34).

27.   الصيف **على الجبال** أجمل منه على الشاطئ.

Summer **in the mountains** is much more beautiful than on the beach.

28.   السفينة **بين الأمواج** كالريشة في مهب الريح.

The ship **amidst the waves** is like a feather in the wind.

29.   رأيت زيداً **وهو خارج**.

I saw Zayd **going out**.

30.   رأيت زيداً **يخرج**.

I saw Zayd **going out**.

31.   لزيدٍ **في النحو** كتاب.

Zayd **in grammar** (or **syntax**) is brilliant like a book.

The denotative of state or what Fischer called the circumstantial accusative can be demonstrated in the following exercises,

" فَخَرَجَ مِنْهَا **خَائِفًا**." (*The qur'ān*, 28:21)

a. "So Moses left the city, **fearful and wary**" (Haleem, p.246).

b. "He therefore got away therefrom, looking about, **in a state of fear**" (Yūsuf 'Alī, p.471).

c. "So he escaped from there, looking about **in a state of fear**" (al-Hilālī and Khan, p.518).

The lesson to be learnt in general about translation can be seen in translation (a), it is clear that the TT can use anaphoric and cataphoric references, even when the ST has different type of referencing. Before explaining this point, one needs to see what the interlinear translation says, 'He went out from it, fearful': now in the ST the anaphoric reference 'he' and 'it' are replaced in the TL by the nouns these two pronouns are referring back to, i.e. 'Moses' and 'the city'. In translation (b) only the adverbial object 'therefrom' or ''there' in translation (c) has been the TL equivalent or substitute for 'it' in the ST. Both styles in both translations (a) and (b) are definitely acceptable, as they both refer to the same subject or object.

Here is another exercise which shows the denotative of state or the circumstantial accusative in Arabic and its English equivalence.

"وَأَرْسَلْنَاكَ لِلنَّاسِ رَسُولاً." (The qur'ān, 4:79)

a. "We have sent you **as a messenger** to people" (Haleem, p.58).

b. "And We have sent you **as a Messenger** to (instruct) mankind" (Yūsuf 'Alī, p.99).

c. "And We have sent you (O Muhammad) **as a Messenger** to mankind" (al-Hilālī and Khan, p.122).

Just an incidental comment, as this book is focused on syntax only, translation (a) is most appropriate due to its choice of the word 'people' as it is closer to the ST.

"وَلاَ تَعْثَوْاْ فِي الأَرْضِ مُفْسِدِينَ." (The qur'ān, 2:60)

293

a. "and do not **cause corruption** in the land" (Haleem, p.9).

b. "and do **no evil nor mischief** on the (face of the) earth" (Yūsuf 'Alī, p.10).

c. "and do not act **corruptly, making mischief** on the earth" (al-Hilālī and Khan, p.13).

In order to demonstrate the TL equivalence of the denotative of status even more here are more exercises on this theme.

"أَيُحِبُّ أَحَدُكُمْ أَن يَأْكُلَ لَحْمَ أَخِيهِ مَيْتًا." (*The qur'ān*, 49:12)

a. "and would any of you like to eat the flesh of your **dead** brother?" (Haleem, p.339)

b. "Would any of you like to eat the flesh of his **dead** brother?" (Yūsuf 'Alī, p.644)

c. "Would one of you like to eat the flesh of his **dead** brother?" (al-Hilālī and Khan, p.700)

Here we have the Arabic object which is the denotative of state or the circumstantial accusative but its equivalence may not necessarily be from the same word class. This does not mean that such translations are inappropriate but rather that they correspond in their implementation on the TL grammar which is essential but not at the expense of changing the meaning of the ST. This means that the word class may change when translating from one language to another. Moreover, at the lexical level translation © seems most appropriate as it keeps closer to the ST without changing the meaning in the TL – e.g. 'one of you' in translation (c) is closer to the ST than 'any of you' in translations (a) and (b).

Here is yet another exercise,

"إِلَيْهِ مَرْجِعُكُمْ جَمِيعًا." (*The qur'ān*, 10:4)
a. "It is to Him you shall **all** return" (Haleem, p.128).

b. "To Him will be your return" (Yūsuf 'Alī, p.234).

c. "To Him is the return of **all** of you" (al-Hilālī and Khan, p.270).

d. "To Him you shall **all** return" (*my translation*).

Another exercise about this theme regarding the denotative of state or the circumstantial accusative is this,

"فَانفِرُواْ ثُبَاتٍ أو انفِرُوا جميعاً." (*The qur'ān*, 4:71)
a. "March [to battle] **in small groups** or **as one body**" (Haleem, p.57).

b. "either go forth **in parties** or go forth **all together**" (Yūsuf 'Alī, p.98).

c. "either go forth (on expedition) **in parties**, or go forth **all together**" (al-Hilālī and Khan, p.120).

A further exercise is the following,

"وَنَزَعْنَا مَا فِي صُدُورِهِم مِّنْ غِلٍّ إِخْوَانًا." (*The qur'ān*, 15:47)
a. "and We shall remove any bitterness from their hearts: [They will be like] **brothers**" (Haleem, p.163).
b. "And We shall remove from their hearts any lurking sense of injury: (they will be) **brothers**…" (Yūsuf 'Alī, p.305).

c. "And We shall remove from their breasts any deep feeling of bitterness (that they may have). (So they will be like) **brothers**…" (al-Hilālī and Khan, p.342).

The exercise above shows the circumstantial accusative or the denotative of state clearly. But at the lexical level, the SL word صدور and its most appropriate equivalence is under investigation, whether to use 'hearts' or 'breasts'. Culturally English people talk about the 'heart' more when it comes to 'having grudge or bitterness against someone' than the 'breast' or 'chest'. Therefore translations (a) and (b) are more appropriate.

The penultimate exercise is the following,

" ثُمَّ أَوْحَيْنَا إِلَيْكَ أَنِ اتَّبِعْ مِلَّةَ إِبْرَاهِيمَ حَنِيفًا." (*The qur'ān*, 16:123)

a. "Then We revealed to you [Muhammad], 'Follow the creed of Abraham, **a man of pure faith**' " (Haleem, p.174).

b. "So We have taught you the inspired (Message). 'Follow the ways of Abraham **the True in Faith**' " (Yūsuf 'Alī, p.325).

c. "Then, We have sent the revelation to you (O Muhammad saying): 'Follow the religion of Ibrāhīm (Abraham) *Hanif* (**Islāmic Monotheism – to worship none but Allāh**)' " (al-Hilālī and Khan, p.366).

Here translations (a) and (b) have been more successful as the denotative of state is clearer.

" وَمَا نُرْسِلُ الْمُرْسَلِينَ إِلاَّ مُبَشِّرِينَ وَمُنذِرِينَ." (*The qur'ān*, 6:48)

a. "We send messengers only **to give good news and to warn**" (Haleem, p.83).

b. "We send the Messengers only **to give good news and to warn**" (Yūsuf 'Alī, p.147).

c. "And We send not the Messengers but as **givers of glad tidings and as warners**" (al-Hilālī and Khan, p.176).

d. "And We send messengers only as **heralders and foreboders**" (*my translation*).

With this exercise the whole group that demonstrate the SL denotative of state or the circumstantial accusative, alongside its TL equivalence. Now it is time to see the objective complement for distinction in Arabic syntax and its English equivalence.

9.3.9. Objective complement for distinction التمييز

al-Rājiḥī (1988, pp.272-73) explains that objective complement for specification or distinction explains an indeterminate or undefined noun, such as 'something full of <u>what</u>" or "a number of what" as in the following examples:

1.   اشتريت كيساً قمحاً.
I bought a bag **of grain**.
2.   اشتريت فداناً قصباً.
I bought an acre **of bamboo** (or, cane).
3.   رأيت خمسة عشر طالباً.
I saw **twenty-five** students.

Also, al-Rājiḥī finds that the objective complement for distinction explains an undefined clause, such as "<u>from what aspect</u> something has become" or "filled <u>with what</u>". Here are few examples:

4.   إزداد زيد علماً.
Zayd has become **a scholar**.
5.   ما أكرم زيداً خلقاً.

297

How generous Zayd is **in his manners**.

6.   لله در زيد عالماً.

How **scholarly** Zayd is (due to God).

7.   كفى بالله شهيداً.

God is the best **witness**.

8.   حسبك الله وكيلاً.

It is enough that God is the best **protector**.

9.   امتلأت القاعة طلاباً.

The hall is full **of students**.

10.   ازدحمت الشوارع ناساً.

The streets are crowded **with people**.

11.   قال الله عز من قائل.

God, **the most exalted**, says.

So, the objective complement used for distinction usually explains an ambiguous word, and can be recognized by the phrase 'full of <u>what</u>' or a 'number of <u>what</u>'. As soon as the translator or student identifies this objective complement, its TL equivalence becomes straightforward.

Here are few exercises that show how the objective complement for distinction is in Arabic and what its English equivalence is.

(The qur'ān, 7:142)" وَوَاعَدْنَا مُوسَى ثَلَاثِينَ لَيْلَةً وَأَتْمَمْنَاهَا بِعَشْرٍ فَتَمَّ مِيقَاتُ رَبِّهِ أَرْبَعِينَ لَيْلَةً."

a. "We appointed **thirty nights** for Moses, then added ten more: the term set by his Lord was completed in **forty nights**" (Haleem, p.103).

b. "We appointed for Moses **thirty <u>nights</u>**, and completed (the period) with ten (more): thus was completed the terms (of communion) with his Lord, **forty <u>nights</u>**" (Yūsuf 'Alī, p.187).

c. "And We appointed for Mūsā (Moses) **thirty <u>nights</u>** and added (to the period) ten (more), and he completed the term, appointed by his Lord, of **forty <u>nights</u>**" (al-Hilālī and Khan, p.220).

298

The English equivalence of the Arabic objective complement for distinction is straightforward as seen in translations (a-c) and no difference among them with regards to this particular object. Here are more exercises to clarify how this SL object has its TL equivalence.

" فَمَن يَعْمَلْ مِثْقَالَ ذَرَّةٍ خَيْرًا يَرَهُ (7) وَمَن يَعْمَلْ مِثْقَالَ ذَرَّةٍ شَرًّا يَرَهُ." (The qur'ān, 99:7-8)

a. "whoever has done an atom's-weight **of good** will see it, but whoever has done an atom's-weight **of evil** will see that" (Haleem, p.431).

b. "Then shall anyone who has done an atom's weight **of good**, see it! And anyone who has done an atom's weight **of evil**, shall see it" (Yūsuf 'Alī, p.801).

c. "So whosoever does **good** equal to the weight of an atom (of a small ant) shall see it. And whosoever does **evil** equal to the weight of an atom (or a small ant) shall see it" (al-Hilālī and Khan, p.846).

It is slightly problematic to see how this objective complement for distinction in Arabic is conveyed in the TL. To demonstrate how the objective complement for distinction in Arabic works and what its English equivalence is here is another exercise.

" وَاشْتَعَلَ الرَّأْسُ شَيْبًا." (The qur'ān, 19:4)

a. "and my hair is ashen **grey**" (Haleem, p.190).

b. "and the hair of my head does glisten **with grey**" (Yūsuf 'Alī, p.358).

c. "**grey hair** has spread on my head" (al-Hilālī and Khan, p.402).

d. "And my hair has turned **grey**" (*my translation*).

Syntactically, as seen above in these translations the objective complement for distinction in Arabic may not have the same position in its English equivalence, i.e. not necessarily assuming the same position in the structure of the SL sentence as that in the TL. Lexically speaking, the SL word رأسي has its TL equivalence as either 'my hair' or 'my head' as to which is one is better. At the word level obviously 'my head' or 'the head' (the latter to be more precise) is more appropriate. But at the sentence level, and consequently the text level, such word may have to change to fit the context. Therefore, another possible version of translation (d) would be, 'and my head has turned (become) grey'. Another interesting point is the verb اشتعل whose equivalence is literally 'to be lit', but it is a collocation in Arabic to say 'the head is lit up grey' but such a linear and literal translation might sound awkward in English. That is why it is overlooked.

More exercises about the objective complement for distinction are here.

" وَفَجَّرْنَا الْأَرْضَ عُيُونًا." (*The qur'ān*, 54:12)

a. "[We] burst the earth **with gushing springs**" (Haleem, p.350).

b. "And We caused the earth to gush forth **with springs**" (Yūsuf 'Alī, p.666).

c. "And We caused **springs** to gush forth from the earth" (al-Hilālī and Khan, p.724).

d. "And We made the earth burst **with springs**" (*my translation*).

The interesting point here is the structure of the SL sentence which has two types of objects: 'the earth' and 'springs', and certainly its closest equivalence in English is seen in translation (a). However, the addition of the adjective 'gushing' in that translation is necessary as it is connotative in Arabic but not so in English. At the structural level, the ST has one subject, one verb and two objects; but is it the case in the TT in all these translations? Certainly not. The reason is that students and translators need to produce the TT that is structurally sound in the target language and not to follow the SL grammar blindly. Translation (a) uses one verb 'to burst' which is the most appropriate to the ST but the adjective 'gushing' is interpreted.

A further exercise is this one.

"أَنَا أَكْثَرُ مِنكَ مَالًا وَأَعَزُّ نَفَرًا." (*The qur'ān*, 18:34)

a. "I have more **wealth** and a larger **following** than you" (Haleem, p.185).

b. "More **wealth** have I than you, and more honour and power in (**my following of) men**" (Yūsuf 'Alī, p.347).

c. "I am more than you **in wealth** and stronger **in respect of men**" (al-Hilālī and Khan, p.390).

d. "I am **wealthier** than you are, and **my following** is more powerful" (*my translation*).

Admittedly, translation (d) does not follow syntactically the same structure as that of TL, and perhaps another version would be 'I am wealthier and stronger (or more powerful) in men'. It is clear that translation (a) has overlooked the element of 'strength' in the ST

301

which is not necessarily connotative to mean in number but in power. That element is certainly present in translation (c), see p.101 where the SL word عزيز is translated as 'exalted'. Now here that element of power or strength is implied in the comparative adjective أعز. Also, there is an unnecessary addition in translation (b) – i.e. 'more honour'.

A further interesting point is that translators of (b) and (c) often has the TL equivalence derived from the verb 'to exalt', whenever that adjective or its morphological derivations (whether inflectional or derivational morphemes) occur in Arabic.

Another exercise is this,

"إِنَّهَا سَاءَتْ مُسْتَقَرًّا وَمُقَامًا." (*The qur'ān*, 25:66)

a. "It is **an evil home, a foul resting place!**" (Haleem, p.230).

b. "Evil indeed is it **as an abode, and as a place to rest in**" (Yūsuf 'Alī, p.438).

c. "Evil indeed it (Hell) is **as an abode and as a place to rest in**" (al-Hilālī and Khan, p.486).

d. "It (Hell) is **the worst place ever to settle in and reside at**" (*my translation*).

It is clear that translation (d) gives the equivalence of the objective complement for distinction is the two infinitive structures 'to settle in' and 'to reside at'; another possible version to keep the same structure as that in the TL is, 'It is the worst habitat and place of residence'. It is essential to note that the SL verb ساء 'to worsen' is not seen to in the translations (a), (b) and (c). It is evident that the SL structure alongside its full meaning is conveyed which is unfortunately overlooked in these three translations, though the meaning of that verb is partly covered in the equivalents 'evil' and 'foul'.

The penultimate exercise is the following,

" وَسِعَ رَبِّي كُلَّ شَيْءٍ عِلْمًا." (*The qur'ān*, 6:80)

a. "My Lord encompasses everything **in His knowledge**" (Haleem, p.86).

b. "My Lord comprehends **in His Knowledge** all things" (Yūsuf 'Alī, p.152).

c. "My Lord comprehends **in His Knowledge** all things" (al-Hilālī and Khan, p.182).

d. "My Lord encompasses **all the knowledge** about everything" (*my translation*).

The exercise with all the translations (a-d) is self-explanatory and requires no syntactic analysis for the students and translators to benefit from. The final exercise in this group about the objective complement for distinction is this one,

" وَأَمَّا مَنْ آمَنَ وَعَمِلَ صَالِحًا." (*The qur'ān*, 18:88)

a. "while those who believed and did **good deeds**" (Haleem, p.189).
b. "But whoever believes, and works **righteousness**" (Yūsuf 'Alī, p.354).

c. "But as for him who believes (in Allāh's Oneness) and works **righteousness**" (al-Hilālī and Khan, p.398).

d. "But whoever believes and does **a good deed**" (*my translation*).

Now having given a quick glance at the objective complement for distinction or specification it is time to move another interesting factor

303

in grammar which has an effect on the structure of the SL and consequently its TL equivalence will be affected. It is the vocative in Arabic and its English equivalence.

9.3.10. Vocative

al-Rājihī (1988, p.278) writes that the vocative (or the person/thing called المنادى as Cachia calls it, p.98) is considered in the SL as an object by some scholars, and the connotative meaning is "*I am calling you*". Therefore, Its TL equivalence is easy to find. Here are few examples,

1.   يا عليُّ أقبل. يا فاطمةُ أقبلي.
Ali, come. Fatima come.

2.   يا راضي أقبل.
Raḍī, come.

3.   يا هؤلاء أقبلوا.
Hey you all, come.

4.   يا من فعل الخير أبشر.
You the good-doer (or Samaritan), rejoice.

5.   يا رجلان أقبلا.
You two men, come.

6.   يا مجدّون أبشروا.
You hard-workers, rejoice.

7.   نصرك الـله يا قائداً عظيماً.
God has helped you, **great leader**, achieve victory.

8.   يا فاعلَ الخير أقبل.
Good-doer (or Samaritan), come.

9.   يا كريماً خلقُه أبشر.
You the well-behaved, rejoice.

10.   يا قومِ توحدوا.
People, unite.

11.   يا أبتِ

Father!

12.   يا فرحةَ قلبي...

My heart, rejoice...

13.   يا بنَ أمٍ...

You son of...

14.   يا اللـه!

Oh, God!

15.   يا أيها الإنسان تأدب.

Hey man, behave.

16.   يا للمؤمنِ للمظلوم.

Faithful, rescue the oppressed (or the one treated badly).

17.   يا لهذا للضعيف.

You, rescue the weak.

18.   يا للعارِ

What a shame!

19.   يا للعجبِ

Why!

My,

How strange!

How wonderful!

20.   يا لله من المنافقين

God, punish the hypocrite.

So the connotative meaning in the SL is "I am calling...", and its vocative acts as

an object to that connotative verb. Its TL equivalence is similar to that in the SL,

as clearly demonstrated in the above examples along with their equivalence.

Lamentation الندبة

Lamentation in the SL, al-Rājiḥī (1988, p.294) points out, is a form of vocative

for the person who is suffering or victimized. Its TL equivalence

1.   وا زيدُ.

Oh, **Zayd!**

2.   وا رأسي.

Ouch, **my head!**

3.   وا زيداه.

Oh, **Zayd!**

4.   وا عبد الحميداه.

Oh, 'Abd al-**H**am**ī**d!

5.   وا أخاي.

Oh, **your brother!**

6.   وا أخاه.

Oh, **his brother!**

7.   وا أخاها.

Oh, **her brother!**

8.   وا أخاهما.

Oh, **his two brothers!**

9.   وا أخاهمُو.

Oh, **their brother!**

So this is a similar vocative with the connotative meaning "I am calling…" due to

pain and lamentation and not for help and to mean, "Alas!"

Finally, here are few exercises that elaborate the Arabic vocative and its English

equivalence, as well as the TL element of lamentation and its TL equivalence.

"قُلْ يَا أَيُّهَا الْكَافِرُونَ." (*The qur'ān*, 109:1)

a. "Say [Prophet], '**Disbelievers**' " (Haleem, p.441).

b. "Say, **O you** that reject Faith!" (Yūsuf 'Al**ī**, p.811).

c. "Say: (O Muhammad to these *Mushrik**ū**n* and *K**ā**fir**ū**n*): '**O** *Al-K**ā**fir**ū**n*
(**disbelievers** in All**ā**h, in His Oneness, in His Angels, in His Books, in His
Messengers, in the Day of Resurrection, and in the *Al-Qadar*)" (al-Hil**ā**l**ī** and
Khan, p.852-53).

306

The vocative here is evident in both the ST and the three TTs. At another level, however, one might think that translation (c) is extremely exegetic to the extent that it is unacceptable. But it is acceptable, here one is reminded of de Beaugrande when he talks about the seven standards of textuality, and in particularly about acceptability as a standard of textuality. Here the translator of (c) is certainly aware of his audience, that his audience are people who might know what the transliterations mean. This is a kind or 'foreignising' as Lawrence Venuti (1995) and before him the German theologian and philosopher Friedrich Schleiermacher in his lecture about different methods of translation in 1813 (cited by Jeremy Munday, 2001) who prefers 'foreignising' to 'domestication' in translation. This is in a way what has happened in translation (c) with the loan words transliterated and then explained. The translator of (c) gives a full explanation of the verse, and keeps its foreignness by using these loan words. However this technique of paraphrasing shows a weakness on the side of the translator as he has not found a good TL one-to-one equivalence to the lexis in the SL.

A further exercise about the SL vocative and its TL equivalence is useful.

(The qur'ān, 3:37)"كُلَّمَا دَخَلَ عَلَيْهَا زَكَرِيَّا الْمِحْرَابَ وَجَدَ عِندَهَا رِزْقاً قَالَ يَا مَرْيَمُ أَنَّ لَكِ هَـذَا
."

a. "Whenever Zachariah went in to see her in her sanctuary, he found her supplied with provisions. He said, '**Mary**, how is it you have these provisions?' " (Haleem, p.37).

307

b. "Every time he entered (her) chamber to see her, he found her supplied with sustenance. He said: 'O **Mary**! Whence (comes) this to you?"

c. "Every time he entered *Al-Mihrāb* to (visit) her, he found her supplied with sustenance. He said: 'O **Maryam (Mary)**! From where have you got this?' " (al-Hilālī and Khan, p.73).

Translation (c) at the lexical level has used to the two names of the Lady: 'Mary' or 'Maryam'. As usual using the loan foreign word from the ST and then its TL equivalence, most appropriate one. This style is in a way doubling the translator's task for no obvious reason. Another issue is to see that the translator also has found no equivalence for the SL word محراب so he has given the loan word with no explanation as to what that loan word means. This is yet another weakness in this translation. Whereas translations (a) and (b) are most appropriate with regards to the proper names and the equivalent of the SL word mentioned above – by using the proper names known in English culture and the two equivalents of that that words, i.e. 'sanctuary' and 'chamber'.

Another exercise about the SL vocative and its TL equivalence is this one.

"إِذْ قَالَ اللـه يَا عِيسَى إِنِّي مُتَوَفِّيكَ" (*The qur'ān*, 3:55)

a. "God said, '**Jesus**, I will take you back and raise you up to Me' " (Haleem, p.38).

b. "Behold! Allah said: 'O **Jesus**! I will take you and raise you to Myself" (Yūsuf 'Alī, p.62).

c. "And (remember) when Allāh said: 'O **ʿĪsā (Jesus)**! I will take you and raise you to Myself " (al-Hilālī and Khan, p.76).

Here is a further exercise.

"إِذْ قَالَ يُوسُفُ لِأَبِيهِ يَا أَبَتِ." (The qur'ān, 12:4)

a. "Joseph said to his father, '**Father**' " (Haleem, p.145).

b. "Behold! Joseph said to his father: '**O my father!**' " (Yūsuf 'Alī, p.268).

c. "(Remember) when Yūsuf (Joseph) said to his father: '**O my father!**' " (al-Hilālī and Khan, p.304).

It is evident that the SL vocative and its TL equivalence is straightforward.

"وَإِذْ قَالَ مُوسَى لِقَوْمِهِ يَا قَوْمِ اذْكُرُواْ نِعْمَةَ اللـهِ عَلَيْكُمْ." (The qur'ān, 5:20)

a. "Moses said to his people, '**My people**, remember God's blessing on you" (Haleem, 70).

b. "Remember Moses said to his people: '**O my people!** Call in remembrance the favour of Allah unto you' " (Yūsuf 'Alī, p.122).

c. "And (remember) when Mūsā (Moses) said to his people: '**O my people!** Remember the Favour of Allāh to you' " (al-Hilālī and Khan, p.146).

The vocative in all three translations is fine but it would have been more appropriate if its TL equivalence is 'O people!' or even 'People!'. On the addition/deletion technique in translation it is clear the verb 'remember' is an addition. Such addition is not required. It is redundant as it is repeated in both translations (b) and (c), though in a different form in 'remembrance' in the former translation (b). Therefore, translation (a) is most appropriate. Another exercise about the SL vocative and its TL equivalence is this,

" رَّبَّنَا إِنَّنَا سَمِعْنَا مُنَادِيًا." (The qur'ān, 3:193)

309

a. "**Our Lord!** We have heard someone calling us to faith" (Haleem, p.49).

b. "**Our Lord!** We have heard the call of one calling (us) to Faith" (Yūsuf 'Alī, p.83).

c. "**Our Lord!** Verily, we have heard the call of one (Muhammad) calling to Faith" (al-Hilālī and Khan, p.104).

A further exercise is here.

"وَإِذْ قَالَ إِبْرَاهِيمُ رَبِّ أَرِنِي كَيْفَ تُحْيِي الْمَوْتَى ". (*The qur'ān*, 2:260)
a. "And when Abraham said, '**My Lord**, show me how You give life to the dead" (Haleem, p.30).
b. "Behold! Abraham said: '**My Lord!** Show me how You give live to the dead" (Yūsuf 'Alī, p.47).
c. "And (remember) when Ibrāhīm (Abraham) said, '**My Lord!** Show me how You give life to the dead' " (al-Hilālī and Khan, p.59).

The penultimate exercise that students and translators may benefit from regarding the vocative and its TL equivalence is this,

"قُلْ يَا أَهْلَ الْكِتَابِ تَعَالَوْاْ إِلَى كَلِمَةٍ سَوَاء بَيْنَنَا وَبَيْنَكُمْ ". (*The qur'ān*, 3:64)
a. "Say, 'People of the Book, let us arrive at a statement that is common to us all' " (Haleem, p.39).
b. "Say, 'O People of the Book! Come to common terms as between us and you' " (Yūsuf 'Alī, p.63).
c. "Say (O Muhammad): '**O people of the Scripture** (Jews and Christians): Come to a word that is just between us and you" (al-Hilālī and Khan, p.78).

It is amazing that the word الكتاب 'the book' and not 'the scripture' is used earlier by translator (a) (see page 214 in this research); whereas translator (c) has used earlier 'the book'. The reason being that on page 148 it refers to *The qur'ān* whilst here it refers back to the Bible and the Torah. The final exercise is about lamentation in the SL and its TL equivalence.

" قَالَتْ يَا وَيْلَتَى أَأَلِدُ وَأَنَا عَجُوزٌ ". (*The qur'ān*, 11:72)

a. "She said, '**Alas for me!** How am I to bear a child when I am an old woman" (Haleem, p.141).

b. "She said: '**Alas for me!** Shall I bear a child, seeing I am an old woman' " (Yūsuf 'Alī, p.260).

c. "She said (in astonishment): '**Woe unto me!** Shall I bear a child while I am an old woman' " (al-Hilālī and Khan, p.296).

The SL vocative and even lamentation have straightforward TL equivalence as we have seen this chapter and in these exercises. Now it is time to see how 'exception' as a rule in SL grammar, which is also called 'restriction' has found its TL equivalence.

9.3.11. Exception and Restriction المستثنى

Fischer uses the above term as an equivalent to المستثنى (pp.168-70); also the equivalence of the term in Cachia's view is 'restriction (see pp.19-20). Scholars, al-Rājiḥī (1988) points out, consider exception or restriction as a kind of object for the verb 'to exclude' (p.300). The TL equivalence for the exception is similar to that in the SL, therefore there is no difficulty in identifying it in both languages. Here are examples to elaborate this point,

311

1.   جاء الطلاب إلا زيداً.

    Students came <u>save for</u> **Zayd**.

2.   رأيت الطلاب إلا عمراً.

I saw all students <u>except</u> **'Amer**.

3.   مررت بالطلاب إلا عمراً.

I came by all the students <u>except</u> **'Amer**.

4.   دخل الضيوف القاعة إلا كلابَهم.

The guests entered the hall, <u>except</u> **their dogs**.

5.   ما حضر الطلابُ إلا زيدٌ.

No students <u>but</u> **Zayd** were present.

6.   ما حضر الطلابُ إلا عمراً.

No students were present <u>except</u> **'Amer**.

7.   ليست له معرفةٌ إلا الظنَّ.

    He has no knowledge <u>but</u> **suspicion**.

8.   ما لي إلا زيداً صديق.

I have no friend <u>except</u> **Zayd**.

9.   **ما المخلصُ إلا يعمل لوطنه.**

No one is loyal, <u>except</u> **when he works for his country**.

10.   ما عُوقب مُجدٌ إلا الذي أهمل فعقابه رادع.

No hard worker is punished <u>except</u> **the one** who is complacent, and who would be punished severely.

11.   **سألتك بالله إلا ساعدتني.**

I beg you <u>but</u> **to help me**.

Here the phrase 'By God' is connotative in the TL.

12.   حضر الطلابُ غيرَ زيد. (أو سوى زيدٍ).

Students were present <u>except</u> **Zayd**.

13.   حضر الطلاب ما عدا عمراً.

Students were present <u>save for</u> **'Amer**.

14.   حضر الطلاب ما خلا زيداً.

Students were present <u>except</u> **Zayd**.

Fischer (p.169) gives the equivalence to these two words خلا، عدا as to mean 'what goes beyond...'.

15.   حضر الطلاب ما حاشا زيداً.

Students were present <u>except</u> Zayd. (Meaning, 'who did not condescend'.)

16. ما جاءني أحد إلا حماراً.

'<u>No</u> one came to me <u>but</u> an ass' (al-Rājihī, p.254). [*my emphasis*]

Here are few exercises about the exception in Arabic and its English equivalence.

" فَشَرِبُواْ مِنْهُ إِلاَّ قَلِيلاً مِّنْهُمْ ". (*The qur'ān*, 2:249)

a. "But they all drank [deep] from it, **except for a few**" (Haleem, p.28).

b. "But they all drank of it, **except a few**" (Yūsuf 'Alī, p.44).

c. "Yet, they drank thereof, all, **except a few of them**" (al-Hilālī and Khan, p.55).

So the TL equivalence here for the exception or restriction is either 'except for a few,' 'save a few' or 'but for a few'. Another similar exercise is this,

" فَسَجَدَ الْمَلَائِكَةُ كُلُّهُمْ أَجْمَعُونَ (30) إِلاَّ إِبْلِيسَ أَبَى". (*The qur'ān*, 15:30-31)

a. "and the angels all did so. **But not Iblis**: he refused to bow down like the others" (Haleem, p.163).

b. "So the angels prostrated themselves all of them together: **Not so Iblīs**: he refused to be among those who prostrated themselves" (Yūsuf 'Alī, p.303).

c. "So the angels prostrated themselves, all of them together. **Except *Iblis* (Satan)** – he refused to be among the prostrators" (al-Hilālī and Khan, p.341).

In all translations the exception or restriction is clearly seen; so the syntactic analysis is easy in all of them. Moreover, an interesting

313

lexical comment is about the use of the loan word 'Iblis' which is uncommon in translation (a). Here is a similar exercise about the exception,

"وَالَّذِينَ يَرْمُونَ أَزْوَاجَهُمْ وَلَمْ يَكُن لَّهُمْ شُهَدَاء إِلَّا أَنفُسُهُمْ" (*The qur'ān*, 24:6)

a. "As for those who accuse their own wives of adultery, but have no other witnesses" (Haleem, p.220).

b. "and for those who launch a charge against their spouses, and have (in support) no evidence **but their own**" (Yūsuf 'Alī, p.420).

c. "And for those who accuse their wives, but have no witnesses **except themselves**" (al-Hilālī and Khan, p.467).

Also, the exception is straightforward above. Here is a further exercise.

"مَا لَهُم بِهِ مِنْ عِلْمٍ إِلَّا اتِّبَاعَ الظَّنِّ" (*The qur'ān*, 4:157)

a. "with no knowledge to follow, **only** supposition" (Haleem, p.65).

b. "with no (certain) knowledge, **but only** conjecture to follow" Yūsuf 'Alī, p.113).

c. "They have no (certain) knowledge, they follow nothing **but** conjecture" (al-Hilālī and Khan, p.136).

"فَذَكِّرْ إِنَّمَا أَنتَ مُذَكِّرٌ (21) لَّسْتَ عَلَيْهِم بِمُصَيْطِرٍ (22) إِلَّا مَن تَوَلَّى وَكَفَرَ". (*The qur'ān*, 88:21-23)

a. "So [Prophet] remind them: you only task is to remind, you are not there to control them. As **for those who turn away and disbelieve**..." (Haleem, p.419).

b. "Therefore do you give admonition, for you are one to admonish. You are not one to manage (men's) affair. But **if any turn away and reject Allah**..." (Yūsuf 'Alī, p.783).

c. "So remind them (O Muhammad) – you are only one who reminds. You are not a dictator over them – **save the one who turns away and disbelieves**" (al-Hilālī and Khan, p.833).

Unlike translations (a) and (b), translation (c) shows how restriction or exception is dealt properly – i.e. 'save the one who...'. Another interesting exercise is this,

"فَلَبِثَ فِيهِمْ أَلْفَ سَنَةٍ إِلَّا خَمْسِينَ عَامًا". (*The qur'ān*, 29:14)

a. "He stayed among them for fifty years **short of** a thousand" (Haleem, p.253).

b. "and he tarried among them a thousand years **less fifty**" (Yūsuf 'Alī, p.482).

c. "and he stayed with them a thousand years **less** fifty years [inviting them to believe in the Oneness of Allāh (Monotheism), and discard the false gods and other deities]" (al-Hilālī and Khan, p.529).

It is evident that exception is used in both the ST and the three TTs. The penultimate exercise here is this,

" وَلاَ تَقْرَبُواْ مَالَ الْيَتِيمِ إِلاَّ بِالَّتِي هِيَ أَحْسَنُ ". (*The qur'ān*, 6:152)

a. "Stay well away from the property of orphans, **except with** the best [intentions]" (Haleem, p.92).

b. "And come not nigh to the orphan's property, **except to** improve it" (Yūsuf 'Alī, p.165).

c. "And come not near to the orphan's property, **except to** improve it" (al-Hilālī and Khan, p.196).

The final exercise about the TL exception or restriction is this,

" لاَ نُكَلِّفُ نَفْسًا إِلاَّ وُسْعَهَا ". (*The qur'ān*, 6:152)

a. "W do **not** burden any soul with **more than** it can bear" (Haleem, p.92).

315

b. "no burden do We place on any soul, **but that** which it can bear" (Yūsuf 'Alī, p.165).

c. "We burden not any person, **but that** which he can bear" (al-Hilālī and Khan, p.196).

Restriction or exception is more evident in translations (b) and (c). Now with exception and restriction we come to the last chapter about Arabic syntax and its English equivalence, i.e. vituperative or wonder, praise and blame in Arabic grammar.

9.3.12. Wonder, praise and blame, or vituperative التعجب والمدح والذم

Cachia uses the TL equivalent of 'wonder,' 'surprise' and 'blame' (pp.75-6); whereas at other places he calls that Arabic term as the latter part of the title of this chapter – 'vituperative' (pp.86, 87).

1.   ما أجمَلَ السماءَ.
How beautiful is the sky!

2.   ما أجمَل استغفارَ المؤمنِ.
How wonderful is the Faithful who asks God's forgiveness!

3.   أجمِلْ أن يزورَنا زيدٌ
How wonderful it is to have Zayd visiting us.

4.   أجمِلْ أنك ضيفُنا.
How wonderful is that when you are our guest.

5.   نِعمَ القائد خالد.
    What a good leader Khalid is!

6.   نعم ما تفعلُ الخيرُ. (subject)
What a good thing to do good to others!

316

Fischer's equivalence is to mean 'how perfect' or 'how wonderful' (pp.139-40).

7.   نعمَ مَن تصادقُ زيدٌ.

What a good friend Zayd is.

8.   بئس ما يقول الكذبُ.

How evil lying is.

Damn all the lies. (socio-cultural translation)

Fischer's equivalence is 'how evil', 'how bad', or 'what an evil thing' to give the

negative connotation of such term (pp.139-40).

9.   بئس خلقُ طالب العلم الإهمالُ.

How awful negligence is (or, complacency) if it is part of the scholar's manners.

10.   ساء خلقاً الإهمالُ.

How terrible complacency is if it is part of one's manners.

Fischer gives its equivalence as 'how evil, bad' (p.140).

11.   حبذا الصدقُ. (subject)

How wonderful honesty is.

Fischer's equivalence is 'how lovely' and 'how wonderful' (pp.140-41).

12.   لا حبذا الكذب.

How terrible lying is.

13.   حَسُنَ طالباً زيدٌ.

How really wonderful Zayd is as student.

Fischer's equivalence is 'how beautiful, magnificent' (p.140).

14.   خَبُثَ الرفيقُ الشيطانُ.

How sly Satan is.

317

These are the different forms of vituperative or wonder, praise and blame. Here are few exercises that elucidate how these forms have their TL equivalence. Here is the first exercise about praise in Arabic and its English equivalence.

" نِعْمَ الْمَوْلَى وَنِعْمَ النَّصِيرُ." (The qur'ān, 8:40)

a. "the **best** protector and the **best** helper" (Haleem, p.112).

b. "**the Best** to protect and **the Best** to help" (Yūsuf 'Alī, p.204).

c. "(what) an **Excellent** Maulā [Patron, Protector and Supporter] and (what) an **Excellent** Helper!" (al-Hilālī and Khan, p.236).

d. "The Best Protector and the Best Supporter" (my translation).

Here is another exercise about praise in Arabic and its English equivalence.

" إِن تُبْدُواْ الصَّدَقَاتِ فَنِعِمَّا هِيَ." (The qur'ān, 2:271)

a. "If you give charity openly, it is **good**" (Haleem, p.31).

b. "If you disclose (acts of) charity, even so it is **well**" (Yūsuf 'Alī, p.49).

c. "If you disclose your Sadaqāt (alms-giving), it is **well**" (al-Hilālī and Khan, p.61).

The final exercise about praise in the ST and its TT is this,

" وَحَسُنَ أُولَـٰئِكَ رَفِيقًا." (The qur'ān, 4:69)

a. "**what excellent** companions these are" (Haleem, p.57).

b. "Ah! **What a beautiful** fellowship!" (Yūsuf 'Alī, p.98)

c. "And **how excellent** these companions are!" (al-Hilālī and Khan, p.120)

Having finished with the exercises that deal with praise in Arabic alongside its English equivalent, let us see the exercises that show blame.

"بِئْسَ لِلظَّالِمِينَ بَدَلًا." (*The qur'ān*, 18:50)

a. "What a bad bargain for the evildoers!" (Haleem, p.186).

b. "Evil would be the exchange for the wrong-doers!" (Yūsuf 'Alī, p.349)

c. "**What an evil** is the exchange for the *Zālimūn* (polytheists, and wrong-doers)" (al-Hilālī and Khan, p.392).

A similar exercise about praise in both Arabic and English is below,

"بِئْسَمَا اشْتَرَوْاْ بِهِ أَنفُسَهُمْ." (*The qur'ān*, 2:90)

a. "**Low** indeed is the price for which they have sold their souls" (Haleem, p.11).

b. "**Miserable** is the price for which they have sold their souls" (Yūsuf 'Alī, p.15).

c. "**How bad** is that for which they have sold their ownselves" (al-Hilālī and Khan, p.18).

"سَاء مَثَلاً الْقَوْمُ الَّذِينَ كَذَّبُواْ بِآيَاتِنَا." (*The qur'ān*, 7:177)

a. "**How foul** is the image of those who reject Our signs!" (Haleem, p.107).

b. "**Evil** as an example are people who reject Our Signs" (Yūsuf 'Alī, p.194).

c. "**Evil** is the parable of the people who rejected Our *Ayāt* (proofs, evidences, verses and signs, etc.)" (al-Hilālī and Khan, p.227).

Again ساء is used here in Arabic, see it is dealt with earlier in pages 305 and 320 in this book. It is to mean '**how terrible** an example those who...'. Also, as usual translation (c) uses the loan word *Ayāt* which is mistransliteration even, it should have been *Āyāt* but its TL equivalence is rather confusing. The translator seems undecided as to which equivalent to you so he puts them all and given an open-ended list of equivalents. It is the issue of paraphrasing in translation with its exegetic tendency, a technique commonly used the translator of (c). The penultimate exercise about praise in Arabic and its appropriate equivalence is this,

"قُلْ بِئْسَمَا يَأْمُرُكُمْ بِهِ إِيمَانُكُمْ." (*The qur'ān*, 2:93)

a. "Say, '**How evil** are the things you belief commands you to do' " (Haleem, p.12).

b. "Say, '**Vile indeed** are the behests of your Faith" (Yūsuf 'Alī, p.15).

c. "Say, '**Worst indeed** is that which your faith enjoins on you" (al-Hilālī and Khan, p.18).

The final exercise to finish this group is this,

"وَمَأْوَاهُمْ جَهَنَّمُ وَبِئْسَ الْمِهَادُ." (*The qur'ān*, 13:18)

a. "Hell will be their home, and their bed wretched" (Haleem, p.155)

b. "their abode will be Hell – **what a bed of misery!**" (Yūsuf 'Alī, p.288).

c. "Their dwelling-place will be Hell; and **worst indeed** is that place for rest" (al-Hilālī and Khan, p.323).

The vituperative in the last translation (c) is clear, and possibly the most appropriate translation it is.

Conclusion

Lexical issues and syntactic analysis are usually the first barrier students and professional translators encounter. Lexical issues are mainly concerned with word choice and complicated wording in the SL, which would in turn create a problem of finding a similar effective equivalence in the TL, and that is at word level. But when it comes to syntax the situation becomes more complex and more demanding in both the SL and TL. There are certain words in Arabic, for instance, whose meaning and function change according to their positions in a clause or sentence.

A problematic word in Arabic is ما, which depending on its functionality, can be either deleted completely in translation when it is redundant or fully translated as 'not', 'thing' or *wh*-structure, based on its function in the unit. It is obvious that syntax in the SL plays a major role in deciding on which equivalent to use. It is true that the word ما in the SL is polysemous, but how the student or professional translator can decide on which meaning to choose depends heavily on its syntactic aspect. Precise syntactic analysis of the ST certainly helps the student or translator see the function of that particular word and therefore decide which meaning or function is most appropriate for it in the context.

It is noticeable that the syntactic aspect or analysis of these types of nouns helps to identify which position such nouns have, i.e. acting as

321

subject or object. Failure to recognise that aspect certainly leads to making major unacceptable errors in translation.

We have seen that there are variations of the relative pronoun 'who' in the SL, but such variations have either 'who' or 'whoever' in the TL. But when the relative pronoun is referring to inanimate objects, or fauna and flora, the word 'what' or 'which' is the most appropriate equivalence, whilst at times 'that' is the best choice – this usually depends on how far the relative pronoun in the TL is from its referent.

The TL equivalence of verbal nouns in the SL is an utterance, a preposition, phrase or phrasal verb. This, it is shown, depends on the meaning of the verbal noun in the SL first. Further, in most cases verbal nouns in the SL are used for exclamation; and their equivalence has become problematic, because its form in the TL varies between an utterance, a preposition, phrasal verb and phrase. The student or professional translator needs to understand fully the sense of the SL verbal noun, before attempting to find its TL equivalence.

The TL equivalence of any SL interrogative is more or less straightforward and should not be problematic. But compound nouns in the SL do not usually correspond to those in the TL in category. What is known as compound nouns in the TL are completely different and have different functions altogether, but we are not here to explain this grammatical feature in the TL as the basis of this book is to discuss the structure and functionality of the SL, not the TL, that will help in finding the most appropriate TL equivalence.

In short, it is essential to identify the status or position of the word in the SL before one can attempt to find its equivalence in the TL; so analysing the syntax accurately in the SL is the key to finding its most appropriate equivalence. We have seen that clearly in the five forms of the verb, defective nouns with certain endings, defective verbs in the present and past tenses, redundant prepositions and semi-prepositions, and finally in pronouns and certain nouns in the SL. This syntactic analysis of the functionality of these various words is done first for the purpose of finding their appropriate TL equivalence. The syntactic analysis should not be done at word level, but at sentence level in order to see what the function of the word in the structure of the SL sentence is.

What is the next step in such research or the one that students can take, it is to do more exercises, as the saying goes, 'practice makes perfect'. An interesting exercise is to ask students to compare other translations of the holy verses by other official or professional and highly experienced translators and see if such translations are further away from the ST or closer and more truthful than the ones this book has discussed. Those interested in the research of the translations of *The qur'ān*, whether students or translators, are advised to visit the following useful website http://www.comp.leeds.ac.uk/ prepared by Noorhan Abbas and Dr. Eric Atwell. It must be pointed out that none of the translations included in the exercises are taken from that website, but from hard copies of the three translations that are used in this book. However, the website is certainly good to compare various translations, and eight of them are there. Alternatively this is a window for further research that can be done by a dedicated researcher who will first analyse them lexically and then syntactically as the case has been in several places in this book.

Bibliography

Baker, M. (1992). *In other words: A coursebook in translation*. London and New York: Routledge.

British National Corpus, retrieved from
    http://corpus2.byu.edu/bnc/

Cachia, P. (comp.) (1973). *The monitor: A dictionary of Arabic grammatical terms - Arabic/English, English/Arabic*. London: Longman; Beirut: Librairie du Liban.

  http://www.comp.leeds.ac.uk/

Cruse, D. A. (2000). *Meaning in language: An introduction to semantics and pragmatics*. Oxford: Oxford University Press.

De Beaugrande, R. and Dressler, W. (1981). *Introduction to text linguistics*. London: Longman.

Diaz Cintas, J., Matamala, A. and Neves, J. (2010). *New insights into audiovisual translation and media accessibility*. Amsterdam and New York: Rodopi.

Diaz Cintas, J. (ed.) (2009). *New trends in audiovisual translation*, Bristol, Buffalo and Toronto: Multilingual Matters.

Dickins, J., Hervey, S. and Higgins, I. (2002). *Thinking Arabic translation: A course in translation method: Arabic to English*, London and New York: Routledge.

Fischer, W. (2002, 3rded.). *A grammar of classical Arabic*, translated from German by Jonathan Rodgers. New Haven and London: Yale University Press.

Haleem, M.A.S. A. (2004/2010). *The qur'ān: A new translation*. Oxford: Oxford University Press.

Hans Wehr, (1976). *A dictionary of modern written Arabic*, J. Milton Cowan (ed.). New York: Spoken Language Services, Inc.

al-Hilālī, M. T. D. and Khan, M. M. (n.d.). *The noble qur'ān: English translation of the meanings and commentary*. Madinah: King Fahd Complex.

al-Karmi, H. (1997/1999). *Al-mughni al-akbar* [sic] *English/Arabic*. Beirut: Librairie du Liban.

Khuddro, A. (Winter, 1993). Poems by Philip Larkin translated into Arabic, *al-Arbi'āiyyūn journal*.

------ (October 1997). Media translation, *Turjuman*, 6 (2), pp.115-130.

------ (April, 2000). Subtitling in Arabic, *Turjuman*, 9 (1), pp.31-37.

------ (May 2009). Subtitling triangle: Technique and practice. In F. M. Federici (Ed.), *Translating voices for audiovisuals*. Roma: ARACNE editrice S.r.l.1st edition.

Lyons, J. (1981). *Language and linguistics: An introduction*. Cambridge: Cambridge University Press (ed. 1999).

Munday, J. (2001). *Introducing translation studies*. London and New York: Routledge.

Newmark, P. (1981). *Approaches to translation*. Oxford: Pergamon Press (ed. 1986).

One thousand and one nights, retrieved from www.alwaraq.net. Also, *The Arabian Nights: Tales of 1,001 Nights* by Penguin Publishing House and *1001 Arabian Nights* by Sir Richard Francis Burton (Translator).

Pöchhacker, F. (2004). *Introducing interpreting studies*. London and New York: Routledge.

al-Rājiḥī, A. (1988). *The implementation of [Arabic] syntax*. Beirut: Dār al-Nahḍa al-ʿArabīyya.

Ryding, K.C. (2005). *A reference grammar of modern standard Arabic*. Cambridge: Cambridge University Press, ed. 2008.

Singleton, D. (2000). *Language and the lexicon: An introduction*. London: Arnold, a member of the Hodder Headline Group.

al-Thaʿālibī's *Yatīmat al-Dahr*. Retrieved from *www.alwaraq.net*.

al-Thaʾālibī *Fiqh al-Lugha*. Retrieved from *www.alwaraq.net*.

Venuti, L. (1995). *The translator's invisibility: A history of translation*. London and New York: Routledge.

Yūsuf ʿAlī, ʿA. (2007). *The holy qurʾān*. Kuala Lumpur:
    Islamic Book Trust.

Zakī, ʿI. (2003). *Tears on the Slopes of Glory*. Amman:
    Dar al-Irshad liʾl-Nashr.

Appendices

Appendix I: Varieties, analysis of STs translated from English into Arabic

Unlike the rest of the chapters which discuss the analysis of the Arabic syntax with Arabic as SL and English as TL, this appendix discusses mainly examples from *English* into *Arabic*; and therefore it cannot be considered as one of the main parts of the book.

The use of the conjunction أو 'or' in the SL and its equivalence

It is noticeable that the use of the conjunction أو 'or' can make nouns change slightly.

Here is an example by Fischer,

رمي بسهم أو سهمين.

He shot **an arrow or two.** See Fischer (p.177).

رمى بسهم أو اثنين. (back translation)

It is clear that this back translation shows how the TL (English) in the above example has a different style to that in the SL, which repeats the noun سهم; that repetition is connotative and therefore is ignored totally. However, it must be noted that if we were to reverse this, make the English as the SL and the Arabic as the TL, seen in the back translation, it is clear that the translator seems to be influenced by the

English style, this is a common error. Here is another example with English as the SL and Arabic as the TL:

I will meet you in **an hour or two.**

سألتقيك في ساعة أو اثنتين. (literal translation)

سألتقيك في ساعة أو ساعتين. (semantic or even communicative translation)

Another similar recurrent mistake with the use of the conjunction و 'and' when translating from English into Arabic, e.g.

The shop is far from here, about **two and a half kilometres.**

المتجر بعيد من هنا، نحو كيلومترين ونصف الكيلومتر.

This session will last one and a half hours.

سوف تستغرق هذه الجلسة ساعة ونصف الساعة.

Two clauses links with the conjunction و

Here is an example by Fischer, though used in a different context his book,

نموتُ معك ونحيا.

We shall die and live **with you.**

See Fischer (p.207), though that example is used there in a different context.

Notice how the complement which is linked to both verbs, has occurred immediately after the first verb in the SL (Arabic), but immediately after the second verb in the TL (English).

The use of the word غير to be mean 'the opposite of'

A recurrent error many Arab students make is the use of the word غير as in the phrase 'the dishonest man' with its appropriate equivalence 'الرجل غير الصادق'.

See Fischer (p.206) when he discusses this type of phrase beautifully there.

Gender related matters when translating from English into Arabic

It must be noted that sometimes the adjective may not agree with its feminine noun, so it will be masculine. One can say إمرأة حنون 'an affectionate woman' and not حنونة. Also, the example 'وامرأتي عاقر' 'and my wife is barren' (The qur'ān, 3:40). Also, Fischer (2002, p.71) in his book *A grammar of classical Arabic* has noted, "Adjectives that specifically refer to feminine qualities, as a rule, do not take the feminine ending: إمرأة طالق ...| 'divorced women [sic]'...."

Homonyms in Arabic

Two words which are either spelt similarly can have two different meanings, such as 'قط' meaning 'never' which means 'not ever', but the SL word 'قط' can also be read mistakenly to mean 'a cat'. Another example is the verbal phrase ' لم ينم' meaning 'did not sleep' or 'لم ينمّ' but the shadda or doubling of the letter 'م' is not shown, and the latter may either mean 'to show'/'to indicate' or 'to slander'.

331

Polysemous words in English and their Arabic equivalence

It is of benefit to point yet another problematic word in translation which is the

polysemous adjective 'good', a common error in translation from English into

Arabic, here is an example by Ryding of this modifier,

- ‏'طبيب أسنان جيد.'‏

'A *good* dentist' (p.213). [*emphasis in original but my italics*]

Here Ryding is doing a translation of the Arabic, but in Arabic the word 'good' is

not often used to describe a doctor or dentist. A good translation from English

into Arabic would have been ‏'طبيب أسنان شاطر/ماهر'‏. Here is another example, 'a

good boy' with its most appropriate Arabic equivalence ‏'ولد صالح'‏ or ‏'ولد مطيع'‏

and *not* ‏'ولد جيد'‏.

Appendix II: Practicals

Foreword:

The practicals below are chosen from the media to test one's translation ability independently, with little help and preparation of the terms and collocations in the STs and their TL equivalence before starting the task of translating. It is proven through experience that when one translate a text without preparing its terms and collocations, problems arise quickly. The first step is to read the ST thoroughly, then prepare all its terms and expressions and try to find their working TL equivalence before starting one's translation. If this is done the process of translation becomes relatively easy.

If this book is to be given to students as a textbook, the instructor needs to provide students first with the practicals, without giving them the terms with their *working* TL equivalence, provided here after each practical, in order to make students prepare their own list of expressions, terms and collocations when wearing the hat of the researcher, see Preface.

Practical One

The Guardian, Wednesday 26 September 2012 22.29 BST

Editorial - **Europe's austerity protests: mad as hell**

In all the dozens of summits and meetings held over the past couple of years about how to keep the euro show on the road, one subject has been notably absent. Amid all their talk of haircuts (on debt values) and tranches (of loans), European leaders have barely talked about the people who are bearing the brunt, first of the crisis and then of the throat-clearing that passes for firefighting in Brussels. This is not accidental. The euro project has relied upon draining the politics out of the inherently political: the very existence of a 17-nation economic union without a common treasury is testimony to that.

Especially amid austerity, however, it is impossible to ignore the politics. More than 200,000 demonstrators took to the streets of Athens on Wednesday. Thousands besieged parliament in Madrid on Tuesday. Last week more than half a million people marched in cities across Portugal to protest against cuts in social security. This is a pan-southern-European pushback against austerity, while the package is still being negotiated. The political strains are causing old regional fissures to re-emerge. One fifth of the population of Catalonia, 1.5 million people, marched last week in what can only be interpreted as a surge of separatist sentiment. For them it is not just the contract with Brussels and Frankfurt that needs to be renegotiated, but the contract with Madrid – in other words, the constitution. With regional elections coming up on 25 November, this is not something Madrid can ignore. Initially they wanted to collect their own taxes, which they would share with Madrid. When that was rejected, the price of peace escalated. Popular outrage over Catalan money going elsewhere, amid health and education cuts, is fuelling demands that the money stays put.

On Thursday the prime minister, Mariano Rajoy, unveils an austerity budget which is meant to pre-empt Brussels' conditions. When Spain is finally forced to ask for a bailout, it can say that the conditions demanded are the ones that it is already enacting. But this will only rub more salt into the wounds at home. With his absolute majority, Mr Rajoy was meant to be the leader who could deliver the austerity necessary to secure a future national bailout. That no longer looks certain, which is why Spanish bond yields went soaring yesterday. This in turn will hasten the outcome both Madrid and Brussels have been stalling on.

The Greeks and the Spaniards are committed Europhiles. No one has forgotten the history of coups and dictatorships from which membership of the EU served as a release. The EU has not stopped being the future. But its funds can no longer be called structural. Destructural funds are nearer the mark for millions of ordinary citizens. And everyone in the EU will pay the price.

335

'Europe's austerity protests'
English Terms with their working TL equivalences

Austerity protests	احتجاجات ضد التقشف
Summits	اجتماعات القمة
to keep show on the road	حتى يظل العرض أو الموضوع ساخناً
tranches of loans	دفعات كبيرة لتسديد القروض
bearing the brunt	يحتمل كل الضغط
drain politics out of ...	تفريغ السياسة من...
take to the streets	النزول إلى الشارع
besieged parliament	محاصرة البرلمان، تطويقه
marched in cities	خرجوا في مسيرات في المدن
cuts in social security	تقليص نفقات الأمن الاجتماعي
pushback against austerity	الرد ضد إجراءات التقشف
the package is still negotiated	لا يزال يتم التفاوض على حزمة الـ...
the political strains	الضغوط السياسية
old regional fissures	تصدعات إقليمية قديمة
a surge of separatist sentiment	موجة من مشاعر الانفصالية
needs to be renegotiated	ثمة حاجة إلى إعادة التفاوض بشأنها
collect their own taxes	جباية ضرائبها
the price of peace escalated	ارتفاع في ثمن السلام
popular outrage	
fuelling demands	ما زاد في المطالبات
the money stay put	أن تبقى الأموال في مكانها
history of coups and dictatorships	تاريخ الانقلابات والأنظمة الدكتاتورية
its funds	أموالها
nearer the mark	أقرب إلى المطلوب
pay the price	دفع الثمن
health cuts	تقليص نفقات الصحة
talk of haircuts	الحديث عن تقليص النفقات

Practical Two

Saudi Gazette - Kingdom Hospital embarks on ambitious expansion plan

Last Updated : Wednesday, September 05, 2012 12:23 AM

RIYADH — The Kingdom Holding Company (KHC) has unveiled an ambitious expansion plan for the Riyadh-based Kingdom Hospital. The SR550-million project will be carried out on a plot of land acquired by the company recently on the southern side of the present hospital. "The expansion is in line with the company's strategic local investment strategy," said Prince Alwaleed Bin Talal, Chairman of Kingdom Holding Company. The magnitude of the project reflects Kingdom Hospital's commitment to provide high quality care, combining clinical skills and cutting edge technologies, said a company statement.

Talal Ibrahim Al-Maiman, Executive Director for Development and Domestic Investments at KHC, said: "Kingdom Hospital together with Consulting Clinics and Pharmacies is determined to maintain their leading position as a premiere health care provider locally and regionally. Our investment in the health sector will have rewarding returns to KHC's investors."

Dr. Fayez Takieddine, Executive Director, Kingdom Hospital and Consulting Clinics, said: "The expansion is in keeping with its mission of providing quality medical care and exceeding patient satisfaction. Kingdom Hospital will expand its varied services in coordination with leading medical centers of the world."

With growing demand for healthcare in Saudi Arabia over the next two decades, the new project is expected to increase patients' access to evidence-based healthcare with more than 1 million outpatient visits a year, the KHC statement said. "The project demonstrates a rethinking of the use of the physical and technological infrastructure and design to improve the patient's experience and to enable the hospital's clinical and administrative staff to work in an environment that exemplifies their professional and medical expertise," it added. The project will be developed over the next three years with a total built-up area of 85,000 square meters. In addition to specialized outpatient clinics that can accommodate one million patient visits annually, the new expansion will add 150 private rooms for in-patients and state-of-the-art operating rooms and areas for day surgical procedures. With the expansion, the hospital's Emergency Department and Trauma Center will double in size to accommodate more than 100,000 visitors.

Kingdom Hospital in northern Riyadh is one of the most advanced private hospitals in Saudi Arabia. Established in 2000, the hospital completed its first expansion in 2011 doubling its bed capacity and adding a heart center equipped with advanced facilities, a pediatric ward, a surgical ward and a special pavilion for patients who want healthcare services in a luxurious environment. It is accredited by the Central Board for Accreditation of Healthcare Institutions (CBAHI).

The hospital recently finalized a merger plan with Consulting Clinics (CC), which is located at the intersection of Takhassussi and Makkah roads. Established in 1986 by Dr. Mustafa Ghandour and Dr. Fayez Takieddine, CC started with only six consultants and four departments. Today, it boasts of over 40 consultants covering all medical fields and has over 150,000 registered patient files.

"With the finalization of the merger, KH and CC will be offering advanced and specialized medical services that shall be announced in due course," the KHC statement said. It also revealed a comprehensive plan to establish a network of medical centers throughout Riyadh with moves to start such services countrywide in the future. — SG

English Terms with their working TL equivalences

unveiled an ambitious expansion plan	كشف النقاب عن خطة توسع طموحة
a plot of land	قطعة أرض
in line with	يتماشى مع
Local investment strategy	استراتيجية الاستثمار المحلي
the magnitude of the project	ضخامة المشروع
commitment to provide high quality care	الالتزام في تقديم أفضل رعاية صحية
cutting edge technologies	أحدث التقنيات
leading position	مكانة رائدة
health sector	قطاع الصحة
as a premiere health care provider	على أنه المورد الأساسي للرعاية الصحية
rewarding returns to investors	عائدات مجزية للمستثمرين
expansion in keeping with its mission	التوسع بحيث يتماشى مع مهمتها
providing quality medical care	تقديم الرعاية الصحية الممتازة
exceeding patient satisfaction	يفوق رضا المريض
varied services	خدمات متنوعة
in co-ordination with leading medical centres	بالتنسيق مع المراكز الطبية الرائدة
with growing demand for healthcare	مع ازدياد الطلب على الرعاية الصحية
increase patients' access to	زيادة إمكانية حصول المرضى على الرعاية
evidence-based healthcare	رعاية صحية تستند إلى الأدلة
outpatient visits	زيارات مرضى العيادات الخارجية
the project demonstrates a rethinking	يبين المشروع عملية إعادة التفكير في
physical and technological infrastructure	البنية التحتية والتقنية
hospital's clinical and administrative staff	العاملون في المستشفى من إداريين ومن الكادر الطبي
total built-up area of x square metres	تشغل المباني كلها مساحة كذا مترا مربعة
specialised outpatient clinics	عيادات متخصصة للمرضى غير المقيمين
accommodate one million patient visits	يوفر زيارة مليون مريض
private rooms for in-patients	غرف خاصة للمرضى المقيمين
state-of-the-art operating rooms	غرفة جراحة متطورة جدا

Arabic/English syntax in translation

areas for day surgical procedures مساحات للإجراءات الجراحية النهارية

Emergency and Trauma Centre مركز الطوارئ والحالات الخطرة

double in size to accommodate more than...

ازداد حجمها إلى الضعف لكي تلبي احتياجات أكثر من...

doubling its bed capacity تضاعف استيعابها للأسرّة

a heart centre equipped with advanced facilities

مركز طبي مجهز بأفضل المعدات المتطورة

paediatric ward جناح الأطفال

the hospital recently finalised a merger plan

لقد انتهى المستشفى من خطة اندماج

Practical Three

The New York Times

International Herald Tribune   OPINION OP-ED COLUMNIST   Reading, Math and Grit

By JOE NOCERA Published: September 08, 2012

Early in his acceptance speech Thursday night, President Obama gave a nod to his administration's backing of education reform. "Some of the worst schools in the country have made real gains in math and reading," he said, calling on the country to add 100,000 math and science teachers in the next decade. Then he moved on to other topics, like foreign policy and Medicare, that he clearly views as more vital to the campaign as it enters the home stretch.

It is hardly a surprise that education isn't a heated subject in the presidential race. Not when the economy is still sluggish, and the fight over the role of government so central. Besides, Republicans and Democrats alike have tried to fix education: George W. Bush with "No Child Left Behind," and Obama with his administration's "Race to the Top." Those "real gains" notwithstanding, progress remains fitful and frustrating. Too many disadvantaged children remain poorly educated. Too many high school graduates don't attend - or drop out - of college, which has become the prerequisite for a middle-class existence.

Which is why the publication of a new book, entitled "How Children Succeed," written by Paul Tough, a former editor of the Times Magazine, is such a timely reminder that education remains the country's most critical issue. In "How Children Succeed," Tough argues that simply teaching math and reading - the so-called cognitive skills - isn't nearly enough, especially for children who have grown up enduring the stresses of poverty. In fact, it might not even be the most important thing.

Rather, tapping into a great deal of recent research, Tough writes that the most important things to develop in students are "noncognitive skills," which Tough labels as "character." Many of the people who have done the research or are running the programs that Tough admires have different ways of expressing those skills. But they are essentially character traits that are necessary to succeed not just in school, but in life. Jeff Nelson, who runs a program in partnership with 23 Chicago high schools called OneGoal, which works to improve student achievement and helps students get into college, describes these traits as "resilience, integrity, resourcefulness, professionalism and ambition." "They are the linchpin of what we do," Nelson told me. Nelson calls them "leadership skills." Tough uses the word "grit" a lot.

On some level, these are traits we all try to instill in our children. (Indeed, Tough devotes a section of his book to the anxiety of many upper-middle-class parents that they are failing in this regard.) But poor children too often don't have parents who can serve that role. They develop habits that impede their ability to learn. Often they can't even see what the point of learning is. They act indifferently or hostile in school, though that often masks feelings of hopelessness and anxiety.

What was most surprising to me was Tough's insistence, bolstered by his reporting, that character is not something you have to learn as a small child, or are born with, but can be instilled even in teenagers who have had extraordinarily difficult lives and had no previous grounding in these traits. We get to meet a number of children who, with the help of a program or a mentor who stresses character, have turned their lives around remarkably. We meet Dave Levin, the founder of KIPP, perhaps the best charter school chain in the country, whose earliest graduates run into problems when they get to college - only 21 percent of them had graduated after six years, according to Tough - and then begins stressing character traits to turn things around.

'Reading, math and grit'
English Terms with their working TL equivalences

Obama's administration	إدارة أوباما
Backing of education reform	دعم الإصلاح في التربية والتعليم
calling on the country to add more teachers	يناشد البلاد على زيادة عدد المدرسين
worst schools in the country	أسوأ المدارس أداء في البلاد
foreign policy	السياسة الخارجية
more vital to the campaign	أكثر أهمية للحملة
as it enters the home stretch	مع دخولها الساحة الداخلية
education is not a heated subject	التربية والتعليم ليس موضوعا ساخنا
in the presidential race	في السباق على الرئاسة
the economy is still sluggish	لا تزال حركة الاقتصاد بطيئة
the fight over the role of the government	الصراع على دور الحكومة
Democrats and Republicans alike	الديموقراطيين والجمهوريين على حد سواء
try to fix education	محاولة إصلاح التعليم
No Child left behind	لن نترك طفلا وراءنا
Race to the Top	السباق إلى القمة
Real gains notwithstanding	مكاسب حقيقية تستحق الذكر
progress remains fitful and frustrating	يظل التقدم متذبذبا ومثبطا للعزيمة
too many disadvantaged children	الكثير من الأطفال البائسين
to remain poorly educated.	أن يبقى تعليمهم دون المستوى.
high school graduates	خريجو الثانوية العامة
drop out of college	الطلاب الذين تركوا مدارسهم
How Children Succeed	كيف يفلح الأطفال
former editor of the Times	محرر سابق في جريدة التايمز
Such a timely reminder	إنه يذكر في الوقت المناسب
Education remains the country's most critical issue	يبقى التعليم القضية الأكثر حساسية في البلاد
cognitive skills	مهارات معرفية
enduring the stresses of poverty	يحتمل ضغوط الفقر

Tapping into a great deal of recent research

يعتمد على كمية كبيرة من الأبحاث الحديثة

the most important things to develop in students

الأمور الأكثر أهمية التي يجب أن يتم تطويرها للطلاب

non-cognitive skills مهارات غير معرفية

people running the program الأشخاص الذين يديرون البرنامج

character traits صفات الشخصية

One runs a program in partnership with يشارك في إدارة برنامج مع

students get into college الطلاب الذين ينضمون إلى الكلية

traits such as resilience, integrity, resourcefulness

صفات مثل المرونة والاستقامة وسعة الحيلة

professionalism and ambition المهنية والطموح

these traits are the linchpin of what we do

هذه الصفات هي العصب المساعد لما نقوم به

Traits to instil in our children صفات نعلمها لأطفالنا

he devotes a section of his book كرس جزءا من كتابه

Parents can serve that role يمكن أن يقوم الأبوان بهذا الدور

To act indifferently or hostile in school اللامبالاة والعدائية في المدرسة

His insistence, bolstered by his reporting إلحاحه مدعوما بتقريره

Teenagers to have extraordinarily difficult lives

المراهقون الذين يعيشون حياة صعبة للغاية

No previous grounding in these traits دون وجود أرضية أصلا لهذه الصفات

A mentor who stresses character مرشد يؤكد على الشخصية

To turn their lives around remarkably يغير حياتهم بصورة ملحوظة

run into problems when they get to college يصادف مشاكل حين دخوله الكلية

Practical Four

Saudi Gazette - Sunday, 09 September 2012   APEC leaders vow freer trade to bolster growth

VLADIVOSTOK, Russia – China will ensure steady and robust growth by boosting domestic demand and rebalancing its economy to help counter the obstacles hindering a global recovery, President Hu Jintao pledged Saturday to Asia-Pacific leaders gathered for a regional summit.

Asia remains the biggest driver of global growth, despite a decline in Chinese growth to a three-year low of 7.6 percent in the second quarter, and Beijing is struggling to create enough jobs and cope with the adverse impact of the debt crisis on its own economy, Hu acknowledged.

"The global economy has reached a critical juncture, and we face the arduous task of overcoming major difficulties standing in the way in order to achieve full recovery and ensure steady growth," Hu told business leaders gathered on the sidelines of the Asia-Pacific Economic Cooperation (APEC) summit in this Russian Far East seaport.

Revitalizing trade and growth is an urgent priority for APEC, whose aim is to dismantle barriers and bottlenecks that slow trade and business while nurturing closer economic ties. Both China and host Russia pledged to do what they can to support those aims.

China's own growth has slowed as the government curbed bank lending to counter a property market bubble and soaring prices, just as the deepening debt crisis in Europe slammed demand for its exports. "Economic growth is facing notable downward pressure," Hu said. "Some small and medium-sized companies are having a hard time, and exporters are facing more difficulties." Hu, who is due to step down as China's top leader following a Communist Party congress this fall, promised to "ensure the continuity and stability" of the country's economic policies. "We will boost domestic demand and maintain steady and robust growth as well as basic price stability," he said. China's effort to wean itself from heavy reliance on export-driven growth has helped to rebalance its trade and will generate $10 trillion in demand for imports during the five-year period from 2011-2015, Hu said.

Russia's hosting of the APEC summit highlights a renewed focus on developing its neglected but resource-rich Far East. Putin has showcased his country's aspirations to play a more active role in the Pacific Rim region. President Vladimir Putin promised regional business leaders that they can count on Russia, which has long focused mainly on supplying oil and gas to Europe, to be a reliable energy supplier.

Moscow also has ambitious plans to develop its railroads, roads, seaports and airports in the resource-rich but long neglected east of the country to provide a bridge between Asia and Europe, Putin said. "The first and main thing we're going to do is develop transport infrastructure," he told regional business leaders.

Clinton welcomed Russia's recent admittance to the World Trade Organization. America's exports to Russia could double or even triple as the country implements its commitments to open its markets further, while Russia itself could raise its GDP by about 11 percent in the long run, she said, citing World Bank estimates. "Fostering a balanced and stable economy is a challenge too sweeping and complex for countries to approach in isolation," Clinton said. "If we do this right, globalization can become a race to the top, with rising standards of living and more broadly shared prosperity."

APEC economies – both huge and tiny, rich and poor – account for about half of world economic activity. Given its status as an organization governed by consensus, its annual summit is not known for major policy breakthroughs.

But a sharp decline in growth of trade in the 21-economy APEC region this year — from 12 percent in December to 4.6 percent in May — underscores the importance of pushing ahead with trade initiatives, the APEC Policy Support Unit, an independent data analysis and research unit, said in a report issued Friday.

The APEC leaders meet Saturday and Sunday for an "informal retreat" where they are expected to approve various initiatives, including one that will cut tariffs on environmental-related goods — such as waste-water treatment technologies — to 5 percent by 2015. They also are expected to endorse measures for ensuring food security, protecting supply chains and beefing up emergency preparedness. – AP

'APEC leaders vow freer trade to bolster growth'
English Terms with their working TL equivalences

Leaders vow freer trade to bolster growth	الرؤساء يتعهدون بتجارة حرة بصورة أكبر لتعزيز النمو
Steady and robust growth	نمو ثابت وقوي
President pledged	تعهد الرئيس
regional summit	قمة إقليمية
biggest driver of global growth	أقوى دافع للنمو العالمي
a decline in growth	تضاءل في النمو
three year low growth	أبطأ نمو منذ ثلاث سنوات
in the second quarter	في الربع الثاني
the adverse impact of the debt crisis	التأثير الشديد على أزمة المديونية
the global economy	الاقتصاد العالمي
to reach a critical juncture	يصل إلى منعطف خطير
Standing in the way	تقف عائقا في الطريق
to achieve full recovery	لتحقيق انتعاش كامل
ensure steady growth	لضمان النمو المستمر
leaders gathered on the sidelines of the summit	اجتمع الرؤساء على هامش اجتماع القمة
revitalising trade and growth	تفعيل التجارة والنمو
an urgent priority for APEC	أولية عاجلة لمجموعة دول الإيبك (منطقة آسيا والمحيط الهادئ)
the aim to dismantle barriers and bottlenecks	الهدف هو إزالة العوائق والمنغصات
to slow trade and business	إبطاء التجارة والأعمال،
closer economic ties	توثيق الروابط الاقتصادية
the government to curb bank lending	تعمل الحكومة على ضبط عملية الإقراض في المصارف
to counter a property market bubble	للتصدي إلى فقاعة سوق العقارات
soaring prices	ارتفاع مذهل في الأسعار
the deepening debt crisis	أزمة المديونية المتفاقمة
slammed demand for its exports	أوقفت الطلب على صادراتها
economic growth	النمو الاقتصادي

facing notable downward pressure	مواجهة ضغط شديد للهبوط
having a hard time	تمر في وقت عصيب
Top leader due to step down	أحد الرؤساء من المقرر أن يتنازل عن منصبه
Stability of the country's economic policies	استقرار السياسات الاقتصادية في البلاد
to boost domestic demand	تعزيز الطلب المحلي
maintain steady and robust growth	الحفاظ على النمو الثابت والقوي
basic price stability	استقرار السعر الأساسي
Effort to wean itself from heavy reliance	بذل جهود بحيث تحول دون اعتمادها الشديد على
export-driven growth	نمو يعتمد على الصادرات
help to rebalance its trade	تسعى لإعادة توازن تجارتها
generate money in demand for imports	توليد الأموال من خلال الطلب على الواردات
A sharp decline in growth of trade	تدهور شديد في نمو التجارة
fostering a balanced and stable economy	السعى إلى اقتصاد متوازن ومستقر
a challenge too sweeping and complex	وهو تحد ساحق ومعقد
for countries to approach in isolation	التعامل مع كل بلد على حدة
to implement its commitments	تنفيذ التزاماتها
to open its markets further	فتح أسواقها بصورة أكبر
in the long run	على المدى البعيد
to count on Russia	الاعتماد على روسيا
a reliable energy supplier	مورّد للطاقة معوّل عليه
to develop transport infrastructure	تطوير بنية تحتية للنقل
rising standards of living	رفع مستويات العيش
more broadly shared prosperity	والمشاركة في الازدهار بصورة أكبر
an organisation governed by consensus	منظمة تعمل بآلية الإجماع
underscores the importance of pushing ahead	يؤكد على أهمية المضي قدما
trade initiatives	مبادرات في التجارة
an independent data analysis and research unit	وحدة مستقلة لتحليل البيانات والأبحاث

a report issued Friday	صدر تقرير يوم الجمعة
an informal retreat	ملاذ غير رسمي
to approve various initiatives	الموافقة على مبادرات مختلفة
to cut tariffs on environmental-related goods	تقليص التعرفة الجمركية للسلع ذات الصلة بالبيئة
waste-water treatment technologies	تقنيات لمعالجة مياه الصرف الصحي
to endorse measures	للموافقة على الإجراءات
for ensuring food security	لضمان الأمن الغذائي
to protect supply chains	لحماية سلسلة الموردين
beefing up emergency preparedness	زيادة الاستعدادات للحالات الطارئة

Practical Five

Saudi Gazette - EDITORIAL

Another Israeli deception

Last Updated : Wednesday, September 26, 2012 1:10 PM

Here we go again. Another leading Israeli politician has made another seemingly moderate suggestion for a Palestinian settlement. This is supposed to make the outside world believe in the carefully-created myth that the Israelis, and not the hapless Palestinians, are the victims and are struggling to find a "reasonable" peace deal which will protect them.

The latest stunt comes from Ehud Barak, the defense minister in Benjamin Netanyahu's coalition government. Barak has proposed that if the peace talks, which have been stalled for four years, can proceed no further, then Israel should simply withdraw from the occupied West Bank and dismantle the "majority" of the settlements.

There are now half a million Jews living in 118 illegal settlements in Palestinian land. This sounds like a major concession. But as ever with the Israelis, you have to read the small print. The main settlements at Ariel, Etzion and Maale Adumim would be kept, along with a few other strategic locations. And guess what! Almost 90 percent of all the illegal settlers are to be found in these three fortified settlements. Ariel even boasts its own university. And Palestinian East Jerusalem is now ringed with Israeli colonies.

These are what Netanyahu describes in such a sinister fashion as "the facts on the ground". And Barak, by offering, in reality, to move some 25,000 settlers and demolish their dwellings, is in truth going a very long way toward solidifying those "facts on the ground". Commentators are saying that Barak has come up with this proposal because he wants to differentiate his Independence Party from Netanyahu's Likud in advance of elections due in just over a year's time. Barak is characterized as a "dove", yet during his time as Prime Minister, he continued the West Bank and Jerusalem expansion programs pursued by all other Israeli governments, before and since.

The unspoken part of Barak's proposal is likely to be that, in return for giving the Palestinians back part of their own land, (albeit wrecked from the building and subsequent destruction of the illegal settlements), Palestinians currently living in Israel and holding Israeli citizenship, should be "encouraged" to move to the West Bank. Maybe they will be offered the chance to take over the homes that Israeli settlers will be forced to vacate. That would pose a problem for the Palestinian authorities!

International public opinion may now be increasingly seeing less take-in in Israeli maneuvers of which Barak's plan is only the latest. However foreign governments, fearful of engaging with the real issues confronting the Palestinians, can use such "reasonable" proposals, as a smokescreen, behind which they cannot be seen busily doing nothing.

Why can't one world leader call it as it is? Ehud Barak is behaving like a mugger who has stolen your wallet at gunpoint, then offered to give you back the small change, provided that you agree to let him keep the bank notes, the credit cards and promise to be suitably grateful for his generosity, and assure him that you will not subsequently go to the police.

'Another Israeli deception'
English Terms with their working TL equivalences

seemingly moderate suggestion	يبدو أنه اقتراح فيه اعتدال
A Palestinian settlement	تسوية فلسطينية
hapless Palestinian	الفلسطينيون المساكين
a reasonable peace deal	صفقة سلام معقولة
Latest stunt	آخر محاولة بهلوانية
coalition government	حكومة الائتلاف
defence minister	وزير الدفاع
peace talks	محادثات سلام
talks stalled for four years	محادثاتُ توقفت قبل أربع سنوات
proceed no further	ولم تخطُ خطوة أخرى إلى الأمام
withdraw from the occupied West Bank	الانسحاب من الضفة الغربية المحتلة
to dismantle the majority of the settlements	تفكيك معظم المستوطنات
illegal settlements	مستوطنات غير شرعية
a major concession	تنازل كبير
fortified settlements	المستوطنات المحصنة
a few other strategic locations	بضعة مواقع استراتيجية أخرى
such a sinister fashion	بأسلوب مشؤوم
the facts on the ground	الحقائق على الأرض
demolish their dwellings	هدم مساكنهم
come up with this proposal	تقديم هذا المقترح
the unspoken part of this proposal	الجزء الذي لم يتم التكلم عنه في هذا المقترح
to take over homes	الاستيلاء على البيوت
settlers will be forced to vacate.	سوف يجبر المستوطنون على إخلائها
less take-in in Israeli manoeuvres	ألا يخدع كثيرا المناورات الاسرائيلية
fearful of engaging with the real issues	خشية الانخراط في مناقشة القضايا الحقيقية
confronting them	مواجهتهم
as a smokescreen	مجرد تمويه أو تعمية

behaving like a mugger

Steal your wallet at gunpoint
give you back the small change
the credit cards
another deception

التصرف مثلما يتصرف اللص
يسرق محفظتك بعد تصويب
المسدس عليك
ثم يعطيك بعض الفكة
بطاقات إئتمان
خداع آخر

END

Printed in the United States
By Bookmasters